EXPLAINING EURO-PARALYSIS

ST ANTONY'S SERIES

General Editors: Alex Pravda (1993–97), Eugene Rogan (1997–), both
Fellows of St Antony's College, Oxford

Recent titles include:

Mark Brzezinski
THE STRUGGLE FOR CONSTITUTIONALISM IN POLAND

Peter Carey (editor)
BURMA

Stephanie Po-yin Chung
CHINESE BUSINESS GROUPS IN HONG KONG AND POLITICAL
CHANGE IN SOUTH CHINA, 1900–25

Ralf Dahrendorf
AFTER 1989

Alex Danchev
ON SPECIALNESS

Roland Dannreuther
THE SOVIET UNION AND THE PLO

Noreena Hertz
RUSSIAN BUSINESS RELATIONSHIPS IN THE WAKE OF REFORM

Iftikhar H. Malik
STATE AND CIVIL SOCIETY IN PAKISTAN

Steven McGuire
AIRBUS INDUSTRIE

Yossi Shain and Aharon Klieman (editors)
DEMOCRACY

William J. Tompson
KHRUSHCHEV

Marguerite Wells
JAPANESE HUMOUR

Yongjin Zhang and Rouben Azizian (editors)
ETHNIC CHALLENGES BEYOND BORDERS

St Antony's Series
Series Standing Order ISBN 0–333–71109–2
(outside North America only)

You can receive future titles in this series as they are published by placing a standing order.
Please contact your bookseller or, in case of difficulty, write to us at the address below with
your name and address, the title of the series and the ISBN quoted above.

Customer Services Department, Macmillan Distribution Ltd
Houndmills, Basingstoke, Hampshire RG21 6XS, England

Explaining Euro-Paralysis

Why Europe is Unable to Act in International Politics

Jan Zielonka
Professor of Political Science
European University Institute
Florence

in association with
ST ANTONY'S COLLEGE, OXFORD

Published by PALGRAVE
Houndmills, Basingstoke, Hampshire RG21 6XS and
175 Fifth Avenue, New York, N. Y. 10010
Companies and representatives throughout the world

PALGRAVE is the new global academic imprint of
St. Martin's Press LLC Scholarly and Reference Division and
Palgrave Publishers Ltd (formerly Macmillan Press Ltd).

Outside North America
ISBN 0–333–73040–2

In North America
ISBN 0–312–21463–4

This book is printed on paper suitable for recycling and
made from fully managed and sustained forest sources.

A catalogue record for this book is available from the British Library.

Library of Congress Catalog Card Number: 98–15288

10   9   8   7   6
06   05   04   03   02   01

Printed and bound in Great Britain by
Antony Rowe Ltd, Chippenham, Wiltshire

Contents

Acknowledgments

This study has taken many unexpected turns from its inception in 1994. It started as a short analysis of Europe's handling of the nuclear proliferation issue and developed into a comprehensive analysis of the Union's common foreign and security policy. The study was supposed to be accomplished during my one-year sabbatical in Oxford, but it went on for nearly four years, following me back to Leiden, and then to Florence, where I assumed a new position in January 1996. I started this study with Europe's traditional foreign policy agenda and ended with an agenda dominated by cultural and democratic items. I began with a great dose of confidence, but ended with more questions than answers. I intended to develop a comprehensive European strategy for the next millennium, but in the end I decided to recommend only two basic measures: that the Union should fix its ever- shifting borders and that it should dispose of its military aspirations. In my judgment all these changes and turns proved to be for the better rather than for the worse and were chiefly due to the splendid academic environments I encountered at each of the three different institutions. True, the pace and scope of events in Europe kept me permanently alert. The mushrooming literature on the subject was ever inspiring. But the fact that I was given a lot of freedom and resources to accomplish this work has been of fundamental importance, not to mention the rich intellectual environments in which I was able to conduct my research. I am therefore indebted to several individuals and institutions.

My gratitude goes first to the Netherlands Organization for Scientific Research (NWO) for offering me a "Talent Stipendium" to spend a year researching in Oxford. The University of Leiden gave me a generous leave to go to Oxford, and I was welcomed there warmly by the Center for International Studies and St Antony's College. I am also grateful to the European University Institute in Florence and its Robert Schuman Centre for encouraging me to finish this book rather than immediately imposing new commitments on me when I arrived here to assume a chair in Political Science. In each of these institutions there have been numerous individuals providing various kinds of assistance and encouragement that helped me accomplish my work. I would like to mention, in particular, Alfred van Staden from Leiden

University, Alex Pravda, and Adam Roberts from Oxford University, and Yves Mény from the Robert Schuman Centre.

As usual, I owe a special debt of gratitude to colleagues who read early drafts of my chapters, and offered me their insightful advice and critiques. I am especially indebted to Adam Roberts who set me on the right path at the beginning of this project, and to Pierre Hassner who acted as my mentor and tutor throughout the entire process of writing this book. Special thanks go also to Luciano Bozzo, Maarten Brands, Anne Deighton, Christopher Hill, Iver Neumann, Peter Mair, Roger Morgan, Richard Rosecrance, and Karen Smith. I am also grateful to the participants in my seminar devoted to the subject of the book which was held at the European University Institute in Florence in the 1996–97 academic year.

The task of editing my manuscript was a daunting one and Ania Krok-Paszkowska once again manifested her gift as an excellent editor. The final polishing was done by Nida Gelazis and Elizabeth Webb who work with me in Florence, and by Aruna Vasudevan from Macmillan. Alex Pravda, a general editor of the St Antony's Series and Timothy Farmiloe, the Publishing Director of Macmillan's academic division, assured the smooth and speedy production of this book. I am greatly indebted to all of them.

Special thanks go also to Mei Lan, Alexander, and Robert.

Florence,
January 15, 1998

List of Abbreviations

CFE Treaty	Conventional Forces in Europe Treaty
CFSP	Common Foreign and Security Policy
CJTF	Combined Joint Task Forces
COREPER	Committee of Permanent Representatives
CSBM	Confidence- and Security-Building Measure
CSCE	Conference of Security and Cooperation
DG	Directorate General
EC	European Community
EDC	European Defense Community
EEC	European Economic Community
EFTA	European Free Trade Area
EMS	European Monetary System
EMU	European Monetary Union
EPC	European Political Cooperation
ERM	Exchange Rate Mechanism
ECSC	European Coal and Steel Community
ESDI	European Defense and Security Identity
EU	European Union
Euratom	European Atomic Energy Community
FCO	Foreign Commonwealth Office
GATT	General Agreement on Tariffs and Trade
GDP	Gross Domestic Product
NACC	North Atlantic Cooperation Council
NATO	North Atlantic Treaty Organization
NPT	Nuclear Proliferation Treaty
OSCE	Organization for Security and Cooperation in Europe
PLO	Palestinian Liberation Organization
SALT	Strategic Arms Limitation Talks
SEA	Single European Act
TEU	Treaty on European Union
UN	United Nations
UNPROFOR	United Nations Protection Force
WEU	Western European Union
WTO	World Trade Organization

Introduction: Beyond Euro-optimism and skepticism

This book is about Europe's apparent inability to cope with a complex international environment. The focus is not on trade and economics, where the Union is a strong and dynamic actor, but on security, diplomacy, and politics, where the Union is paralyzed. In the 1991 Maastricht Treaty, the European Union proclaimed its ambition to set up a common foreign and security policy (CFSP). Its institutional framework was quickly created, but the common policies envisaged by the Treaty hardly ever get off the ground. The question is: why? Why does the Union fail to live up to the letter and spirit of the Treaty and its broad political expectations? In the search for answers to this basic question the arguments presented in this book draw upon various intellectual schools, academic disciplines and political traditions. I also deal with many issues that are not on the usual EU agendas. Thus, this book is not only about the Union and its institutions but also about culture, identity, democracy, and power politics in present-day Europe. It is not merely about procedures of foreign policy-making, but also about conceptual challenges facing states and politicians. Nor is it simply about instruments of defense and diplomacy, but about ways of justifying and legitimizing common European endeavors. Although the book focuses on the awkward acronym, CFSP, it is in fact about the broader subject of European politics and the changing nature of international relations.

Of course, the aim is not to do justice to all the complex issues mentioned above, but to present a fresh way of thinking about the Union and its foreign policy and security dilemmas. Nor is it my intention to side with one or another of the opposing camps in the on-going controversy over Europe. While I agree with the Euro-enthusiast's claim that common foreign policies can, in principle, enhance Europe's fortune, I also underwrite the Euro-skeptic's warning that common policies make little sense unless they are truly democratic, purposeful and effective. This does not mean that the book avoids taking a bold stance amidst conflicting evidence and the

1

enormous complexity of problems under consideration. Description is followed by prescription – however difficult and controversial.

Five distinct explanations for Europe's failure to create truly common policies will be considered. They originate from different schools of thought on politics and international relations. Their conclusions will bring us to a field uncharted by diplomats and defense experts: cultural identity and democratic legitimacy will be found to be the most crucial factors at the root of the CFSP failure.

The period under consideration is basically between December 1991 (the Treaty of Maastricht) and June 1997 (the Draft Treaty of Amsterdam). The original CFSP design, agreed upon in Maastricht, remains largely intact in the Draft Treaty of Amsterdam. Therefore, the problems analyzed in this book are likely to confront Europe for some time.

THE GRAND DELUSION

"A common foreign and security policy is hereby established" was proclaimed proudly in the 1991 Treaty on European Union.[1] The aim of the Union is "to assert its identity on the international scene ...covering all areas of foreign and security policy." The member states, according to the Maastricht Treaty "shall support the Union's external and security policy actively and unreservedly in a spirit of loyalty and mutual solidarity." They shall also "refrain from any action which is contrary to the interests of the Union or likely to impair its effectiveness as a cohesive force in international relations" and shall "ensure that their national policies conform to the common positions." The European Council has been obliged by the Treaty to ensure "the unity, consistency and effectiveness of action by the Union." Functional consistency should also be ensured between the Union's "external relations, security, economic and development policies."[2]

The language of the Maastricht Treaty is plain and clear. There can be no doubt about the Union's ambitions. "We need to be far-sighted, to think big", declared then-President of the Commission, Jacques Delors, "what we need is a more coherent and committed foreign policy."[3]

The Treaty has been formally ratified, and armed with it the Union has jumped into the fray of post-Cold War international politics from Russia to Yugoslavia, to Turkey, Iraq, Albania, and Rwanda. However, the more the EU got involved, the more criticism it encountered. From one case to another it has become increasingly evident that Europe's common policy is neither coherent nor committed nor, as Delors would have it, far-sighted. In 1996 Tony Judt put it bluntly: "The European Union has utterly failed to bring its members together for any common policy or action in military or foreign affairs... the European edifice is fundamentally hollow, selfishly obsessed with fiscal rectitude and commercial advantage."[4]

Criticism of the CFSP came from all possible corners, including the Union's own officials. In 1995 the European Commission admitted: "The experience of the common foreign and security policy has been disappointing so far."[5] The Commission's report on the first 18 months of the CFSP performance uses such damaging terms as "confusion," "incoherence," and "paralysis."[6] The European Parliament's report underlined "shortcomings" on the institutional front and in the definition of EU's security interests.[7] Presenting a perspective from the European Council, Juan Duran Loriga acknowledged that the CFSP suffers from "inefficiency," "lack of credibility," and "lack of real influence on the international scene," while the EU Commissioner, Hans van den Broek, admitted that "in handling serious political crises the Union has rarely acted as one; we often speak with different voices, giving different answers to the same questions."[8]

Non-governmental security circles have also been critical of, if not altogether frustrated with, the CFSP. "The mood in expert circles is depressed," declared Elfriede Regelsberger and Wolfgang Wessels in 1996, "there is a common opinion that the first experiences with the CFSP are on the whole negative. The handling of the Yugoslavian case is perceived not as an exception to otherwise positive experiences but as highlighting structural deficiencies."[9]

Journalists, as usual, have been more sharp and candid: "Enough Eurobabble," demanded Thomas L. Friedman; Abram de Swaan called the European foreign policy "een benauwende mislukking" (worrying failure); while Charles Bremner talked about "the emptiness of the grand ambitions of the common foreign and security policy enshrined in the treaty."[10]

The list of weaknesses of European foreign policies is long and worrying. They range from operational to conceptual problems. The Union is either unable to formulate its policies or unable to implement policies already adopted. Sometimes procedural and institutional difficulties are at the core of CFSP failures. At other times the Union is simply faced with member states' reluctance to have any common policy whatsoever. Reforms to the initial structure of CFSP could help fortify some of its weaknesses, but as the 1997 Amsterdam European Council demonstrated, the Union is incapable of reforming itself.

Union officials continue to be very active, they meet and talk quite frequently about foreign and security issues, they sponsor initiatives, nominate mediators and distribute economic rewards and sanctions. In the EC foreign and security issues have long been considered to be "untouchable" subjects. In the EU these issues are very high on bureaucratic and political agendas, yet the relationship between (hyper)activity and output is pretty disappointing. As a special report in the Bertelsmann Stiftung observed: "Whilst these actions have been useful, they have not led to increased EU visibility nor really decisive action. The scope has been modest and the added value of CFSP not always apparent."[11]

Member states' unilateral policies, and their failure even to consult other EU partners, have been notorious and striking. The most famous among them was President Mitterand's trip to Sarajevo, straight from the EC Summit in Lisbon and without a word to any of the European heads of state gathered in Lisbon.[12]

The Union's inaction in crisis situations has also been frequent. "Europe slept through the night" complained, for instance, US Assistant Secretary of State, Richard Holbrook during the 1996 Turkish–Greek showdown in the Aegean.[13]

In some cases, such as the Middle East Peace Process, the Union was very active but unable to match the influence of other actors, most notably the United States. In other cases, such as the policy towards Maghreb, the Union was clearly in the driver's seat, yet for years it was unable to come up with a proclaimed policy that would go beyond simple economic aid and address complex issues of development, religion, and democracy in the region.

Comparisons with other international institutions are also insightful. For instance, both NATO and the EU embarked on a policy of eastward enlargement. The NATO enlargement issue appeared on the international agenda later than the EU enlargement issue, and it was also more controversial. Russia utterly opposed NATO enlargement, Western Europeans feared that enlargement would dilute the collective defense component of NATO, and it was never clear how NATO would address the economic and ethnic causes of instability in Eastern Europe. Yet after four years of deliberations, NATO has decided to enlarge: it set the date of enlargement for its 50th anniversary in 1999, and identified Poland, Hungary, and the Czech Republic as its first new members. The idea of the EU enlargement was accepted in principle as early as 1990 and no major objections to enlargement have been raised since. More importantly, the Union put into action an elaborate and extensive framework of Association Agreements and is working on an accession strategy *vis-à-vis* several Eastern European states. Yet for a long time the Union failed to make the most important strategic decisions: it was unable to differentiate among various criteria for admission, identify new members among an ever-growing list of applicants, set a date for enlargement, or decide whether enlargement would be simultaneous or staggered. In December 1997, the Union decided to invite five Eastern European countries plus Cyprus to start negotiations leading to enlargement, but some politicians insisted that the list was too short, while others did not try to conceal their desire to have as few new EU members as possible and as late as possible.[14] Even countries nominally in favor of eastward enlargement, such as Germany, Great Britain, and France, oppose the significant changes to the EU budget implied by enlargement. The fact that during the 1997 Amsterdam European Council the current member states failed to readjust the EU institutions for the purpose of further enlargement complicates the issue even further. As a consequence, it is difficult to expect any post-communist Eastern European country to enter the Union before the year 2005. In the meantime, confusion and destructive public quarrelling is likely to be the order of the day.

Successive chapters will describe in more detail some of the major defects of the Union's policies. The overall picture seems to be clear: CFSP is in a state of paralysis!

This statement requires some qualification. Paralysis may imply many things and it is worth specifying which meaning of paralysis is endorsed in this book and which meanings are rejected. I argue that the Union is in a state of paralysis because it is unable to live up to its Treaty-binding obligations as stipulated, for instance, by Renaud Dehousse and Joseph H.H. Weiler.[15] This does not mean that the CFSP has never enjoyed any success or that the Union as such is impotent. Nor does it mean that the CFSP project is basically flawed or that the Union must live up to some absolute expectations.

First and most obviously, paralysis is not total, in the sense that it is difficult to deny CFSP some successes. However, these successes have been few and the exact impact of the CFSP on the outcomes is unclear. For instance, the EU policy towards South Africa certainly contributed to the collapse of the apartheid regime there, but so did many other factors – domestic ones most notably.[16] Another example: the so-called "Stability Pact" aimed at preventing ethnic and territorial disputes in Central and Eastern Europe is rightly quoted as the CFSP's great achievement.[17] But as some experts have pointed out, the Pact "reinvents the wheel because some countries in Central and Eastern Europe already have negotiated bilateral agreements or are in the process of concluding one."[18]

It is sometimes argued that the CFSP performed well in meeting its "alternative" agenda, that is it helped foreign ministries survive by providing them with a new European mission and it served well as a scapegoat for failures in national politics.[19] The problem is that an "alternative" CFSP agenda was never publicly declared, justified, or approved; it cannot, therefore, be assessed as being either a possible success or failure.[20]

Secondly, CFSP paralysis does not imply that the Union as such is impotent and worthless. With nearly 380 million people, a combined GNP higher than that of the United States, the largest market in the world, a pivotal position in international trade, and the leading position in development assistance and humanitarian aid the Union cannot be dismissed from world affairs – let alone European ones. It is enough to look at the impressive list of applicants for EU membership to conclude that the Union does have some worth. However, my argument is that the Union is unable to live up to its CFSP pretensions as embedded in the Treaty, *despite* its enormous potential and powerful international leverage.[21]

Cynics would argue that the letter of the Treaty should not be taken very seriously. They assert that treaties often contain largely declaratory goals to which the signatories may not be wholeheartedly committed. But does not the abundance of evidence suggest that in the early 1990s the political ambitions of EU's crafters were actually higher than what they ultimately wrote into the Treaty? As Günther Burghardt, a top EU official, put it in 1991:

> In the 1970s and 80s West Germany used to be described as "an economic giant but political dwarf." The same description could have been applied to the Community in the 1980s. But just as the unification of Germany has given the Germans a stronger political voice, so too will the political weight of the Community increase in parallel with its moves to integration. The logic of a CFSP is inescapable and although the Community may only be prepared to move half way at Maastricht there can be no doubt as to the ultimate destination.[22]

Another indication that there is a real commitment to the goals outlined in the Treaty was the result of the 1997 Amsterdam European Council. Since little progress had been made in meeting the EU foreign policy arrangements made six years earlier in Maastricht, the Council could have taken measures to scale down its ambitions at the 1997 Amsterdam meeting. Instead, the 1997 Draft Treaty of Amsterdam reinstated nearly all of Maastricht's foreign policy pretensions.

Thirdly, the paralysis of recent years does not imply that the idea of a common foreign and security policy is by definition absurd.[23] The CFSP might well be a controversial scheme, but the alternatives seem to be even worse. Can one credibly claim that individual European countries can effectively run all sorts of foreign policies on their own? Should we resign ourselves to the idea that the United States is best suited to run foreign policies on Europe's behalf? Or should we rely on a new type of great powers' *directoire* to do the job? To all three questions most people would answer with a resolute "no!" Besides, there is no need to reason in zero-sum terms. The CFSP does not have to preclude foreign policies being run by other actors and it does not need to fulfill all possible international functions. In short, the CFSP makes sense, provided that it is well designed and works in practice. But can it be made to work? Is the paralysis reversible? Of course, improvements can hardly come about spontaneously without a major change in policies, institutions, and concepts. But one should try to identify the major causes of the CFSP "sickness" and then search for the proper "medicine." There is no need for "euthanasia" at this early stage.

Fourthly, paralysis does not necessarily mean that the Union has failed to live up to some imagined (absolute) standards. A common policy is different from a single one practiced by a full-fledged federation and we should not expect the Union to perform considerably better than any of the existing international actors. All international organizations suffer from slow and clumsy decision making. Even individual states are not immune to cumbersome procedures and competence conflicts. The foreign policy of any national or international actor is usually of a neutralizing nature (that is, reactive) rather than of a progressive one (that is, pro-active). In short, there is no point in blaming the Union for failing to produce miracles. This does not mean that it is impossible to assess the efficacy of an international actor nor that we are condemned to total relativism. As John G. Ruggie rightly argued:

In the final analysis, the reality of regimes resides in the principled and shared understandings of desirable and acceptable forms of behavior among relevant actors. Adaptations to new and unforeseen developments, attenuating circumstances, the rationales and justifications for deviations that are proffered, as well as responsiveness to such reasoning on the part of other states, all are critical in assessing the efficacy of regimes.[24]

HISTORICAL PERSPECTIVE

The time frame of any evaluation is always crucial. On the one hand, it may be unfair to judge the CFSP after only four years of formal existence. On the other hand, it could be argued that the process of setting up common foreign policies had already begun in the early 1970s, if not earlier. Is not the CFSP a new name for EPC (European Political Cooperation)? Consensus is still required before making European foreign policies and the CFSP, like EPC, is not equipped with all the instruments needed for action. It is no wonder that its policies are basically declaratory and ineffective.

I will judge the CFSP on its own merits as defined by the Treaty of Maastricht, first, because the Treaty marks a deliberate leap forward towards the creation of a more coherent international unit – the Union – and second because the Union's creation coincided with a major geostrategic change in Europe. The end of the continent's bi-polar division forces us to re-think basic assumptions about foreign and security policies at both Union and nation-state levels. The kind of foreign affairs cooperation reminiscent of the 1970s and 1980s is clearly inadequate in coping with the challenges of the 1990s. Although some of the reasons for Euro-paralysis may not be linked to historical changes, many others nevertheless are linked to the on-going process of transition that began with the CFSP's creation.

This does not mean that the pre-Maastricht history of European cooperation should be ignored. Despite contrasts, dissimilarities, and change, there are also a lot of parallels, similarities and continuity between pre- and post-Maastricht cooperation efforts in the sensitive field of security and foreign affairs. The historical legacy in terms of continuity and common trends can be grouped under three distinct headings: gradualism, pragmatism, and ambiguity. It is this three-fold historical legacy which presents an additional means for judging the CFSP's current design and performance.

First, cooperation in foreign affairs did not emerge overnight, but developed in an incremental and often disguised manner. The European Political Cooperation project was officially launched in 1970 as a cautious and pragmatic means for advancing the issue of cooperation which had already been at the center of political discussions for 20 years. As early as May 1952, six European countries committed themselves to engineering a new political superstructure needed to give direction and legitimacy to the future European Defense Community (EDC).[25] The EDC failed, partly because it was too ambitious, if not revolutionary. However, efforts to act together in the international arena continued in a more muted, modest, and gradual fashion. Although the 1957 Treaty of Rome emphasized economic integration and intra-European interests, it nevertheless provided for a clear international role for the EC by creating a common trade policy that gave the Community the power to initiate association agreements between the EC and third countries and to conclude international treaties. Thus, the legal framework and political legitimacy for conducting external relations by the Communities had been laid down. Setting up the European Political Cooperation project represented a natural extension of common efforts directly into the field of "high-politics." Next, careful steps were taken to extend EPC aims, improve its procedures, and equip it with certain powers in 1973 (the Copenhagen Report), 1981 (the London Report), and 1983 (the Solemn Declaration on European Union). Thus, the Europeans slowly developed their foreign policy aims, from pure "consultations" to policy "coordination" and even "common policies." As far as policy means are concerned, a gradual agreement was reached to go beyond declaratory "common positions" and use, if necessary, trade, aid, and sanctions as foreign policy tools. By degree, the EPC cooperation framework was improved and structured: the role of the EC presidency was elaborated, the Commission was associated, and regular meetings of EC delegates were convened. The Single European Act of July 1987 gave EPC a solid legal basis.[26] It established that EPC could utilize both economic and political instruments and included provisions for the creation of the EPC Secretariat. The Maastricht Treaty on European Union was primarily a clear step forward in terms of joint aims: a common foreign and security policy had become an EU objective. It also improved the organization and structure of European cooperation and created a new policy instrument that went beyond a "common position": common action.[27]

Thus, although the CFSP represented a novel type of cooperative arrangement to cope with novel challenges, it did not simply flash from the sky like lightning. On the contrary, it represented yet another stage in a gradual process of extending common policies into the field of international relations. This has important implications for judging the CFSP's performance. If performance has been weak so far, it is hardly because of any natural *Kinderkrankheit*.[28] As Elfriede Regelsberger and Wolfgang Wessels rightly argued:

> The Maastricht provisions were not imposed [on Europe's governments], but were the products of a common attempt to reinforce and rationalize the pre-existing intergovernmental procedures...The CFSP failed due to the unwillingness of the governments to play by the rules of the game which they themselves established.[29]

Another common historical trend relevant to my argument is the pragmatism of European governments when dealing with the sensitive issue of diplomacy and defense. The prevailing reasoning in recent years has been that it is better to make practical progress in foreign policy cooperation rather than indulge in doctrinal legal battles. Countries were making practical progress in shaping joint policies without being compelled to do so by any specific legal framework. The legal framework was always created post factum. The law was used to sanction an existing practice, and not to create it. For the first 17 years of its existence, EPC did not even have a proper legal basis. It was based on private agreements between foreign ministries to organize regular meetings and observe certain conventions. This lack of a legal framework had not prevented the EPC from taking some bold political steps, such as the Venice Declaration of June 1980 on the Euro-Arab dialogue and the situation in the Middle East.[30] The legal form of EPC only took shape in the mid-1980s with the Single European Act, though the Act did little more than endorse an already existing practice. As Simon J. Nuttall put it:

> The most significant feature of the Single European Act was that it was single: it combined in one legal text provisions for Political Co-operation and amendments to the Community Treaties, thus breaking the taboo of over thirty years. That this came about was in part owing to the fact that the two frameworks had been growing together, helped by the Commission's full association with EPC since 1981 and the series of events which encouraged interaction between EPC and the Community.[31]

Like the Act, the Maastricht Treaty's legal stipulations sanctioned existing practices to the extent that analysts questioned whether or not the CFSP was merely a new name for an old policy – lofty declarations aside.[32] But the prevailing assumption of member countries was that actual foreign policy cooperation would go beyond the required legal commitments.

This means that our method of judging the CFSP's performance in terms of meeting the legal commitments expressed in the Maastricht Treaty is somewhat cautious and conservative. If EPC was ever subject to criticism it was because it did not live up to international challenges and political expectations, and not because it did not fulfill its legal commitments. This book argues that the CFSP does not even live up to its minimal legal commitments – not to mention its failure to live up to various challenges and expectations.

Of course, law and politics cannot be easily separated. After all, EPC has been upgraded and renamed CFSP not because of any legal necessity (that is, a supposedly irreversible march towards federalism), but because historical circumstances required more effective European cooperation in the field of security and foreign policy. If we claim that the Union is paralyzed because it is unable to live up to CFSP pretensions, as stipulated in the Treaty, it does not mean that we have to adopt a narrow legal perspective that ignores politics. Our reasoning suggests, however, that we view the CFSP in more critical terms than the EPC, even if both institutions are proved to be equally declaratory and ineffective. The point is that the official aims of the CFSP are much more advanced than those of the EPC, and for good reason.[33]

Judging the CFSP in terms of legal rather than political criteria may be more appropriate, but it still leaves us with a lot of problems. This is because of the ambiguity of the legal language employed to define any cooperative arrangements in the field of security and foreign policy. The European Defense Cooperation project failed not only because it was too revolutionary, but also because it was too straightforward, especially in its federalist framework. Subsequent efforts to enhance foreign affairs cooperation eventually got off the ground, not only because they were more gradual and modest, but also because they were more ambiguous. I already mentioned the fact that the Treaty of Rome laid down a legal foundation, not only for economic but also for foreign affairs cooperation without actually spelling it out. The Luxembourg Report of 1970, which formally established the EPC, set up a mechanism that was essentially intergovernmental, though it proclaimed in a communitarian manner that the intention was to "give shape to the will to political union." The language of the Maastricht Treaty is plain so far as policy aims are concerned, but there is a great discrepancy between its envisaged means and aims. The language becomes particularly cryptic in regard to the issues of security and common defense: "The common foreign and security policy shall include all questions related to security of the Union, including the eventual framing of a common defense policy, which might in time lead to a common defense."[34]

The ambiguity of successive cooperative arrangements was basically rooted in the persistent differences among European countries concerning the very nature of integration (federalism versus intergovernmentalism), the functional scope of integration (high politics versus low politics) and competing national agendas (for example French and Spanish "anti-Americanism" versus British and Dutch "pro-Americanism"). Ambiguity helped achieve the necessary consensus, but as we shall argue later, it has also prevented the Union from acquiring an equally necessary identity and strategic purpose. It has further complicated the evaluation of cooperative efforts. Should these efforts be judged by federalist or intergovernmentalist standards? If policy aims are vague, how can we determine whether or not they are being ignored or implemented?

The problem of ambiguity must be taken seriously, but we refuse to accept the argument that the Union has no serious commitments owing to the vague language of the Maastricht Treaty. Some analysts would suggest that an anything-goes policy in Europe is effectively sanctioned by the Treaty and no conscious commitment has ever been made to upgrade the previous cooperative effort in the field of defense and diplomacy. If this were so, however, why then were some member states fiercely opposed to the idea of creating a common foreign and security policy for more than 30 years? Why have neutral Finland, Sweden, and Austria been specifically asked to fully subscribe to *all* CFSP provisions before being granted EU membership?[35] As stated earlier, there is no reason to endorse total legal or political relativism.

It is also worth emphasizing that despite the revisions made to the Maastricht Treaty in the Draft Treaty of Amsterdam, it maintains Maastricht's tradition of gradualism, pragmatism, and ambiguity. The Draft's stipulations are vague, the reforms introduced are anything but "revolutionary," and the European Council has been given more freedom to determine how the most important legal stipulations are implemented in practice.[36]

In sum, the paralysis analyzed in this book has a clearly defined meaning. The Union is paralyzed because it fails to live up to the CFSP pretensions initially embedded in the Maastricht Treaty and restated in the Draft Treaty of Amsterdam. Paralysis is neither absolute nor comprehensive, it is neither fatal nor incurable, but it is certainly not healthy. Let us now try to identify possible explanations for the paralysis.

FIVE EXPLANATIONS

Practitioners and analysts have put forward plenty of explanations for CFSP failure. They range from elaborate theories to very simple statements. Different explanations reflect authors' different professional backgrounds and intellectual propensities. Those working within the EU institutional system usually talk about institutional weaknesses behind CFSP failure, while those working within national political systems emphasize divergence of national interests and the EU's democratic deficit. Students of international interdependence focus on the damaging implications of global economic pressures, while students of local or regional communities talk about a weak European cultural identity. Diplomats focus on different issues than security experts. Sociologists, lawyers, and political scientists concentrate on problems related to their own particular disciplines. So far, no single explanation has gained prominence, although institutional arguments have been heard most frequently.

This book has grouped all the different explanations into five distinct categories. The choice was somewhat arbitrary, but the five groups chosen accommodate most of the arguments raised in the ongoing CFSP debate. The first type of explanation presents a "back-to-the future" scenario for Europe: the old-type power game among major European nations is responsible for the EU's failure to develop a common foreign and security policy. With the demise of the Cold War, it is argued, we are back to a Europe of national ambitions, manipulation, and aggression. Countries are searching for security and power amidst growing uncertainties and change. The policies of ever-changing alliances, "ganging up," or even "bullying" are again in vogue. As Pierre Lellouche has forcefully argued:

> Once again, Europe is characterized by a pivotal and strong Germany, a backward and unstable Russia, and a large number of small,

weak states. And again, France and Great Britain are incapable by themselves of balancing German power or of checking Russian instability, let alone restructuring the entire European order around a Franco-British axis...Nationalism, border questions and structural imbalances have been resuscitated [in the post-Cold War Europe].[37]

Is this hypothesis true or false? Are we indeed witnessing the "back-to-the-future" scenario or rather a "forward-to-the-future" one? Is the on-going power politics a sign of renewed hegemonic ambitions or merely of atavistic search for pride and glory by some frustrated (former) empires?

The second explanation does not assume any sinister ambitions on the part of modern states, but it points to a natural divergence of national interests in Europe. European states are not necessarily pursuing power and hegemony, but their interests stem from different historical experiences, geographic locations, patterns of economic interdependence, and cultural links with the outside world. Given this, it is indeed difficult for the diverse EU members to reach common ground in deciding upon foreign and security policies. As Robin Niblett put it: "There remain very few foreign policy issues concerning which EU members bring common interests to the table."[38]

The third explanation argues that the end of the Cold War resulted in profound strategic confusion that blocked otherwise successful efforts towards a common foreign and security policy. States are faced with new and largely unknown challenges, international institutions are undergoing major restructuring, and new political arrangements are slow to emerge under ever-changing circumstances. While the old dispute between Hobbesian, Grotian, and Kantian approaches to international politics is still unresolved, the assertion of romantic and post-modern types of thinking undermine the very foundation of modern rationality. How can a foreign and security policy of the Union get off the ground if Europe does not know what kind of order it intends to have, how to achieve it, and at what price?

The fourth explanation questions the ability of modern European states to cope with a new set of internal and external challenges. European democracies find themselves in a deep structural crisis which effectively prevents them from acting swiftly and cohesively in the international framework. The growing gap between government and the governed feeds a growing sense of cynicism and stimulates disaffection concerning any intergovernmental efforts. The rise of public diplomacy and the media syndrome causes strategic arthritis.

The long-lasting consensus on the basic notions of national interest, the utility of international involvement, and the usual hierarchy of values guiding foreign and security policies is undermined by the assertion of sectarian interest groups. And a dominant state-centric model of democracy makes it difficult to legitimize common European endeavors, especially in the sensitive field of foreign and security policy.

The fifth explanation focuses on the misguided pattern of European integration and the weakness of European institutions. It argues that common foreign and security policies are a victim of EU's ill-structured decision-making process. The disaggregated policy process of institutional regional integration has proved to be especially inadequate for the anticipation and management of military and diplomatic crises. There are also doubts as to whether common foreign and security policy can emerge in a gradual manner in the way that economic integration apparently can; and the "interlocking" institutional framework of various pan-European, Western European, trans-Atlantic and global organizations has proved to be detrimental rather than beneficial to the functioning of the CFSP.

My analysis will partly prove and disprove arguments expressed by all five explanations/hypotheses. Each of the explanations will be found justified to a certain degree, but often in a different sense than initially asserted. The book will also show that some arguments are more valid than others and that the most valid arguments are in fact made up of elements from each of the five explanations. The book will also show the need to go beyond the traditional foreign policy and security agenda, since it is hardly possible to explain CFSP failures by using standard terms and concepts of defense and diplomacy.

In conclusion, the book argues that Euro-paralysis is basically caused by democracy and identity problems. Common policies do not work because they do not really enjoy genuine public legitimacy.[39] Europeans do not have a high degree of natural affinity with these policies and they have virtually no control over them. Traditional foreign policy concerns such as power, institutions, and national interests are found less crucial in explaining CFSP failures.

What can be done? The Union should tell its citizens what the CFSP is all about. It should make some basic strategic choices about its purpose, functions, and territory. One choice suggested in this book is to opt for a civilian power model for the Union, the other is to define the borders of the Union. The long-standing ambiguity about the

Union's geographic reach and functional purpose is shown to be a grave liability.

ANALYTICAL PREMISES

This book is neither truly empirical nor theoretical. It tries to give straight answers to some basic questions without ambition to support each point by either abundant statistical evidence or theoretical models. True, anyone who studies the footnotes will discover that this book has been written with the help of an enormous body of literature in the field of social and political science as well as international relations. Yet I do not take a stance on the on-going academic dispute between contending camps of neo-realists, neo-functionalists, liberal inter-governmentalists, constructivists, positivists, structuralists, and others. Moreover, for the sake of clarity I try to avoid important but often awkward and confusing terms and concepts used by these various theories. I do not even use the word "theory," preferring the much more modest term, "schools of thought," and I label them in a rather impressionistic if not eccentric manner as romantic, post-modern, Grotian, or Kantian. That said, a short explanation about what I think is important. No author is free from methodological and theoretical prejudices, and here comes a catalogue of my own.

Susan Strange has recently observed that "the common sense of common people is a better guide to understanding than most of the academic theories being thought in universities."[40] In her view "the social scientists, in politics and economics especially, cling to obsolete concepts and inappropriate theories."[41] John Lewis Gaddis, for his part, proclaimed that the "failure of international relations theory" is caused by a selective use of variables and arbitrary assumptions: "methodological passing of ships in the night" – as he put it.[42]

This book, however, is not based on such strong, if not absolute premises. I do see that much of the existing statistical data are either banal or misleading, while most of the existing theories claim to be mutually exclusive. I also see how risky it is to make any predictions or claim a monopoly of truth in social sciences. But I try to learn from empirical studies and from diverse theoretical analyses because not doing so would mean that we are totally at the mercy of fortune-tellers and astrologers.[43] It is one thing to expose weaknesses of individual theories, but quite another to claim that theoretical approaches to international politics are inherently deficient. After all, it is impossible to establish what to study and how to study it without referring to theories of some sort. Most of our current insight into the world of politics and diplomacy is rooted in the work of social scientists trying to identify and explain various trends and patterns, correlations, and irregularities.

That said, I have a clear preference for certain theories over others. I favor theories that try to break down, rather than put up, fences dividing different academic disciplines. Susan Strange once used a metaphor of ranchers and farmers to compare trans-border academic travelers with those who toil in restricted disciplinary areas with the help of conventional methods and concepts.[44] I side with the former attitude of ranchers, or even add the third preferred attitude of hunters who explore new conceptual terrain in search for original ideas for hunting.[45]

In the same spirit I do not believe that various theories are contradictory rather than complementary. For instance, I find nothing contradictory in the following three sets of assumptions expressed by three different schools of thought: (1) realism; international politics is about power and self-interest, states continue to be major actors and military power is crucial; (2) liberalism; trade and economics can alter state behavior and so can institutional forms of communication and cooperation; (3) constructivism; structures of international politics are social rather than strictly material and they shape actors' identities, interests and behavior. In short, one can be a liberal-constructivist-realist regardless of what the guardians of individual theoretical temples may think.[46]

And finally, I believe that analyses integrating external and internal factors offer a better understanding of foreign and security policy than approaches relying exclusively on one aspect. In other words, there is nothing wrong with mixing structural and unit levels.[47] As Thomas Risse-Kappen rightly argued: "The 'state world' and the 'society world' need each other."[48] This explains why in a book on foreign and security policy so much attention is devoted to the issue of democracy and culture. States' behavior within the European Union reflects not merely structural power calculations but also "frivolous" or "erratic" electoral calculations and "irrational" cultural pressures.[49]

Such an approach to the study of foreign and security policy may well be called eclectic. But let it be so, if the alternative is theoretical dogmatism and extremism. To those uncertain about the virtue of my analytical premises I offer a quotation from Leszek Kolakowski's essay on "The General Theory of Not Gardening":

Those who hate gardening need a theory. Not to garden without a theory is a shallow, unworthy way of life. A theory must be convincing and scientific. Therefore we need a number of theories. The alternative to not-gardening without a theory is to garden. However, it is much easier to have a theory than actually to garden.[50]

This book was written on a premise that, in the final analysis, gardening is what really counts.

NOTES

1. Treaty on European Union, Title V, Article J. The following quotations come both from Title V and Title I of the Treaty. The Maastricht Treaty was formally adopted in 1993, after a lengthy process of ratification by the national parliaments of member states. In June 1997, a revised Draft Treaty was adopted in Amsterdam by a special Conference of the Representatives of the Governments of the Member States. As far as the CFSP is concerned, the 1997 Draft Treaty departs only slightly from the Treaty of Maastricht. These discrepancies will be pointed out and discussed throughout this book.

2. The Draft Treaty of Amsterdam contains similar stipulations. For instance, the amended Article C of the Treaty states that "the Union shall in particular ensure the consistency of its external activities as a whole in the context of its external relations, security, economic and development policies. The Council and the Commission shall be responsible for ensuring such consistency and shall cooperate to this end. They shall ensure the implementation of these policies, each in accordance with its respective powers."

3. Jacques Delors, "The Role of the European Community in the Future World System", in *The European Community after 1992: A New Role in World Politics?*, Armand Clesse and Raymond Vernon, eds. (Baden-Baden: Nomos, 1991), p. 44.

4. Tony Judt, "Europe: The Grand Illusion", *The New York Review of Books*, (July 11, 1996), p. 9.

5. European Commission, *Report on the Operation of the Treaty on European Union*, SEC(95), Brussels, (May 10, 1995), p. 5.

6. Ibidem, pp. 63–75.

7. "Report on Progress Made in Implementing the Common Foreign and Security Policy" (November 1993–December 1994). Rapporteur: Abel Matutes, Doc. A4–0083/95. See also "Report on the functioning of the Treaty on European Union with a view to the 1996 Intergovernmental Conference implementation and development of the Union". Doc. A4–0102/95/Part I.A, (May 12, 1995), pp. 3–4.

8. Hans van den Broek, "CFSP: The View of the European Commission", and Juan Duran Loriga, "CFSP: The View of the Council of the European Union", in *The European Union's Common Foreign and Security Policy. The Challenges of the Future*, Spyros A. Pappas and Sophie Vanhoonacker, eds. (Maastricht: European Institute of Public Administration, 1996), pp. 25 and 31.

9. Elfriede Regelsberger and Wolfgang Wessels, "The CFSP Institutions and Procedures: A Third Way for the Second Pillar", *European Foreign Affairs Review*, Vol. 1, No. 1 (July 1996), p. 29.

10. See Thomas L. Friedman, "Europe Has 18 More Months to Get Its Bosnia Act Together", *International Herald Tribune*, November 25, 1996; Charles Bremner, "EU foreign policy left in disarray by Balkan and Aegean bungling", *The Times*, February 12, 1996; and Abram de Swaan, "De laatste les", *NRC Handelsblad*, December 28, 1996.

11. "CFSP and the Future of the European Union", Interim Report by the Bertelsmann Stiftung, prepared in collaboration with the Research Group on European Affairs (University of Munich) and the Planning Staff of the European Commission (DG1A), Gütersloh, (July 1995), p. 12.

12. Unilateral policies have been particularly visible in the military field. In the case of Bosnia, for instance, the British government decided unilaterally to reinforce its UNPROFOR forces in May 1995. The incumbent French president, Jacques Chirac, decided to retake a brigade in Sarajevo from Bosnian Serbs. The Dutch minister of defense, Joris Voorhoeve called back close air support when the Srebrnica enclave was under attack by Serbs in July 1995.

13. Richard Holbrook quoted in Bruce Clark, "No escape from destiny – Richard Holbrook explains to Bruce Clark why the US must remain in Europe", *Financial Times*, February 23, 1996.

14. "Spain, Italy, Greece, and Portugal are determined to keep their share of EU regional aid while smaller countries, such as Belgium and Luxembourg, are worried that expanding membership without deepening political integration would undermine their rights." See "EU braced for enlargement war", *Financial Times*, July 14, 1997, p. 2.

15. The argument of Dehousse and Weiler was made in the context of the Single European Act and its Title III provisions on Cooperation in the sphere of foreign policy, but it applies even more to the Maastricht Treaty and the Amsterdam Treaty with their CFSP provisions. According to Dehousse and Weiler many provisions of Title III of the Single European Act are legally binding despite the absence of effective enforcement mechanisms. In their view some seemingly vague terminology such as "the parties shall endeavor to formulate a European foreign policy" create an obligation to act in good faith, which is a recognized concept of international law. Besides, international legal commitments are frequently deprived of enforcement mechanisms other than reciprocity and counter-measures. See Renaud Dehousse and Joseph H.H. Weiler, "EPC and the Single Act: from Soft Law to Hard Law?" in *The Future of European Political Cooperation. Essays on Theory and Practice*, Martin Holland, ed. (London: Macmillan, 1991), pp. 128–31.

16. For a more detailed analysis of EU's successes and failures in South Africa see Martin Holland, *European Union Common Foreign Policy. From EPC to CFSP Joint Action and South Africa* (London: Macmillan, 1995), pp. 218–21.
17. See, e.g., The Reflection Group's Report, Messina, June 2, 1995 and Brussels, December 5, 1995, SN 520/95 (Reflex 21), p. 39.
18. Mathias Jopp, "The Strategic Implications of European Integration", *Adelphi Paper* No. 290 (July 1994), p. 53. See also Jonathan Eyal, "France's False Sense of Security", *The Independent*, January 27, 1994. Jopp also pointed out that the Pact has often been perceived in Eastern Europe as an "arrogant" Western effort to establish a sort of *droit de regard* in the Eastern part of the continent. (The Pact was not intended to deal with problems of Northern Ireland or the Basque country.) Moreover, the Pact failed to address other key aspects of security related to social and economic development.
19. This was suggested in: Knud Erik Jørgensen, "The European Union's Performance in World Politics: how should we measure success?", in *Paradoxes of European Foreign Policy*, Jan Zielonka, ed. (London: Kluwer Law International, 1998), forthcoming.
20. This does not mean that the seemingly sinister argument of Weiler and Wessels is by definition wrong: inaction of EPC (and by extension CFSP) is a virtue, because it managed to avoid Europe getting dragged into all sorts of trouble. After all, there is nothing in the Single European Act (or the Treaties of Maastricht and Amsterdam) which compels the Community/Union to get involved in all possible damaging conflicts. See Joseph Weiler and Wolfgang Wessels, "EPC and the Challenge of Theory", in *European Political Cooperation in the 1980s. A Common Foreign Policy for Europe?*, Alfred E. Pijpers, Elfriede Regelsberger, Wolfgang Wessels and Geoffrey Edwards eds. (Dordrecht: Martinus Nijhoff, 1989), p. 252.
21. Richard Rosecrance recently suggested that the Union had unique and unparalleled foreign policy strengths despite the fact that there has not yet been, and probably there will not be, a common European foreign and defense policy. The claim of this particular book is, however, much more modest. I believe that the Union's foreign policy strengths are very much the function of the vitality and effectiveness of the CFSP, regardless of all the important structural factors underlined by Rosecrance's analysis. See Richard Rosecrance, "The European Union: A New Type of International Actor", in *Paradoxes of European Foreign Policy*, Jan Zielonka, ed. (London: Kluwer Law International, 1998), forthcoming.
22. Günther Burghardt, "Political Objectives, Potential and Instruments of a Common Foreign and Security Policy", in *Global Responsibilities: Europe in Tomorrow's World*, Werner Weidenfeld and Josef Janning, eds. (Gütersloh: Bertelsmann Foundation Publishers, 1991), p. 25. At the time of this publication Burghardt was Director in the General Secretariat of the Commission of the EC.
23. See, e.g., the editorial article, "Euromyths three", *The Times*, February 23, 1996, p. 17, (no author).

24. John G. Ruggie, "Embedded Liberalism Revisited: Institutions and Progress in International Economic Relations", in *Progress in Post-War International Relations*, Emmanuel Adler and Beverley Crawford, eds. (New York: Cambridge University Press, 1991), p. 209.

25. See Edward Fursdon, *The European Defence Community: A History*, (London: Macmillan, 1980), especially pp. 192–9.

26. For a more detailed analysis of this point see Renaud Dehousse and Joseph H.H. Weiler, op. cit., pp. 121–42.

27. Procedural and organizational changes resulting from the Maastricht Treaty included the merging of the General Affairs Council and EPC, the merging of EPC Secretariat into the Council Secretarial, a special directorate (DG1 A) and Commissioner for External Political Affairs, synchronization of procedures with WEU (Western European Union), allowing majority voting in some circumstances, directly involving the COREPER in CFSP work. Chapter 5 will deal with these and other institutional questions in more depth.

28. This was well demonstrated in Mathias Jopp, "Die Reform der Gemeinsamen aussen-und Sicherheitspolitik, Institutionelle Vorschläge und ihre Realisierungschancen," *Integration*, Vol. 3 (July 1995), pp. 133–43.

29. See Elfriede Regelsberger and Wolfgang Wessels, "The CFSP Institutions and Procedures: A Third Way for the Second Pillar", *European Foreign Affairs Review*, Vol. 1, No. 1 (July 1996), pp. 42–3.

30. The declaration has remained the basic "guiding" document for the EC for many years. It stressed the need for Israel to put an end to the territorial occupation which it has maintained since the conflict of 1967, and insisted that the PLO will have to be associated with peace negotiations. The declaration also stipulated that the traditions and common interests which link Europe to the Middle East oblige them to play a special role and now require them to work in a more concrete way towards peace. For a more detailed analysis of the Venice Declaration see Alfred Eduard Pijpers, *The Vicissitudes of European Political Co-operation. Towards a Realist Interpretation of the EC's Collective Diplomacy* (Leiden: University of Leiden, 1990), pp. 147–69.

31. Simon J. Nuttall, *European Political Cooperation* (Oxford: Clarendon Press, 1992), p. 10.

32. See e.g. Anthony Forster and William Wallace, "Common Foreign and Security Policy: a New Policy or Just a New Name?", in *Policy-Making in the European Union*, Helen Wallace and William Wallace, eds. (Oxford: Oxford University Press, 1996), pp. 411–35.

33. Despite mounting political pressure from the federalist camp and the official negotiations mandate prepared by the Milan European Council, the Single European Act failed to create a "common foreign policy," but instead opted for "cooperation in the sphere of foreign policy" making it clear that states are to remain the central, if not exclusive actors, both at the decision-making and at the implementation levels. See Renaud Dehousse and Joseph H.H. Weiler, op. cit., p. 126. In political terms my argument is in line with the concept of "plateau" introduced by Elfriede Regelsberger who suggested that the EPC has become more ambitious over time. The CFSP must simply do better than EPC because

circumstances require it. Moreover, the CFSP cannot use the excuse of *Kinderkrankheit*. See Elfriede Regelsberger, "EPC in the 1980s: Reaching Another Plateau?", in *European Political Cooperation in the 1980s*, Alfred Pijpers et al., eds., op. cit., pp. 3–48.

34.   Article J.4.1 of the Treaty on European Union, Maastricht, December 1991.

35.   During the EU accession negotiations of these countries the Commission questioned the compatibility of the neutrality policy of these countries with the full acceptance of the common foreign and security policy of the Union. At the end of the membership negotiations, a joint declaration was given by the EU member states and the applying countries stating that the new members have to be ready and capable of participating fully and actively in the CFSP from the beginning, of accepting its contents without reservations, and of supporting the policy in force when entering the Union. See e.g. *Helsingin Sonomat*, December 22, 1993.

36.   For instance Article J.7 of the Amsterdam Treaty states that "The common foreign and security policy shall include all questions relating to the security of the Union, including the progressive framing of a common defense policy, in accordance with the second paragraph, which might lead to a common defense, *should the European Council so decide.*" (my emphasis)

37.   Pierre Lellouche, "France in Search of Security", *Foreign Affairs*, Vol. 72, No. 2 (Spring 1993), p. 130.

38.   Robin Niblett, "The European Disunion: Competing Visions of Integration", *The Washington Quarterly*, Vol. 20, No. 1 (Winter 1997), p. 95.

39.   According to opinion polls a clear majority of Europeans support not only a common foreign policy, but also common defense. See, e.g., *Eurobarometer*, No. 44 (Spring 1996), pp. 42–4. However, as I argue later in this book these statistics are rather misleading. It is one thing to give a positive answer to an abstract question: do you support common foreign policies? It is another to underwrite common policies with a check-book, if not "blood, sweat and tears."

40.   Susan Strange, *Retreat of the State. The Diffusion of Power in the World Economy* (Cambridge, Cambridge University Press, 1996), p. 3. Such arguments were recently echoed in many European countries. See, e.g., Alfred van Staden, "Politieke Wetenschap en Politiek Comentaar", *Internationale Spectator*, Vol. 51, No. 2 (February 1997), pp. 100–3.

41.   Ibidem.

42.   According to Gaddis: "Theorists of international relations are using the methods of classical science when they conduct their investigations exclusively along a behavioral, structural, or – within the evolutionary approach – a linear or cyclical axis of analysis. They are excluding other variables and controlling conditions in order to produce theories from which they can forecast events. They know that if they do not impose such exclusions and controls, complications will quickly overwhelm their calculations, and predictability will suffer." John Lewis Gaddis,

"International Relations Theory and the End of the Cold War", *International Security*, Vol. 17, No. 3, (Winter 1992/93), pp. 53 and 55. For a European version of this argument see e.g. Maarten Brands, "The Obsolence of almost all Theories concerning International Relations," *Uhlenbeck Lecture No. 14*, (Wassenaar: The Netherlands Institute for Advanced Study in the Humanities and Social Sciences, 1996), pp. 3–25.

43. This, of course, is not to underestimate the role of historians. However, historians are primarily concerned with the past rather than the present and the future, and they also emphasize chaos and complexity rather than order and regularity. See, e.g., George A. Reisch, "Chaos, History, and Narrative," *History and Theory*, Vol. 30, No. 1 (1991), pp. 1–20.

44. Susan Strange, "Review of K.J. Holsti, The Dividing Discipline. Hegemony and Diversity in International Relations", in *International Journal*, Vol. 42, No. 2 (Spring 1987), pp. 398–401.

45. A good illustration of such preference is presented in John Peterson's study of decision-making in the European Union. According to Peterson "EU decision-making is governed by different dynamics – or 'decisive variables' – at different levels of analysis. Different theoretical models may offer 'best' explanations for decision-making at different levels of analysis. A portfolio of theories is needed to explain EU decision-making, even if a 'one-to-one' fit between theory and level of analysis cannot be guaranteed." See John Petersen, "Decision-Making in the European Union: Towards a Framework for Analysis", *Journal of European Public Policy*, Vol. 2, No. 1 (March 1995), p. 83. See also Michael Clarke, "Foreign Policy Analysis: A Theoretical Guide", in *Domestic Sources of Foreign Policy: West European Reactions to the Falkland Conflict*, Stelios Stavridis and Christopher Hill, eds. (Oxford: Berg, 1996), p. 21.

46. Complementarity between realism and liberalism was well illustrated in Joseph S. Ney, "Neorealism and Neoliberalism", *World Politics*, Vol. 40, No. 1 (October 1987), pp. 234–51. Vast areas of complementarity between realism and constructivism are enumerated in Alexander Wendt, "Constructing International Politics", *International Security*, Vol. 20, No. 1 (Summer 1995), pp. 71–81. See also Christopher Hill, "1939: The Origins of Liberal Realism", *Review of International Studies*, Vol. 15, No. 4 (October 1989), pp. 319–28.

47. For the opposite view see Kenneth Waltz, "Reflections on 'The Theory of International Politics': A Response to My Critics", in *Neorealism and Its Critics*, Robert Owen Keohane, ed. (New York: Columbia University Press, 1986), p. 340.

48. Thomas Risse-Kappen, "Structure of Governance and Transnational Relations: What Have We Learned?" in *Bringing Transnational Relations Back In. Non-State Actors, Domestic Structures and International Relations*, Thomas Risse-Kappen, ed. (Cambridge: Cambridge University Press, 1995), p. 310. See also Daniel Wincott, "Institutional Interaction and European Integration: Towards an Everyday Critique of Liberal Intergovernmentalism," *Journal of Common Market Studies*, Vol. 33, No. 4 (December 1995), pp. 597–609.

49. For theoretical implications of such a premise see, e.g., Friedrich Kratochwil, "Is the Ship of Culture at Sea or Returning?", in *The Return of Culture and Identity in International Relations Theory*, Yosef Lapid, ed. (Boulder: Lynne Rienner, 1995), pp. 201–21.
50. Leszek Kolakowski, *Modernity on Endless Trial* (Chicago: The University of Chicago Press, 1990), p. 240.

1 Power politics, again

As Martin Wight used to say: "Power politics is a colloquial phrase for international politics."[1] And today in Europe we see power politics at their height. Released from Cold War constraints, European states have returned to a familiar pattern of struggling for power, primacy, even hegemony within the region. Everything now seems to be up for grabs in an increasingly anarchic continent where the rules of self interest have come to the fore once more. With this comes the old Hobbesian fear, as small states fear large states and large states fear each other. The search for security through a new balance of power promises only to bring about new conflicts and new alliances. In short, there is no point in hoping for a common foreign and security policy within the European Union.

Is this description true or false? Are we back to a Europe of the national ambitions, manipulation and aggression which produced so much bitterness and misery in the past, especially between 1850–78 and again in 1914–45? There are good reasons to believe that this is indeed the case. Consider the rise of national xenophobia across the entire continent, the fears evoked by German unification, the bullying policy of small countries such as Greece and the "go-it-alone" policy of large countries such as France and Great Britain, the post-Maastricht internal squabbles and the international squabbles about the structure of a new security system, the level of national interest prevailing in policies towards the former Yugoslavia, Russia, the United States, Japan, China – even Albania, Rwanda, and Somalia – and the lack of any common European commitment to the global UN effort. The list is long and worrying.

This chapter will examine the part played by power politics in the behavior of European states. While the existence of this relationship will soon appear to be obvious, we will also see that power politics of today are very different in nature from the power politics of 50, 100, or even 150 years ago. Today European states look and act differently from the states of the 19th and early 20th century; they are also under unprecedented transnational pressures. Nuclear weapons have changed the rules of the power game. Moreover, the hierarchy of aims and values pursued by major European nations has changed. The threats to Europe are many and they are serious, but they are different from those presented by Napoleonic France, the Germany of Wilhelm or

Hitler, and Russia under Catherine, Stalin, or Brezhnev. In short, we are not going "back to the future" as some observers suggest. The parochial arrogance, petty jealousies, and inferiority complexes of some states, and the pathetic claims to glory of others are as deplorable as they are destabilizing, but they do not necessarily lead to the bloody struggle for hegemony, territorial conquest, and ideological subjugation that has marked European history for so many years.

The good news ends here, however. The current power game may well be more tranquil than in the past, but it still may be enough to prevent any common foreign and security policy from emerging. I will therefore try to analyze the origin and rationale of the present revival of power politics and to assess the damage they inflict upon common European endeavors.

THE WORLD OF *REALPOLITIK*

Mainstream international relations specialists recall the ghosts of history for both theoretical and practical reasons. Theoretical reflection stems from a series of assumptions about the nature of international relations.[2] Wars are terrible but are to be expected, the argument goes, since there are no supranational forces to prevent them. Power, which means military power in most instances, determines which states prevail and which fail. The most effective way of preventing either total anarchy or hegemony of the strongest is to seek a balance of power, viewed as analogous with the Newtonian solar system.[3] The structure of the international system is therefore of prime importance, it is argued. This structure is composed of sovereign states that are guided by a rational assessment of their national interests. States have no permanent friends, only permanent interests. Sovereignty is absolute and cannot be shared. Hans J. Morgenthau, one of the greatest proponents of this particular reasoning, put it thus:

> A divided sovereignty is logically absurd and politically unfeasible ... What exists is an international society of sovereign nations. There does not exist a supranational society ... the nation is the recipient of man's highest secular loyalty ... No attempt to solve the problem of international peace by limiting national aspirations for power has succeeded, and none could have succeeded under the conditions of modern state systems ... People are willing and able to sacrifice and die so that national governments may be kept standing.[4]

It is one thing to comprehend the true nature of power politics, and quite another to assess its fateful effects upon modern European history. Large states have clashed attempting to increase their power and territorial acquisition through warfare from the time of Frederick II, Napoleon I, and William II, to that of Mussolini, Stalin, and Hitler. Small states have been forced to fall into one hegemonic orbit or another. Slaughter on a huge scale, migration, and economic deprivation have been common aspects of successive military ventures; and it has not only been the Germans, Russians, British, and French who have championed the politics of brute power and expansion. Sweden, Hungary, Portugal, and Spain have all entertained dreams of conquering large parts, if not all, of Europe in their day. The Netherlands Belgium, and Portugal practiced imperial power politics in Africa and the Far East. Indeed, in a Europe without a common overruling government and a workable collective security system the presence of power politics has seemed unavoidable: it has been the only game to play.

Finding a balance of power as a solution to competition has proved to be a problem in itself, however, as states seeking a balance have clashed with one another over real or imaginary imbalances. There have been other attempts to constrain the excesses of power politics through agreements on certain universal principles of morality and government; the Vienna Congress of 1815 agreed on the principle of legitimacy, the Versailles Settlement of 1919 established the principle of self-determination, and the Yalta meeting of 1945 endorsed the principle of democracy. But all these attempts failed, as nation states refused to sacrifice their national interests on the altar of abstract principles and universal justice. Attempts to ignore power politics altogether have ended in even greater failure. Most notably, in the late 1930s the appeasement politics of Britain and France *vis-à-vis* Nazi Germany ended in the greatest holocaust in human history.

Although power politics did not end in 1945, the argument goes on, there were three crucial factors which dampened their most damaging effects: the bipolar balance of military power on the continent, the "pacifying" domination of the two superpowers within their respective spheres of influence, and the presence of nuclear weapons at the heart of the continent. As a result, Europe embarked upon an unprecedented period of "long peace," although life in the area east of the "Iron Curtain" had little to do with the lofty principles of democracy, legitimacy, and national self determination.

However, now that the Soviet Union has collapsed and the United States is gradually reducing its military commitment to Europe, power politics are at play once more, it is argued, giving rise to chaos, suspicion, and instability. No longer constrained by the Soviet threat and by the stabilizing presence of America, European nations have supposedly begun the race for hegemony and survival. The unification of Germany virtually destroyed any hope of a regional balance developing beyond the direct influence of the US and Russia: there is simply no way to create a balance with a country of 80 million people and with the greatest economic strength on the continent. Although still not a true military power, the acquisition of nuclear weapons is for Germany merely a matter of political decision; the technological and economic capability to do so is already there.

It is therefore not surprising that the principal advocate of the "back to the future" argument, John J. Mearsheimer, declared as early as the summer of 1990: "The demise of the Cold War order is likely to increase the chances that war and major crises will occur in Europe...the basic nature of states is to focus on maximizing relative power, not on bolstering stability."[5] Wars may occur again, it is argued, for the same reasons they so often occurred in modern European history: through the uncertain workings of multi-polar balancing processes that involve both small and large states.[6] The small states of Eastern Europe in particular, released from the Soviet grip but still weak and unstable, may act as catalysts for conflict among large powers. The fact that Germany, the most "suspect" European state, is particularly exposed to instability in the post-communist region complicates the situation even further. The bi-polar European stalemate resulted in "long peace". But now it is feared that the new multi-polar rivalry will result in anarchy, suspicion, hyper-nationalism, military build-ups, and ever-changing alliances. Minor wars will be the order of the day, and the danger of a large continental war will raise its head.

Initially such fears seemed to be greatly exaggerated, but as years passed the evidence began to show that power politics were back in fashion, that small wars were indeed flaring up at the outskirts of Europe, and that the German question was again a source of disquiet in many European nations. As Josef Joffe put it in 1993: "History, it turned out, had not ended with the champagne party atop the breached Berlin Wall in November 1989, the reunification of Germany in October 1990 or the dissolution of the Soviet Union in December 1991. History in fact came back with a vengeance."[7]

There are three cases that are often quoted as being illustrative of the resurgence of power politics on the continent: the diplomatic maneuvers around German unification, the pre-and post-Maastricht bargaining, and the controversies surrounding European involvement in peace-keeping operations.[8] All three are said to bear witness, not merely to Euro-paralysis, but to the conscious politics of manipulation, defiance, egoism, and partisan favoritism.

The full story of the diplomatic maneuvering behind German unification is not yet known, but the facts revealed so far give enough reasons to fear that power politics are indeed back in fashion.[9] In 1955, the United States, Great Britain, and France had pledged themselves by treaty to support German unification. However, when in 1989 the unification emerged as a real prospect France and Great Britain began secretly to conspire against it. President Mitterand, in particular, indulged in a power-balance game of such delicacy that he earned himself the name of the new European Metternich.[10] His visit to Kiev in December 1989, where he stressed the particular responsibility of France and Russia for European stability, proved as controversial as his visit to East Berlin several days later. Mrs Thatcher also went to Moscow in September 1989 to express Britain's apprehension about German unification to President Gorbachev. And she plotted behind Germany's back with France and other European partners about ways of containing the new German power which is, as she put it: "by its very nature a destabilizing rather than a stabilizing force in Europe."[11] Italy and The Netherlands also expressed their misgivings about the prospect of German unification, and took part in secret talks which examined the troubling emergence of a new power center at the heart of the continent.[12]

Although the German government was not truly in control of the largely spontaneous process of unification, it could have done much more to allay the fears and suspicions of its European partners. Instead, Chancellor Kohl indulged in unilateral policies that could hardly be labeled "European," as far as the decision-making process was concerned. Most notably, neither the Chancellor's "10 point" blueprint for unification, announced in November 1989, nor his visit to Moscow in February 1990, to discuss the details of unification with President Gorbachev, had been properly debated with Germany's European allies. Nor was the Chancellor willing to bend to European pressure to rerecognize the Oder-Neisse border in the early stages of unification. President Gorbachev summarized his dealings with Chancellor Kohl in a characteristic fashion: "We have acted in the spirit of the well-known German expression *Realpolitik.*[13]

The pre-and post-Maastricht argument was linked to German unification, as countries tried to use the "European question" as a means of coping with the German question. But Maastricht was not only about Germany, it was about a complex set of issues directly affecting all EU members. And so individual countries began a hard and bitter political bargaining process for the best possible deal, not so much for Europe as for themselves. Formation of ad hoc and cross-cutting coalitions was the order of the day, but some governments did not hesitate to use their veto to protect their real or imaginary national interests. Two opposing camps were often those of France and Great Britain, with their largely incompatible views on many crucial aspects of integration. Germany sided with France as far as deepening of the Union was concerned, but it sided with Britain when it came to the widening of the Union. The Netherlands supported France's federalist creed in the economic, monetary, and political fields, but it joined the anti-French pro-NATO league in the field of defense. Ireland, Spain, Portugal, and Greece were willing to support most of the existing coalitions provided that they endorsed substantial transfers of resources from richer to poorer EU members. Italy tried to play the role of mediator between various competing camps, but in effect complicated the situation even further. The Maastricht Treaty, resulting from this unprecedented international squabbling, contained agreements that were either meaningless or bound to collapse under the strain of competing pressures. The European Exchange Mechanism collapsed under the pressure of financial speculation in September 1992, while the common foreign and security policy provisions proved meaningless when faced with the war in the Balkans. The former case in particular evoked new doubts about "real" German intentions, as the German Bundesbank was clearly implicated in the collapse of the ERM system, resulting in heavy financial losses for Britain, Italy, and France. They all were deserted at a crucial moment, without German help against fierce speculation.

From this point the power struggle within the Union has been played out in the open. The 1994 summit meeting in Corfu failed to elect Jacques Delors' successor: Chancellor Kohl vetoed the candidature of Ruud Lubbers, and Prime Minister Major vetoed the candidature of Jean-Luc Dehaene.[14] Later in 1994, the German idea of a two-tier European Union with a "hard core" of five EU states produced a torrent of criticism, especially from Denmark, Italy, Spain, and Great Britain.[15] Responding to the German initiative the leader of the Italian Northern League, Umberto Bossi, said that Europe was falling under the influence of the "Prussian heel." The German proposal, he argued: "with typical Teutonic arrogance, splits Europe into two camps and puts Italy in the B class."[16] These conflicts only intensified when the European Monetary Union began taking shape in late 1996, with Italy desperately trying to get on board in the first round and Germany trying to prevent it. At the 1997 Amsterdam European Summit, power politics were also difficult to disguise. There was a Franco-German row over the "stability pact" rules linked to the introduction of the EMU. Large and small countries clashed over the new voting rules in the European Union. And there was an open conflict over the Union's defense project, with France and Germany arguing for absorbing the Western European Union, and Britain together with the neutrals stone-walling the initiative. "Welcome to Brussels, Metternich," put cynically *The Economist*, and a Dutch newspaper, *De Volkskrant* talked about "intrigue, blackmail, and a clear demonstration of power-play" within the Union.[17]

The resurgence of power politics is also evident when we look at divergent European approaches to violent conflicts in the Middle East, Africa, and the Balkans. During the Gulf War President Mitterand was repeatedly blamed for omitting to tell his allies of diplomatic initiatives which undercut their own, Germany demonstrated its reluctance to give practical support to its allies, and Belgium even refused to sell Britain ammunition for the purpose of the conflict.[18] France continued its unilateral policies in the Middle East under the presidency of Jacques Chirac, sending its diplomatic envoys to the region without prior consultation with the Union and causing embarrassment for the EU's own envoys there. Italy has been accused of running a kind of private war in its former protectorate, Somalia – much like France in Rwanda. The latter situation brought France and Belgium to the edge of diplomatic crisis when a series of mutual accusations were exchanged between the media of both countries.[19] France's decision to carry out a series of nuclear tests in the South Pacific also infuriated several EU allies; (ten of them voted in favor of a November 1995 UN resolution condemning the tests).

However, the most spectacular show of disagreement was witnessed in connection with the war in the former Yugoslavia. Britain and France, both of which had a tradition of good relations with Belgrade, tried to maintain the status quo in Yugoslavia until the end of 1991, although the "misbehavior" of the Yugoslav army made such a

position untenable for the Germans and the Danes.[20] Germany subsequently decided to recognize Slovenia and Croatia unilaterally, a
move that was met with fury by most European partners. (In the
end, they all reluctantly followed the German lead. From this point,
relations between Europeans steadily deteriorated, with unilateral
policies prevailing over collective ones in most instances of European
involvement. Greece vetoed the EU recognition of Macedonia, and
imposed a unilateral blockade of this small Balkan country despite the
outrage expressed by other EU members.[21] (Some Greek politicians
went as far as to orchestrate a boycott of Dutch and Danish products in
response to open criticism of Greek behavior from Copenhagen and
The Hague.) Greece also vetoed EU investment credits to Albania
because of the so-called "Vorio Epirus question".[22] In May 1993
France and Britain used the UN Security Council to overturn decisions
taken by The Twelve only 12 days earlier, causing fury in Germany,
Italy, and The Netherlands.[23] Italy blocked the EU association agreement with Slovenia because of its own petty quarrel with the country
(Summer 1994).[24] The early British resistance to the Franco-German
initiative for WEU interposition of force in Croatia (Summer 1991)
practically precluded the use of a peace-enforcing military operation in
later stages of the Yugoslav conflict. Great Britain eventually sent its
troops to the Balkans together with France and other EU countries.
Germany, however, resisted to do so until December 1995 while maintaining an assertive political line in dealing with the Balkan conflict.[25]
Germany, France, and Great Britain had also few qualms about abandoning their EU allies when signing the US-led "Joint Action Plan,"
and later joining the so-called "Contact Group," which acted as a kind
of great powers directorate, ignoring consultation with the EU as such.
All in all, European involvement in the former Yugoslavia has shown a
degree of disunity and partisan squabbling unknown for many years.

   The conclusion of this section is therefore obvious: power politics is
back in play. What is less obvious, however, is the precise nature of
power politics as practiced at present. Is it about hegemony or disengagement? Do Europeans entertain imperial ambitions or are they
developing an introverted egoism? Is use of force and territorial
acquisition a part of the current power game? Or should we rather
expect more of the same: fruitless talking, indecision, and rhetorical
threats? Are we heading into yet another deadly European gamble or
merely a bad-tempered family quarrel, that does not call into question
the family's existence? If history indeed is about to repeat itself, will it
resemble an apocalypse or a farce?

A DIFFERENT READING OF RECENT HISTORY

There are good reasons for questioning the "back to the future" argument. First of all, the gloomy picture painted by this argument is probably inaccurate: the United States has not disappeared from Europe altogether, Germany is not aspiring to hegemony, and Russia has replaced the Soviet Union as a source of fear along with its "unifying" effect on the European Union. Although the bi-polar division of Europe is no longer in existence, the pursuit of continental domination through changing alliances, bullying and ganging-up has not (yet) re-emerged.

Secondly, if power politics is about pursuing national interests, what do these interests consist of at present? Territorial geopolitics could well make a great deal of sense in the history of Europe, but is this still the case? Can bullying and conspiring really enhance the power of any post-industrial European state?

Thirdly, one should ask whether power politics based on territorial conquest and aggressive alliances are still a viable military option for EU members. What are the "pacifying" characteristics of nuclear weapons? How do democracy, demography, ecology, mass media, and other factors constrain the use of force on the continent?

Fourthly, the impact of the existing institutional infrastructure on the conduct of power politics should be reviewed. Are institutions such as the EU, NATO, WEU, UN, and OSCE only about disguising the power politics of today or about modifying them? Do the present-day institutional arrangements work any better than their historical predecessors such as the Concert of Europe?

The argument here is about the interpretation of the existing evidence. It is one thing to endorse a set of assumptions about the nature of power politics in Europe, and another to prove that the power politics of today is following in the footsteps of history, towards "*la geopolitique de grand 'papa'*," as François Heisbourg put it.[26] After all, not all, if any, European squabbles necessarily lead to military conflict, not all national ambitions are about imposing regional domination, and not all interstate coalitions are about dividing Europe into new spheres of influence. Some pacifying factors from the Cold War era may be missing, but others are still in place. The relationship between European states turned sour and chaotic over the last few years, but this does not necessarily vindicate arguments based on historical analogy. Nor does it justify preoccupation with the military aspects of power politics at present.

Let us start with the most frightening factor: Germany. At first sight everything seems to confirm Germany's comeback to hegemony: infamous history, accumulated power, and domestic politics. Yet I would suggest that history is one of the principal reasons for believing that there are no hegemonic aspirations in present-day Germany. The war trauma produced a society with a pacifist rather than imperialistic outlook and there is no evidence to support the claim that the young generation of Germans will bring about any change.[27] True, neo-fascist violence has shaken Germany's image in the world. However, careful studies point to the fact that violence against immigrants has not been endorsed by any large sectors of the German public and that, in comparison to other European neighbors, the Germans are not markedly more xenophobic, racist, or fascist.[28] Nor is it possible to claim that German unification awakens the ghosts of history, (those of 1870–71, in particular). After all, the unification was achieved "by telephone and checkbook rather than blood and iron," to use Timothy Garton Ash's words.[29] The unification was largely spontaneous and was not manipulated by either German government following a hegemonic script. In fact, Chancellor Kohl's "10 points program," describing steps towards possible unification after the fall of the Berlin Wall, envisaged two German states for some time to come.

Unification created the most powerful European country, but a country where constitutional patriotism clearly prevails over nationalist chauvinism, and where there is an overall commitment to denuclearization, free trade and multilateralism in international affairs. "Germany is a postmodern nation", said Hans-Peter Schwartz, "that has been purged of the most virulent characteristics of nineteenth and early twentieth-century nationalism: cultivation of historical myths and old hatreds, folk ideology, a tribal mentality, and religious intolerance."[30]

No doubt, Germany has begun to rediscover the notion of national interest, a factor which will lead to a greater assertiveness within Europe before long.[31] It is also obvious that German politicians are not immune to a certain clumsiness, which may at times appear threatening to weaker European partners. Yet there are no grounds for over-reaction to German power simply on principle. As Samuel Huntington once observed: "States and other actors who are powerful can, and do, do evil. But power is also the prerequisite for doing good and promoting collective goods. Almost nothing beneficial in the world happens except by the exercise of power."[32] The valuable aid given by

Germany to Central and Eastern Europe illustrates this point very well. But here we see the hypocrisy of some European commentators who, on the one hand, expect Germany to pay for stabilizing reforms in Eastern Europe, and on the other, accuse Germany of trying to buy-up (read: dominate) Eastern Europe.

Moreover, it is far from certain that Germany is actually so powerful. First of all, Germany is a one-dimensional "soft" power, as it recently reaffirmed its commitment not to acquire atomic, biological, or chemical weapons. The French may fear that the "balance of the Mark and the Bomb" is sliding to the advantage of the former, but the fact remains that for the first time in modern history France has no need to fear German invasion.[33] Even taking the soft power situation, German predominance is not evident. European markets cannot be separated from world markets, and in global terms the relative economic power of Germany is not very impressive.[34] Finally, unification might have enhanced Germany's power in statistical terms, but it is less clear that it likewise enhanced its political and social cohesion – let alone the overall morale of the nation. This is not to suggest that Germany has grown in size but has shrunk in spirit, but to emphasize the limits of Germany's ability to act. In fact, Germany is constantly being accused of being too strong and too weak simultaneously, as for example, the EMS crisis clearly showed.[35]

To summarize, in a Europe of rising nationalism and chaos Germany might prove to be a rather benign European federalist, but the evidence for a return of Germany's hegemonic aspirations is simply not there. The internal European balance of power has indeed shifted in Germany's favor, but this does not imply that Germany is now in a position to manipulate France and other EU members. Besides, it is the global, rather than merely regional, balance of power that will shape the future of the old continent.

This brings us to the alleged abandonment of Europe by the United States. Three factors are often quoted to illustrate this point: the drastic reduction in the US military presence in Europe (from 325,000 to 100,000 soldiers), the competitive pattern of relations between the US and the EU in the field of trade (here, the GATT and WTO squabbles, in particular), and the United States's initial reluctance to engage fully in the Balkan war. Europe is no longer Washington's prime international concern, it is argued. Mounting domestic pressures do not justify any extensive American commitment to Europe. And increasingly, the economic, diplomatic, and even security interests of Europe and the United States are diverging.

Although these arguments are largely correct, and the examples given are true, they hardly prove that America is willing to abandon Europe. Instead, they indicate a readjustment in US policy towards Europe as a result of the recent changes taking place on the continent. The collapse of the Soviet Union should necessitate even fewer American troops in Europe than the current 100,000. With the creation of a single European market, Washington was confronted with a new economic competitor, hence the rush of trade disputes and diplomatic arguments. However, trade disputes do not necessarily lead to a breakdown of long-standing security agreements, as the history of Japanese–American relations demonstrates.

Nor does the war in Yugoslavia suggest US disengagement from Europe. True, the United States decided to deploy ground forces in the Balkans as late as 1995. However, in the early stages of the war Europeans preferred to deal with the Balkans on their own. "We do not interfere in American affairs. We hope they will have enough respect not to interfere in ours" declared the President of the European Commission, Jacques Delors.[36] Later, when American involvement was eventually welcomed, it proved impossible for *all* involved outsiders to agree on a single workable solution to the on-going war, and it would be unfair to blame Washington alone for this deplorable state of affairs. One should also comprehend that the interest shown by the US in Yugoslavia is essentially different in nature from that shown by (Western) Europe as a whole. One cannot but agree with Michael E. Brown that "The United States has two main security interests in Europe: preventing a hegemonic power from establishing effective control over most of the continent, and keeping the great powers in Europe from going to war with each other. Everything else is secondary."[37] In other words, the US policy towards Yugoslavia does not attest to a US policy of disengagement from Europe; rather a policy of selective engagement.

This will not satisfy those Europeans who would like to see a total and unconditional US commitment to security within Europe. Some may even convincingly argue that Washington wants few commitments, but a great deal of influence and prestige on the continent. But when in 1994 President Clinton stressed "the core of our security remains in Europe," he meant it.[38]

The case of Russia is more complicated, not only because the situation there is confused and the future uncertain, but because the pacifying effect of the former Soviet (and by extension the future Russian) threat is not that obvious. While the Soviet threat did indeed enhance transatlantic solidarity, it probably undermined Western European solidarity as it was obvious that a purely Western European defense system would be inadequate to cope with the Soviets.[39] Since Russia is clearly a lesser threat than the Soviet Union, a genuine Western European system may finally get off the ground: bad news for those predicting hegemonic strife in Europe. However, were Russia for one reason or another to turn out to be an equal or even greater threat than the Soviet Union, the NATO stabilizing framework would presumably remain.

The collapse of Soviet rule in Central and Eastern Europe created a power vacuum that could, in principle, become an object of competition among Western European nations. So far, however, there is little to suggest that any of them, even Germany, is willing to jump in and exploit the historic opportunity created by the Soviet withdrawal. The problem of Central and Eastern Europe is that it is largely being left on its own with its many problems and internal conflicts. Western European powers are turning their backs on the region rather than rushing to dominate it. Consider the passive behavior of Western Europe in Yugoslavia, the limited West European economic investment in Central and Eastern Europe and the initial hesitation to develop any meaningful defense links between East and West European establishments. True, German involvement in Central and Eastern Europe is much greater than that of any other EU member, but this says more about the indifference of individual EU members towards the region than about alleged German hegemonic aspirations there. Immediately after the changes of 1989 some Central and Eastern European governments feared the resurgence of "neo-colonialist features" in German policy towards Eastern Europe.[40] Since then, however, they have all come to welcome an increase in German and other Western European involvement in their region.

Finally, there is concern that once again we will witness a Russian-German *rapprochement* dividing Europe into two hegemonic spheres of influence: the Yalta system will be replaced by the Rapallo system.[41] As Jean-Pierre Chevènement put it in 1990:

The balance of forces between these two powers, which act expansionistically towards each other when their individual strength is too divergent, may in the next stage lead to a sort of accord...There is an ancient understanding between the [German and Russian] peoples that has taken on various forms, from Catherine II to Bismarck. In our century there have been new examples of it: everyone will recall Rapallo or the Hitler-Stalin pact.[42]

In a way, such fears were justified when Chancellor Kohl met with President Gorbachev to negotiate the withdrawal of Soviet troops from East Germany, along with the terms of German unification. These negotiations have indeed manifested a great deal of cooperation and understanding between the two countries, but the result of this understanding was not a new Rapallo but a green light for the united Germany to remain a member of the EU and NATO. Now that all Russian troops have departed from German soil Russia is left with little leverage to force Germany into following the path of Rapallo, even if it wanted to.

Of course, there will always be politicians searching for a Russian–German conspiracy behind all new events. For instance, in 1996 two prominent British euroskeptics characterized Chancellor Kohl's ambition for a federal European Union as a "desire to create a federally integrated hard core of states as the Western pillar of a German–Russian condominium to govern the entire continent."[43] But such statements tell more about the peculiar nature of the current political discourse in some states than about the real course of events in Europe. They tell us more about the identity crisis evolving in some European states than about the real substance of Russian–German relations.[44]

Russia will remain a highly unpredictable, if not destabilizing, factor in European politics, but its ability to draw EU members into a hegemonic power game is rather limited. To claim that Stalin or Brezhnev were Europe's great "pacifiers" is to simplify the situation enormously. The Soviet threat indeed resulted in a gigantic American military presence on the continent. However, the disappearance of the Soviet threat allowed for a rescaling of the US presence without breaking the transatlantic security partnership. The Russian threat is less than the Soviet one, but it is and will probably stay sufficient to keep Europeans on guard.

In conclusion, the "back to the future" scenario is based on a misreading of recent history and a misinterpretation of current developments. The many quarrels and divisions that Europe is undergoing at present are not about hegemony. They are about petty parochialism and many other factors which will be discussed later on these pages. In principle, there is no reason to assume that a hegemonic power struggle will somehow re-emerge. But how do we know this for certain?

What makes us think that the struggle for territorial domination and military supremacy will not return? And why do Germany, France, or Spain act in the way they do rather than follow the *realpolitik* script? This brings us to the role of nuclear weapons and policy goals in guiding the behavior of modern European states.

POWER POLITICS' NEW STYLE

There is one simple reason why major European countries do not act in the same way as the great powers of the past: they have no interest in doing so. Modern states of Western Europe have come to realize that their power and well-being is affected more by the state of their economy and "human capital" than by territorial conquest, international ganging-up, and other forms of military adventurism. The grand failure of the Soviet Union, having practiced old-style hegemonic politics, but having neglected economic efficiency and personal creativity, leaves little doubt as to the right choice for a modern country. A system of open trade, together with technological progress, has offered states new ways of changing their status: through economic growth and intellectual vitality rather than through military conquest. Why should Germany embrace militarism and hegemonic expansion if its policy of economic growth and diplomatic multilateralism has elevated it to its highest ever status within Europe?

Old-style power politics was guided by three basic assumptions: (1) territorial geopolitics is of prime importance, (2) the use of force is a viable and visible option, and (3) states are autonomous entities following their respective national interests. All three assumptions are now irrelevant or obsolete.

In the past, territorial gains seemed particularly attractive. Territory used to be a crucial economic asset, especially for self-sufficient agrarian states and industrial states heavily dependent on natural resources. It has also been valued for barriers such as mountains, rivers, and marshes which act as natural defenses. However, with the increased range and accuracy of modern weapons the defensive value of territory has become less important, if not obsolete. Nor is territory any longer an economic asset for the modern, post-industrial states of Europe.[45] Technological know-how together with the skills and motivation of the workforce are today the most crucial assets, none of which are obtainable by territorial gains, especially those involving conquest by force. As Richard Rosecrance rightly argued:

Free movement of capital and goods, substantial international and domestic investment, and high levels of technical education have been the recipe for success in the industrialized world of the late twentieth century. Those who depended on others did better than those who depended only on themselves... The most advanced nations shifted their efforts from controlling territory to augmenting their share of world trade... Countries are downsizing – in function if not in geographical form... Imperial Great Britain may have been the model for the nineteenth century, but Hong Kong will be the model for the 21st... These findings are a dramatic reversal of past theories of power in international politics.[46]

Military power is still required for defensive purposes, but the wisdom of acquiring military power for any imperial or hegemonic purposes is now being questioned. Here the economic argument comes to the fore once more: military power is regarded not as a means to economic well-being, but as an alternative to it.[47] Nor is military power of much use in the war of ideas, as the fall of the Soviet military superstate, with its grandiose ideological pretensions, has shown. The use of military power to intimidate, blackmail, and bargain from a position of strength is now regarded as morally wrong, at least among Western European countries. And the use of military power in situations that are not threatening in the most fundamental sense is now constrained by powerful democratic and demographical factors that exist in all post-industrial modern European states. In other words, the public of Western Europe is currently unwilling to tolerate the smallest human casualties for the sake of somewhat abstract goals such as the balance of power or regional domination. If soldiers' lives can be placed at risk only in extreme situations then one can surely forget about hegemonic power games which, as we know from history, require the discretion to use force with equanimity.[48]

On top of that come strategic arguments related to nuclear weapons.[49] First of all, nuclear weapons make large conventional forces irrelevant, and enable states to concentrate attention on their economy rather than on their military. Secondly, nuclear weapons bend strategic forces to one end: deterring attacks on a country's vital interests. Nuclear weapons are not well suited as an instrument of territorial geopolitics, for instance. Thirdly, nuclear weapons have made the price of war among major European states prohibitive: the balance of power has been transformed into a balance of terror. This also applies to Europe's periphery: the great powers of today are not inclined to dabble in peripheral wars with the readiness of the great powers in the pre-nuclear era because the risk of escalation is too high. Fourthly, nuclear weapons change the nature of old-style alliance politics, since nuclear states do not need each other's help to provide an effective deterrent.

Old-style hegemonic power politics was traditionally the domain of great powers: large, autonomous, independent states of Europe ruled by small elites seeking to gain advantage through manipulating the balance of power and striking secret alliances. These elites had absolute discretion and indeed little difficulty in defining their national interests, based as they were on the security, prestige, and territoriality of their respective states. At first sight, politics in today's Europe still looks the same: nation states remain the predominant international actors. Foreign and security policies are still more exclusively the domain of small governmental elites than economic policies, for instance, and these elites are still more than happy to manipulate in the name of their respective national interests. This simple comparison is, however, misleading. With the passage of time, various sub-national and transnational pressures have gradually intensified, changing the nature of European states, the meaning of national interests, and the process of foreign policy making. On the one hand, governmental elites have lost full control of their foreign policies because of increasing mobility of people, money, military equipment, and intelligence information, and on the other, because of domestic democratic pressures.[50] The demands of democratic politics forces the elites to open up the foreign policy-making process, to increase the number of foreign policy goals, and, at the same time, to reduce the number of foreign policy instruments suitable for meeting these goals. (Consider, for instance, the fore-mentioned public reluctance to use military force as an instrument of foreign policy.) The highly interdependent external environment, on the other hand, limits the ability of the elites to externalize domestic pressures through unilateral national actions. Consequently, the art of conducting foreign and security policy becomes more complex, and takes on a different nature. In short, Metternich and Bismarck would find it impossible to operate in the very complex political environment of today.

States as a whole are also affected by all these cross-cutting pressures from within and without, from below and above. In order to satisfy a wide range of domestic and international expectations they are constantly forced to compromise between sovereignty and integration, national interests and multilateral arrangements. Although many interests and values can still be defined in national terms, they are at the same time larger and smaller, global as well as municipal, cosmopolitan as well as provincial. As a result, the nation state has shifted from its traditional position of supremacy to the intermediate position necessitated by the constraints and demands of both sub-national and international interests.[51] The power game which used to be dominated by a competition between nation states is now taking place on at least three levels: transnational, national, and on a local community level.

The pressure of practical considerations has also intensified, confusing the notion of national interest even further. There is tension between the pursuit of security and military power (high-politics) and the pursuit of welfare and affluence (low-politics). There is tension between cultural identity and economic interpenetration, between disarmament and employment security, between a free market of people and goods and immigration policies. All these problems are beyond the control of national governments and can hardly be managed by old style manipulation à la Bismarck and Metternich.

Moreover, over the last few decades Europeans have developed closely-knit institutional networks to cope with the pressures created by interdependence. Some of these institutions were specifically designed to be a constraint upon old-style power politics if not to get away from power politics altogether. It is easy to show that the latter effort has largely failed: European powers are still attempting to manipulate the workings of international institutions. But the style and substance of this manipulation has clearly changed. In other words, the institutionalization of hegemonic politics à la Concert of Europe is no longer taking place, despite all structural similarities.[52] This is partly because the present-day European institutions rely heavily on formal procedures and an extensive organizational framework for conflict resolution rather than merely on the assumed compatibility of interests among states. As I will show in another chapter, present-day institutions are designed to increase the transparency and predictability of states' behavior and they offer incentives to concentrate on absolute (collective) gains rather than merely on relative (national) ones. These reassuring effects prevent the formation of balancing coalitions and inject an element of order into an otherwise chaotic international environment.[53]

The changes mentioned above do not necessarily imply an end of power politics; they merely signal the death of old-style power politics.[54] War has not become obsolete, but modern Western European countries have few incentives to go to war at present. Military power is still of crucial importance, but with nuclear deterrents in place, competition for power takes place chiefly in the field of economics. Nation states still play a major role in Europe, but they look and act differently from Wilhelm's Germany or the France of Napoleon. Given the absence of supranational authority Hobbesian anarchy still prevails; but a dense network of institutional cooperation constrains the "go-it-alone" policy of "self-help." States still seek a stabilizing balance of power, but are unwilling to fill all the power vacuums that are arising at Europe's periphery, especially if this involves "blood, sweat, and tears."

As Pierre Hassner recently observed:

> It is a fact that the two classic mechanisms linking local conflicts and external powers – escalation and intervention – have become much more difficult to use. The two mechanisms which have generalized conflict – the interplay of diplomatic-military alliances before 1914 and the ideological confrontation of the interwar period and during the Cold War – are absent...Increasingly, international relations are made up of the combination of at least three types of processes: the *interaction* of strategies (in particular diplomatic and military), the *interdependence* of interests (in particular economic) and the *interpenetration* of societies (in particular from a demographic and cultural point of view).[55]

However, states have only limited control over the second and third types of processes; foreign policy establishments are not well suited for coping with economic, cultural, and demographic problems; and the traditional methods of power politics, such as the use of force and secret diplomacy, will be of little help in addressing the interdependence of economic interests and interpenetration of societies.

Hassner goes further and asserts that the third type of international process – interpenetration of societies – is assuming an increasing importance in comparison with the classic categories and that it rebounds on them by giving rise to new economic turmoil and new risks of violence. Given the fact that this third societal process is more diffuse and difficult to control, where would a new Bismarck or Metternich begin?[56]

HEGEMONIC ATAVISM

Old-style power politics makes little sense in the present climate and there is considerable evidence to suggest that Europeans now understand and play by a new set of rules. However, there are also examples of hegemonic atavism that need to be explained. Time and again we are confronted with cases of national bullying which fuel prejudice about the imperial aspirations of some states. Why is this the case? Why do some states still choose to act like great powers of the past in spite of the fact that this is damaging for both Europe and for the states concerned?

Four reasons seem to present themselves. First, old-style hegemonic politics is often used to legitimize an unpopular government. In several European states, especially larger ones, an imperial image and a tough nationalist stance go down very well with certain sectors of the public. French and British politicians are particularly good at overstating the primacy of their national interests in Europe and at proclaiming a right to European leadership, even though their perspectives on the European leadership usually differ.

Secondly, old-style power politics is still frequently practiced outside Europe; some European countries are clearly implicated in this respect in Africa, Middle East, and Latin America. Consider, for instance, the French, Portuguese, and Belgian military involvement in Africa, or the British response to the invasion of the Falklands.[57] Moreover, manipulation by a "concert" of great powers is a common way of dealing with Third World conflicts, be it via the UN Security Council, the G-7 countries, or bilateral or trilateral national arrangements. However, this practice of acting with a unilateral iron fist outside Europe suggests that the same pattern may also be at play within Europe itself.

Thirdly, in Europe itself, some countries are more modern than others in the sense that they cherish economic welfare more than national myths, and cultivate cosmopolitan rather than tribal values. As a consequence, "less" modern countries, such as Greece, manifest a more traditional attitude to power politics than "ultra" modern countries such as The Netherlands and Denmark. This is not to ignore the complexity of Greece's geopolitical situation, but to indicate a difference in political culture and strategic priorities.

Fourthly, a peculiar legacy of the Cold War has allowed some states to pursue a policy of playing off and ganging-up with impunity. In fact, many French people would argue that their policy of allying Germany to France and Europe, of building up a "third" European force with Moscow, and of resisting American and even British influence on the continent has been quite advantageous for France. President Mitterand's mega-diplomacy of 1989–92 suggests an effort to carry these policies through to the post-Cold War era. (In a similar fashion, Britain's special relationship with Washington and Germany's with Moscow – albeit very different – allowed for some independent balancing arrangements to be made over the heads of other Europeans.)

Do these reasons for continued hegemonic atavism give grounds for concern? As far as the common foreign and security policy is concerned, the answer is "yes." The Greek bullying policy in the Balkans has undermined EU efforts to tame nationalistic fever and territorial claims in the region. The self-images of France and Britain, seeing themselves as major powers with a global mission, have hampered common European efforts in the Third World. And their habit of deriding other Europeans for the sake of domestic electoral campaigns has made it difficult to strike collective deals in Brussels even when most needed. But atavism remains what it is: a resemblance to a remote hegemonic ancestor, not a pattern dominating present-day politics. The end of the Cold War made Mitterand's policy à la Metternich look awkward and inadequate. In 1994 the French government openly distanced itself from the traditional "concert of great powers" politics of Mitterand. France is to conduct its security policy "no longer by playing one state against another, but in reuniting, for the first time in the tormented history of the old continent, a *mutualization of power*, in service of the defense of Europe and a security common to the states engaged in its construction."[58]

Similarly there is little trace of the old "sinister" conspiracy between the United States and Great Britain which used to take place behind Europe's back. Now, Washington converses with several European power centers simultaneously, including Bonn, Paris, and Brussels.

Former colonial countries will continue to interfere in Third World politics, but the persistence of bad imperial habits in Africa does not imply a resurgence of hegemonic habits in Europe. France and Great Britain, in particular, will hang on to their image of being great powers with the same knock-for-knock diplomacy practiced in Europe and elsewhere. But German unification has only confirmed what was already becoming obvious when the two countries failed to regain control of the Suez Canal in 1956: Britain and France are unable to play the hegemonic politics of days gone by; their occasional assertiveness is indicative of a defensive rather than an offensive reflex.

Greece, and possibly other less modern EU members, will indulge in parochial bullying tactics with their neighbors; but if things were to get out of hand, the EU has enough leverage to constrain this sort of misbehavior.

In short, hegemonic atavism is a factor hampering the creation of a common foreign and security policy, but hegemonic atavism is not the same as hegemonic politics *per se*.

CONCLUSIONS

In this chapter I have looked for evidence of hegemonic politics in post-Cold War Europe, but have only found traces of hegemonic atavism. I have examined the possible existence of a "back to the future" scenario, but have concluded that the "forward to the future" scenario is more likely. The demise of bi-polar stability is acknowledged, but several pacifying factors are still at work at present. The growing network of mutual interdependence between EU members, the decreasing salience of territorial issues, the presence of multi-sectoral institutional arrangements and the restraining effect of nuclear weapons suggest that Metternich or Bismarck would be unable to orchestrate a comeback on the post-Cold War European stage.[59]

Of course, we can know none of these things for certain, especially if we are trying to consider the distant future. But the absence of hegemonic politics at present makes it difficult to argue that old-style power politics will somehow re-emerge in the future to fit into a dogmatic theoretical framework. Two events may change this, however: a dramatic shift to xenophobic populism in one of the major European states or total anarchy on the most sensitive EU borders – North Africa, Central Europe, and the Baltic states. I will later examine the prospects of such developments occurring. For now, it is safe to assume that none of these dramatic developments is likely in the next couple of years.

Although the "back to the future" scenario is unlikely, I have already established the existence of a group of factors that are hampering the creation and smooth functioning of the Union's common foreign and security policy: hegemonic atavism based on pride and global pretensions, bad habits from the Cold War years, pre-modern values and interests, and parochial opportunism. This hegemonic atavism has much in common with the question of identity and legitimacy which is discussed in this book somewhat later. States indulge in hegemonic politics not because it serves their external interests, but because it helps them to maintain the old image of pride and glory, so dear to their respective electorates. Hegemonic politics may well be an obstacle to stability, modernity, and development, but it gives some people a peculiar sense of security and confidence because it represents a familiar pattern of reasoning and behavior. Hegemonic politics may well be about parochial arrogance, petty jealousies, and inferiority complexes, but it is closed to popular self-images, traditional if not old-fashioned hierarchy of values, and a familiar rhetoric of self-importance. The identity requirement should be taken seriously, but it is doubtful whether cultivating national myths and parochial arrogance is the best way of addressing the identity issue. It is also doubtful whether the price of indulging in hegemonic politics is worth paying. This chapter shows that hegemonic atavism can hardly bring about respect, wealth, or influence to any European country, but it can well retard their development and damage the existing framework of international cooperation.

This chapter also suggests another crucial conclusion. If hegemonic politics makes little sense at present, there is no reason to prepare the Union for a traditional super-power status. One of the often mentioned rationales for the existence and further development of the Union is a need to compete in an ancient-type power struggle among the giants of today. If European nations are not to be crushed by mighty powers such as Russia, China, Japan, and the United States, they have to unite and aggregate strength under the banner of the European Union. The Union needs, the argument goes, to become a full-fledged superpower with not only economic, but also military might: a civilian power can hardly cope with an uncivilized world. As Giovanni Jannuzzi put it in 1992:

> While the world has become increasingly multipolar, with the emergence of a number of new and independent centers of power, the growing size and complexity of the problems to be faced allow only a limited number of "giants" to act effectively in foreign politics, at least on a world scale. Under such conditions, the European Community must emerge – in the transition from a bipolar to a multipolar world – as an actual superpower... If the EC succeeds in the coming years in acquiring a center for political decision-making and in expanding its competence to security, then it will be a full superpower, albeit of a specific and somewhat anomalous nature.[60]

However, in this chapter I have argued that this opinion is based on a false reading of today's power politics. None of the "giant" states are doing exceptionally well at present, rather the states with virtually nothing – limited territory, contained population figures, no natural resources and no military leverage – are advancing. Most successful states are competing by "down-sizing" and not by "up-sizing." They do not aspire to become giants in terms of size and manufacturing strength, but in terms of marketing, design, and financing. Nor do they aspire to geopolitical hegemony and military preponderance. In fact, significant efforts are made to reduce military expenditure and cut down security commitments. It is therefore difficult to see why the Union should aspire to a type of power that is of little utility in present-day competition. In today's complex international environment the Union can best enhance its competitive position by investing in its people rather than in constructing an old-fashioned type of empire with ever growing geographic size, manufacturing strength and military reach. Likewise the Union would be well advised to open its borders to goods, services and people from other competitors rather than to consolidate its borders, embark on protectionist policies and clash head-on with other powers, be it in economic or military terms. If it is argued that old style power politics does not serve the current interests of such countries as France, Germany, Greece and Great Britain, it must also be concluded that it is wrong for the European Union. The utility of the civilian power concept should therefore be rehabilitated. I will try to do this in the conclusion of this book.

NOTES

1. Martin Wight, *Power Politics* (Harmondsworth: Penguin, 1986), second edition, p. 23.
2. This particular school of thought is called realism. For a detailed description of the traditional realist perspective see Hans J. Morgenthau, *Politics Among Nations. The Struggle for Power and Peace* (New York: Alfred A. Knopf, 1960), p. 630. A modern version of realism is presented in Robert O. Keohane, ed., *Neorealism and Its Critics* (New York: Columbia University Press, 1986).
3. This view was already predominant in Europe in the 18th century. See Adam Watson, "European International Society and Its Expansion", in Hedley Bull and Adam Watson, eds., *The Expansion of International Society* (Oxford: Clarendon Press, 1992), p. 24.
4. Hans J. Morgenthau, *Politics Among Nations*, op. cit., pp. 327, 501 and 512.
5. John J. Mearsheimer, "Back to the Future. Instability in Europe After the Cold War", *International Security*, Vol. 15, No. 1 (Summer 1990), pp. 52 and 55.

6. See Jack Snyder, "Averting Anarchy in the New Europe", *International Security*, Vol. 14, No. 4 (Spring 1990), p. 9.

7. Josef Joffe, "The New Europe: Yesterday's Ghosts", *Foreign Affairs*, Vol. 72, No. 1 – "America and the World" – (1993), p. 29.

8. Recently, the run-up to the European economic and monetary union also has been seen as the re-emergence of hegemonic politics. See especially Martin Feldstein, "EMU and International Conflict" *Foreign Affairs*, Vol. 76, No. 6 (November / December 1997), pp. 60–73.

9. Timothy Garton Ash, *In Europe's Name – Germany and the Divided Continent* (London: Vintage, 1994), pp. 344–57. See also Volker Gransow and Konrad H. Jarausch, *Die Deutsche Vereinigung. Dokumente zu Burgerbewegung, Annaherung und Beitritt* (Cologne: Wissenschaft und Politik, 1991).

10. See, e.g., Paul Fabra, "Mitterand-Metternich", *Le Monde*, June 3, 1991.

11. Margaret Thatcher, *The Downing Street Years* (London: Harper Collins, 1993), p. 791.

12. See Marta Dassu, "The Future of Europe: The View from Rome", *International Affairs*, Vol. 66, No. 2 (April 1990), p. 305. Also M.C. Brands, "Een tijd vol misvattingen: de vereniging van Duitsland", *Internationale Spectator*, Vol. 44, No. 5 (May 1990), pp. 268–72.

13. See Gorbachev's statement at the joint press conference on July 16, 1990, quoted in Timothy Garton Ash, *In Europe's Name*, op.cit., p. 352.

14. As Ruud Lubbers put it: "The implicit veto of Kohl [against Lubbers] led to the *explicit* veto of Major [against Dehaene]." See Ruud Lubbers' interview with Derk Jan Eppink, in *NRC Handelsblad*, July 1, 1994.

15. See Victor Smart and Rory Warson, "A Chorus of Disapproval", *The European*, September 9–15, 1994.

16. Umberto Bossi quoted in Donald MacIntyre and Steve Crawshaw, "Major to Reject Franco-German Vision of Europe", *The Independent*, September 6, 1994.

17. The British comment was made in the context of the Intergovernmental Conference in the run up to the Treaty of Amsterdam and focused specifically on the CFSP provisions. See *The Economist*, September 14, 1996, p. 28. The Dutch comment compared the smooth decision-making process under the US leadership in NATO, and the conflict-ridden decision-making process within the EU. See Jos Klassen, "NAVO bedriegt met besluit vooral zichzelf," *de Volkskrant*, July 9, 1997.

18. See Trevor C. Salmon, "Testing Times for European Political Co-operation: The Gulf and Yugoslavia, 1990–1992", *International Affairs*, Vol. 68, No. 2 (April 1992), pp. 233–53.

19. See Jean-Paul Marthoz, "A Marriage of Unequal Partners Hits the Rocks", *The European*, July 15–21, 1994.

20. See an interview with Hans-Dietrich Genscher in *Der Spiegel*, July 5, 1991.

21. See Spyros Economides, "Riding the Tiger of Nationalism: The Question of Macedonia", *The Oxford International Review*, Vol. IV, No. 2 (Spring 1993), pp. 27–9.

22. See James Pettifer, "Albania, Greece and the Vorio Epirus Question", *The World Today*, Vol. 50, No. 8–9 (August–September 1994), pp. 147–9.

The conflict concerns the Greek minority in Southern Albania which produced clashes between Greek irredentists and Albanian nationalists throughout the 1990s, and subsequent governmental reprisals by Athens and Tirana.

23. On May 10, 1993 EC foreign ministers agreed to continue to support the Vance-Owen Plan. However, after the Bosnian Serbs had rejected the Plan, the two permanent European members of the UN Security Council, plus Spain as a regular member, agreed in Washington with the USA and Russia on a new plan of action. They did so without prior consultation with other EU states. See Mathias Jopp, "The Strategic Implications of European Integration", *Adelphi Paper* No. 290 (1994), p. 46.

24. Officially the argument was about financial compensation for Italians expelled from Slovenia in the aftermath of World War II. But relations between Italy and Slovenia had deteriorated by May 1991 as a result of territorial claims made by several Italian politicians from Liberal and Socialist parties. See John Zametica, "The Yugoslav Conflict", *Adelphi Paper* No. 270 (1992), p. 48.

25. On December 4, 1995 the German Parliament voted to send 4,000 troops to Bosnia. In October 1996 it was reported that Germany and France had made advanced preparations for a joint peacekeeping force in Bosnia once the mandate of the existing NATO-led peace force expired. (See "Bonn Moves Ahead With Paris on New Bosnia Force", *International Herald Tribune*, October 18, 1996, p. 5.) However, in the early stage of the conflict Germany was pushing hard for military intervention while insisting that it should not include its own military forces. Anthony Foster and William Wallace reported that at one ministerial meeting in September 1991 the German foreign minister made a passionate speech insisting that troops be sent to Yugoslavia, to which his British counterpart is reported to have replied "You mean you want to send our troops." See Anthony Foster and William Wallace, "Common Foreign and Security Policy: A New Policy or Just a New Name?", in *Policy-Making in the European Union*. Helen Wallace and William Wallace, eds. (Oxford: Oxford University Press, 1996), p. 434.

26. François Heisbourg, "The European-US Alliance: Valedictory Reflections on Continental Drift in the Post-Cold War Era", *International Affairs*, Vol. 68, No. 4 (October 1992), pp. 665–78. Also François Heisbourg, "Sécurité: l'Europe livrée à elle même" *Politique Étrangère*, Vol. 59, No. 1 (Spring 1994), pp. 247–60.

27. See the results of opinion polls published in Peter R. Weilemann, *Zwischen Nationalem Interesse und Europäischem Engagement – Innenpolitische Akseptanz, Institutionelle Reform und die Europapolitischen Vorstellungen der Deutschen* (Bonn: Konrad Adenauer Stiftung, October 1993). Also Philip Everts, "Gaat Duitsland zijn eigen weg?", *Transaktie*, Vol. 23, No. 2 (1994), pp. 172–95.

28. See Manfred Kuechler, "Germans and 'Others': Racism, Xenophobia, or 'Legitimate Conservatism'?", *German Politics*, Vol. 3, No. 1 (April 1994), pp. 47–74.

29. Timothy Garton Ash, "Germany's Choice", *Foreign Affairs*, Vol. 73, No. 4 (July–August 1994), p. 65.

30. Hans-Peter Schwarz, "Germany's National and European Interests", *Daedalus*, Vol. 123, No. 2 (Spring 1994), p. 103.
31. See Jürgen Nötzold and Reinhard Rummel, "Europäische Interaktionen und deutsche Interessen," in *Sicherheitspolitik Deutschlands: Neue Konstellationen, Risiken, Instrumente*, (Baden-Baden: Nomos Verlagsgesellschaft, 1992), pp. 797–812. See also Wolfgang F. Schlör, "German Security Policy", *Adelphi Paper* No. 277 (1993), pp. 23–31.
32. Samuel P. Huntington, "Why International Primacy Matters", *International Security*, Vol. 17, No. 4 (Spring 1993), p. 70.
33. See Dominique Moïsi, "Die Mark und die Bombe", *Die Zeit*, December 9, 1988.
34. See Richard K. Betts, "Wealth, Power, and Instability", *International Security*, Vol. 18, No. 3 (Winter 1993/94), pp. 35–77, and Kenneth N. Waltz, "The Emerging Structure of International Politics", *International Security*, Vol. 18, No. 2 (Fall 1993), pp. 44–79.
35. See M.C. Brands, "Op Zoek Naar een Nieuw Duits Buitenlands en Veiligheidsbeleid", *Internationale Spectator*, Vol. 47, No. 4 (April 1994), p. 173.
36. Quoted in Owen Harries, "The Collapse of 'The West'", *Foreign Affairs*, Vol. 72, No. 4 (September–October 1993), p. 49.
37. Michael E. Brown, "Over Where? Defining a Sustainable US Role in Europe", paper presented at the Second Annual European Conference, "Europe and America After the Cold War", Oxford University, September 2–3, 1994 (unpublished), p. 24. According to Brown, the United States has an interest in preventing hegemonic rule in Europe because a hegemond would have control over a substantial portion of the world's economic and industrial output. Such power would constitute an existential threat to American security.
38. "Excerpts from Speech: Binding Broader Europe", *New York Times*, January 10, 1994.
39. This was well argued in Alfred E. Pijpers, *The Vicissitudes of European Political Cooperation* (Leiden: University of Leiden, 1990), p. 80.
40. For instance, in May 1990 the Czechoslovak Minister of Foreign Affairs, Jiri Dienstbier, warned that Germany might become the new regional hegemond: "[The vacuum in the East] will perhaps be filled soon economically by a strong united Germany, and in view of the glaring inequality to the disfavour of the East European countries economically, that filling could display undeniably neo-colonial features." See Jiri Dienstbier's speech at Harvard University, May 16, 1990 as quoted by Renata Fritsch-Bournazel, "German Unification: Views From Germany's Neighbours", in *German Unification in European Perspective*, Werner Heisenberg, ed. (London: Brassey's Centre for European Policy Studies, 1991), p. 80.
41. See Michel Debré, "Quand Rapallo peut remplacer Yalta", *Le Monde*, November 14, 1989. The secret Rapallo agreement was signed between Germany and the Soviet Union in 1922. According to E.H. Carr, the act of signing was more important than the formal content of the treaty. Rapallo was a symbolic, but nonetheless crucial event. It showed, first, that a defeated Germany and a weakened and besieged Soviet Union

could re-enter the heart of international politics as major forces, and secondly, that in a world of Machiavellian politics, neither widely differing social structure nor equally diverging, even conflicting, ideologies were absolute barriers to strategic alliances. See E.H. Carr, *The Bolshevik Revolution* (Harmondsworth: Penguin, 1933), Vol. 3, pp. 375ff.

42.   Jean-Pierre Chevènement's speech at the Institute des Hautes Etudes de Défense Nationale, May 21, 1990, quoted in Renata Fritsch-Bournazel, *Europe and German Unification* (New York and Oxford: Berg, 1992), p. 130. See also Jean-Pierre Chevènement, *France-Allemagne: parlons franc* (Paris: Plon, 1996).

43.   William Cash and Iain Duncan-Smith, quoted in Philip Stephens, "Britain's Bitter Blast from the Past", *Financial Times*, May 25, 1996.

44.   Philip Stephens in the above quoted article about the anti-German campaign in the British press presents the view of Giles Radice, Labor MP. According to Radice, nasty headlines and ugly cartoons about Germany's alleged hegemonic aspirations are about Britain's own identity and the uncertainty about Britain's place in the new world.

45.   As Richard H. Ullman put it: "In advanced, industrialized states, land itself is of much less economic value than what enterprising individuals might build upon it, or the education and skills – the "human capital" – that the society routinely provides to them, and which they can carry in their heads wherever they go." See Richard H. Ullman, *Securing Europe* (London: Adamantine Press, 1991), p. 27. This does not undermine Laurence Martin's statement that "none of the multiple, interlocking, space-defying relationships made possible by modern communications can serve human purposes unless they are ultimately integrated in the service of individuals and, as these individuals have to live somewhere, they look to a territory based entity to coordinate and advance their interests." See Laurence Martin, "Chatham Chouse: The Way Forward", *The World Today*, Vol. 50, No. 4 (April 1994), p. 62.

46.   Richard Rosecrance, "The Rise of the Virtual State", *Foreign Affairs*, Vol. 75, No. 4 (July–August 1996), pp. 45–61. See also Paul Krugman, *Development, Geography, and Economic Theory* (Cambridge, MA: The MIT Press, 1995), pp. 31–65.

47.   See John Garnett, "The Role of Military Power", in *Perspectives on World Politics*, Richard Little and Michael Smith, eds. (London: Routledge, 1991), second edition, p. 70.

48.   As Edward N. Luttwak put it: "Historically, there have been tacit preconditions to great power status: a readiness to use force whenever it was advantageous to do so and an acceptance of the resulting combat casualties with equanimity, as long as the number was not disproportionate... Great powers normally relied on intimidation rather than combat, but only because a willingness to use force was assumed. Moreover, they would use force undeterred by the prospect of ensuing casualties, within limits of course." See Edward N. Luttwak, "Where Are the Great Powers?", *Foreign Affairs*, Vol. 73, No. 4 (July/August 1994), p. 23.

49.   Here I draw especially on Kenneth N. Waltz, "The Emerging Structure of International Politics", *International Security*, Vol. 18, No. 2 (Fall 1993), pp. 44–79.

50. See Edward L. Morse, "The Transformation of Foreign Policies: Modernization, Interdependence and Externalization", *World Politics*, Vol. XXII, No. 3 (April 1970), pp. 371–92.
51. See Hanns W. Maull, "Europe and the Changing Global Agenda", in *The New Europe: Politics, Government and Economy since 1945*, Jonathan Story, ed. (Oxford: Blackwell, 1993), p. 146.
52. As Philip Zelikow argued: "The structures needed for a new Concert of Europe are already in place." See Philip Zelikow, "The New Concert of Europe", *Survival*, Vol. 34, No. 2 (Summer 1992), p. 13. See also Charles A. Kupchan and Clifford A. Kupchan, "Concerts, Collective Security and the Future of Europe", *International Security*, Vol. 16, No. 1 (Summer 1991), pp. 114–16, and Richard N. Rosecrance, "Trading States in a New Concert of Europe", in *America and Europe in an Era of Change*, Helga Haftendorn, ed. (Boulder, CO: Westview Press, 1993), pp. 127–45.
53. This point was strongly emphasized in Robert O. Keohane's critique of John J. Mearsheimer's "back to the future" argument. See Robert O. Keohane, "Correspondence: Back to the Future, Part II – International Theory and Post-Cold War Europe", *International Security*, Vol. 15, No. 2 (Fall 1990), pp. 192–4. Mearsheimer's views on the issue are further elaborated in John J. Mearsheimer, "The False Promise of International Institutions", *International Security*, Vol. 19, No. 3 (Winter 1994/95), pp. 5–49.
54. For a powerful illustration of how increased economic interdependence shapes the security dilemma see Beverly Crawford, "The New Security Dilemma Under International Economic Interdependence", *Millennium*, Vol. 23, No. 1 (1994), pp. 25–55. As Crawford put it: "Interdependence reduces threats because it weakens incentives for military conquest. But interdependence increases vulnerabilities and threatens to weaken the state because military resources are increasingly found in global commercial markets over which states have little control." (p. 25).
55. Pierre Hassner, "An Overview of the Problem", in "War and Peace: European Conflict Prevention", *Chaillot Paper* No. 11, Nicole Gnesotto, ed., (Paris: Institute for Security Studies, Western European Union, 1993), p. 7.
56. I paraphrase Michael Howard's question in his review of Henry Kissinger's book, *Diplomacy* (New York: Simon & Schuster, 1994). See Michael Howard, "The World According to Henry", *Foreign Affairs*, Vol. 73, No. 3 (May/June 1994), p. 140.
57. But even in these cases there are some new features which make them somewhat different from previous approaches. See, e.g., Diego A. Ruiz Palmer, "French Strategic Options in the 1990s", *Adelphi Paper* No. 260 (1991), pp. 25–7. According to Ruiz Palmer: "None of the extra-European crises in which France has been militarily involved have directly threatened the country's vital interests, but their diversity shows how France's self-image, international standing and economic well-being can be affected by events in the developing world." (p. 26).
58. François Léotard, "Preface", in *Livre blanc sur la défense* (Paris: La Documentation Française, 1994), p. 5. I am grateful to Anand Menon

for bringing to my attention Minister Léotard's statement in his preface
to the French defense White Paper.

59.   Most of these factors had already been at work for some time, and the
       end of the Cold War made their existence all the more striking. See
       especially Wolfram F. Hanriender, "Dissolving International Politics:
       Reflections on the Nation-State", *American Political Science Review*,
       Vol. 72, No. 4 (December 1978), pp. 1276–87.

60.   Giovanni Jannuzzi, "Scope and Structure of the Community's Future
       Foreign Policy" in *Toward Political Union. Planning a Common Foreign
       and Security Policy in the European Community* Reinhardt Rummel, ed.,
       (Baden-Baden: Nomos, 1992), p. 289. The emergence of a European
       superpower was projected most forcefully by Johan Galtung, *Europe in
       the Making* (New York: Crane Russak, 1989), pp. 22–36.

2 Divergent traditions and conflicting interests

Hegemonic politics are dead, major threats are gone, yet Europe seems to be heading for a prolonged period of anarchy. The countries of the European Union have divergent national interests and they cherish different visions of Europe. Why should they compromise on their images of themselves and of Europe in the absence of unifying external pressures that vanished with the fall of the Berlin Wall?

The previous chapter delivered a hopeful message that unity on the continent is not likely to be imposed through coercion: no major European country aspires to hegemonic domination at present.[1] But can unity emerge on the basis of voluntary compromises of sovereign and independent states? What are the binding factors among the EU states that would allow for a common foreign and security policy to get off the ground? Are they not vague, artificial, and abstract; poor products of bureaucratic engineering in Brussels? As William Pfaff put it:

> A European Union in economic and social matters is possible because its members have common economic and social interests, as well as a historical and cultural community. But the members of the European Union do not have a common view of their foreign policy interests, or any geopolitical conception of a world role for Europe. There is a common interest in collective security against external aggression, an interest in peace, a concern to defend the values of western political civilization. That does not add up to a foreign policy.[2]

This chapter will try to establish whether Europe indeed lacks strong binding factors that could lay a basis for common policies in the sensitive fields of diplomacy and defense. But it will also raise the question: are individual national interests in Europe so divergent as to preclude any meaningful cooperation? Is not national posturing more about symbols rather than substance of international affairs?

My conclusion will trace the evolution in policies of individual EU members, and the rather flexible nature of the proclaimed national interests even before 1989. The end of the Cold War further transformed, if not destroyed, the long-standing hierarchy of interests and

55

values behind national foreign policies. Traditional diplomatic and military concerns have become largely irrelevant and states are moving towards a new European order in haste and confusion. This creates a historic window of opportunity for skillful political engineering that would put all distinct national policies in one European line.

However, there are powerful external and internal pressures that keep European countries apart. Europe is no longer confronted with a single overwhelming Soviet threat. New threats, weaker, fragmented, and diffused as they are, would probably be unable to maintain a strong sense of shared purpose and clearly-defined common European interests. Newly created economic, political, and cultural opportunities outside EU borders are not felt equally in all corners of the continent. In short, the external environment confronts individual EU members with different sets of risks and benefits: a poor basis for common European endeavors.

Domestic pressures also stimulate disunity among EU members. Time and again individual governments feel compelled to sacrifice a common European line under the pressure of their domestic electorate. After all, national rather than European loyalties and identities prevail among the peoples on the continent. The latter problem, I will argue, represents the greatest challenge to common foreign and security policies. Citizens' willingness to transfer political loyalty to supranational units, to water down national identity, to abandon historical memories, and to compromise on unique and distinct self-images may prove decisive in shaping the balance between cooperation and conflict on the continent. As Ole Weaver put it: "Identity became a security issue, it became high politics."[3] The problem is that loyalties, images, and identities are often vague, fluid, and irrational; as such they can hardly be dealt with by legal treaties, institutional maneuvers, and military commands. It will therefore be difficult to create a workable harmony of national policies within the Union.

Before evaluating the forces behind unity and disunity among states of the European Union, this chapter will try to establish what exactly the policies of individual member states are about. First, what are individual countries' visions of themselves, and secondly what are their visions of Europe. The problem facing individual governments is how to benefit from European exchange while maintaining as much autonomy and national tradition as possible. From the perspective of the Union, the problem is how to generate a mutually beneficial pattern of cooperation in the face of competing efforts by individual states to manipulate the European system for their own benefit.[4]

NATIONAL POLICIES: CONVERGENCE VERSUS DIVERGENCE

Several years ago Walter Laqueur described the foreign policies of major states in Europe in terms of clinical psychiatry.[5] France was the case of paranoia (complaints about oppression by the United States and Germany) with occasional fits of megalomania, over-aggressive, and defiant behavior. Britain was the case of maladaptation to surroundings combined with the relatively rare symptom of claustrophilia, the wish to insulate itself. Italy was a mixture of severe symptoms of various illnesses, including regression, restlessness, semi-purposive overactivity with handwringing, and inability to sit or lie still, physical and emotional depletion, and fatigue. Laqueur did not suggest that Europe needs great shrinks rather than great statesmen to get it out of, as he put it "a melancholic picture of fragmentation, internal squabbles, and aimlessness."[6] Instead, he argued that policies of European states can seldom be seen as logical, consistent, and rational. As Joanne Wright put it in her study of France: "The key to understanding and explaining French security behavior is ambiguity... France has been a maverick actor in post-war European security since de Gaulle and in this sense France's behavior has remained consistent."[7]

The problem looks even greater when one tries to group various policies of EU countries in a systematic and orderly manner. The end result is chaos, complexity, and despair. It is virtually impossible to trace fixed patterns of coalitions and rifts between EU members. If some countries share a similar perspective on some issues, they differ on others. Consider, for instance, the very different nature of experiences as far as war and foreign occupation are concerned. Or try to explain why Denmark (together with France, Italy, and Greece) wanted to send troops to Albania in 1997, while Sweden (together with Britain and Germany) was opposed to it.[8]

Of course, some patterns of convergence and divergence exist, but they are inconsistent, vague, and unstable. For instance, there are large countries and small countries in the European Union, there are the rich and the poor, the realist and the moralist, the interventionist and the anti-interventionist (or neutral), the original six and the latecomers, the insiders and the outsiders, the federalist and the intergovernmentalist, the Atlantic and the Mediterranean, those obsessed with Germany and those ambivalent towards it, those with socialist governments and those with conservative ones, and the unitary nation states and the states with powerful regions. Each European country belongs to several groups at the same time, opposing some countries on some issues and joining them on other issues. Similarities go hand in hand with dissimilarities, and some countries do not easily fit into any of the above-mentioned categories.

The category of large countries, for instance, would include Germany, France, and Great Britain; between them they contribute three-fourths of the Western European defense expenditure. All three countries have a tendency to settle European matters by private bargains among themselves, and maintain a largely independent policy towards the US and many Third World states. However, Germany lacks important power features of Great Britain and France: nuclear weapons, membership in the UN Security Council, and the eagerness and freedom to use German soldiers for peace-keeping operations abroad.[9] In the security field Germany has proved to be a less individualistic and assertive actor than a small country such as Greece.

France and Britain may look similar in hard-core power terms, and if one trusts government statements, they even share common "interests, assets, view of Europe, hopes and fears for the outside world."[10] With the end of the superpower-dominated Cold War both countries have re-emerged as leading military actors able to operate worldwide. They played similar roles in the Gulf War and in the UN peace-keeping operations in Bosnia and embarked on joint defense projects in the field of nuclear doctrine, air command, training for peace-keeping and a new frigate design.[11] However, it is evident that a mutual distrust of each other's motives, deeply rooted in their history and culture, as well as other factors prevent any substantial Franco–British cooperation from getting off the ground.[12] A good illustration of a mutual stereotype image is provided by a former British defense minister, Alan Clark. Commenting on a new "entente" between the two countries in the Autumn of 1994, Clark observed that "French diplomats may periodically sidle up (if they want something), but the reality is one of deliberate and pervasive espionage, unscrupulous leaking of diplomatic papers, hostile briefings on persons and products in third countries, and systematic obstruction in Brussels."[13] In Clark's view efforts aimed at bridging the existing gap between "devious, nationalistic and single-minded" France and "hesitant, ingratiating and inconsistent" Britain are pointless and based on *"idées reçues."*[14] Although in 1997 both countries elected socialist governments, their mutual suspicion has largely remained.

France and Germany, on the other hand, provide a striking example of how cultural stereotypes and historical animosities can be mitigated by skillful diplomacy and political will.[15] Not only have the two countries managed to establish and maintain an unprecedented level of mutual cooperation throughout the second half of this century, but they also acted as a "magnetic core" for successive stages of European integration. But even this unique European partnership is now under strain primarily because the end of the Cold War has benefited Germany more than France. The change in the relative power status between the two countries has broken their long-standing domestic political consensus on Europe. Especially in France, the gap is widening between "those who cling to the Union as the best way to limit and supervise Germany's new influence – but from a position of weakness, no longer of strength – and those who, fearing that Germany would dominate the Union and would become a cage for France, would like to regain some of the independence they see as having been frittered away."[16] Moreover, the end of the Cold War has imposed different security agendas on Germany and France. While Germany looks at the power vacuum in the East and the unrest inside Russia with growing alarm, France believes that its stability is being directly affected by the spill-over of Islamic radicalism in North Africa. Even if the assertive type of Franco–German partnership is to survive the current strains, it will probably exert "magnetic repulsion" rather than the usual "magnetic attraction" on other countries.[17] In the uncertain post-Cold War circumstances, more and more states fear a Franco–German domination in Europe, "the Mulhouse-dendertrein" as Ruud Lubbers, a former Dutch Prime Minister, put it.[18]

Britain seems even more concerned with the power of united Germany than France, but unlike France it attempts to balance Germany outside rather than inside the EU framework.[19] This is basically because Britain, unlike France, seems to see the Union as a means of enhancing German domination rather than a means of containing it.[20] That said, German and British policies do converge on certain issues, even though they are guided by an opposite rationale. For instance, both Germany and Great Britain strongly support the Union's enlargement eastward. However, Britain hopes that such enlargement would water down the deepening process of the Union, while Germany insists that deepening and widening should go hand in hand. Similarly, Germany and Great Britain insist on maintaining strong transatlantic links. But while Britain seems to view its relations with Washington as an alternative to European politics, Germany tries to combine its transatlantic partnership with the existence of the Franco–German core and support for common European policies.

The group of the three large European countries is thus very much diversified if not divided. The picture gets even more complex if one adds Italy and Spain to the group of large countries.[21] Similar diversity of national approaches is present in the group of small European countries.

Small countries such as Belgium, The Netherlands, and Denmark distrust any idea of a great powers' concert or directorate. They also share a similar geo-strategic situation as compared to other small countries such as Portugal, Greece, and Ireland. Yet Belgium concluded that the Maastricht treaty could go further in embracing common foreign and security policies and it quickly joined Eurocorps. Denmark concluded that the treaty already went too far and requested a special opt-out in the field of defense. The Netherlands neither joined the Eurocorps like Belgium nor requested opt-outs from the Maastricht treaty like Denmark; it remained focused on NATO and skeptical about the ability of Europe to play a serious role in defense.[22]

If historical case studies show how difficult it is to establish a fixed pattern of convergence and divergence among EU states, the same could be said about the findings of empirical political science research. For instance, Frank Pfetsch classified foreign policies of EU countries according to several types of integration, ranging from an independent national policy to a uniform supranational or federative policy.[23] He found that individual policies are determined by the views that countries have on the ultimate form of an integrated Europe (the more national considerations prevail the looser the Union is supposed to be), and by the experiences of various countries with certain forms of government (quasi-federal states tend to favor supranationalism). But his findings basically confirm the existence of cross-cutting inter-state coalitions based on a mixed complementarity of interests, tactical alignments, and various domestic political developments.

On top of this complex picture of interactions, there is also an element of change as individual EU members seldom stick to one line of policy for many consecutive years. Tactical changes in policy are taking place all the time as a result of diplomatic trade-offs and leadership mutation at home. France proved particularly good at trading political concessions for major European posts, while Greece proved particularly vulnerable to domestic leadership changes: each time Andreas Papandreou assumed the post of Prime Minister there was an earthquake in the Greek Ministry of Foreign Affairs. Strategic changes in policy are not that frequent, but nevertheless take place in response to long-term structural trends in the domestic and international environments. Decolonization of the Third World and decommunization of the Second World produced the most dramatic strategic shifts in the policy of most EU members. Less dramatic but nevertheless substantial policy shifts were also caused by economic and technological developments.

THE PULLING EFFECT OF EUROPE

Although the pattern of convergence and divergence among EU states is very confused, three general observations seem proper. First, confusion does not imply conflict: no major antagonisms can be traced between EU members, and there is a significant degree of consensus among them. Secondly, foreign and security policies of individual EU countries are more and more preoccupied with the problems of Europe at the expense of the outside world. And thirdly, divergence in national policies is increasingly caused by cultural and psychological pressures rather than by economic and security ones.

Although EU members often clash head-on in the world of diplomacy, they offer neither a security nor an economic threat to one another. As Christopher Hill put it: "There are innumerable differences of view and divergences of behavior [within the EU], but no serious antagonisms with battle-lines drawn and minds closed. Alliances that do occur tend to be highly informal, issue-centered, and shifting. New ideas and proposals are continually possible, and sometimes succeed."[24]

Moreover, the current scope of political convergence among EU states is also significant, especially when compared to previous years. Students of European Political Cooperation recall that when the then six EEC members met for the first time in late 1970 to discuss foreign policy issues, there were strong doubts as to whether similar meetings would follow at all.[25] Today, diplomats from EU countries meet about 100 times a year for political and security consultations, and adopt over 100 joint statements, communiqués, and declarations.[26] The scope of the so-called *domains réservés* (that is, subjects to be excluded from EU consultations and handled individually by EU members) is shrinking, while the scope of the so-called *acquis politique* (that is, subjects enjoying EU consensus) is increasing. Voting patterns at the United Nations also confirm a substantial degree of political convergence: EU unanimity is reached in almost 50 percent of UN resolutions put to vote. If one considers that Greece alone is responsible for more than half of dissenting votes, then the picture of EU convergence looks even better.

True, the political significance of the EU consensus should not be overstated. As Alfred Pijpers illustrated in his study of EPC, Europe's long-standing consensus on the Arab–Israeli conflict had hardly contributed to peace and stability in the Middle East.[27] However, the political significance of disagreements among EU members should not be overstated either. They are often about minor issues or tactical games, with only one dissenting country preventing consensus from being reached.

The second observation concerns the impact of the external environment on national policies of EU countries. The on-going changes in the international milieu suggest that unilateral policies do not pay and that the EU cooperation framework is indispensable in addressing the current needs and concerns of individual states in Europe. In other words, turning one's back on Europe and pursuing unilateral policies in a non-European framework is not as attractive (or easily available) an option as it used to be. For instance, British foreign policy used to operate independently within three interlocking circles: the highest priority was the Empire and Commonwealth, followed by the special relationship with the United States; while Europe was only in third place. Today, a truly unilateral policy is hardly an option for Britain. As David Howell, long-standing Chairman of the (Parliamentary) Foreign Affairs Select Committee, put it: "Britain alone cannot achieve very much except in 'club' mode."[28] And there is evidence that despite all political problems, many British diplomats see the EU club as the most important for Britain, if only because of the predominant pattern of economic links, the weakening of the "special" Atlantic relationship, and the shrinking scope of the old colonial commitments.[29]

Unlike Britain, The Netherlands was a founding EC member, but until the late 1980s it continued to cherish a maritime, basically anti-continental outlook. Time and again it even showed an aversion to continental problems that at the time were dominated by the East–West conflict. The Dutch were always more involved in defending human rights in the Third World than in Eastern Europe. They preferred Atlantic rather than European frameworks of security cooperation. And they were more eager to spend money for development aid to the South than for arms against possible threats to Europe from the East. But the unification of Germany, the liberation of Eastern Europe and the weakening of the Atlantic alliance demanded a dramatic shift in priorities, away from overseas towards continental Europe. Dutch officials subsequently announced "the end of the Third World" and promised to focus their attention on the center of Europe, and Germany in particular.[30]

Another case of Europe's "magnetic" pulling force is presented by the three neutral countries: Austria, Finland, and Sweden. Unlike Britain and The Netherlands, the three neutrals had no tradition of colonial engagement that would keep them away from Europe, but they maintained a distance from the continent because of Soviet pressure and their overall reluctance to be drawn into the "dirty business" of power politics along the East–West divide. However, the end of the Cold War removed the Soviet pressure and increased a feeling of political and economic marginalization. In security terms, all three countries began to fear falling into a gray zone, exposed to instabilities in the East and deprived of the security commitment of the West.[31] Subsequently, all three joined the European Union and subscribed to the CFSP provisions that are clearly in conflict with their official status of neutrality.

A growing preoccupation with Europe does not imply an abandonment of global links by EU members, and there are states such as Norway and Switzerland that resist Europe's magnetic pulling force. But the preoccupation, if not obsession, with Europe is a common foreign policy feature in all EU states. Europe has become a major battleground where national policies meet and part. Or, as Knud Erik Jørgensen put it, "The EU calendar constitutes the European time frame from which national and domestic calendars are derived."[32]

But what exactly determines individual national policies in Europe? What are states after when shaping their position within the European Union? How do we know that convergence is on the increase amidst so many cases of divergence?

In principle, there are four basic sources of foreign policy objectives: (1) the security requirement of survival and territorial integrity, (2) the economic requirement of prosperity, (3) the national leadership's requirement of legitimacy, and (4) the cultural, psychological, and ideological requirement of the people of each country for prestige and status in the world.[33] The security needs are the most important for all states, but with the end of the Cold War EU countries can afford a more laid-back approach to security. The survival and territorial integrity of EU states is not at stake at present. As a popular argument goes: there are no longer threats but merely risks to the security of individual states in Europe.

Economic needs remain at the center of national foreign policies, but economic well being is only partly dependent on the performance of individual governments. As William Wallace put it: "In the increasingly interdependent economy the concept of 'national economic interest' is less and less definable."[34]

National leaders' search for political legitimacy is as crucial as ever in shaping foreign policies. With economic power largely in the hands of private multinational firms and domestic administration partly in the hands of local authorities, foreign and security policy remains the most important monopoly of central national governments. No other area of public life offers politicians a greater opportunity for manipulation and public relations exercise. With the exception of the defense industry, there are hardly any pressure groups able to influence foreign policies of individual states. Bureaucrats employed by international organizations are clearly weaker than national foreign affairs establishments. In such a situation, it is not surprising that foreign policies of EU countries are frequently more about improving the image and popularity of national leaders than about enhancing true national and European interests.

And finally, there is the requirement of status, prestige, identity, and self-image in foreign and security policy. These factors seem the most resistant to all the recent changes on the continent. Countries still cultivate old stereotypes and myths, they persist in old diplomatic habits and manners, they indulge the same prejudices, and dream the same dreams as if nothing happened around them since 1989 or even earlier. Britain's foreign and security commitments today are far different than in Lord Derby's time more than a century ago. Yet, in Whitehall one can still hear Lord Derby's whispering: "we can trust none of these European governments."[35] Most Nordic countries are now loyal EU members, but they still cultivate a self-image of the enlightened, anti-militaristic region that is superior to the old Catholic continent.[36] Negative cultural and historical stereotypes persist especially among neighbors. The French or the Dutch may well work closely with the Germans, yet mutual suspicion shapes their policies as much as the mutual compatibility of their interests. The Belgians are not on good terms with the Dutch, nor the Portuguese with the Spaniards even though there are no grounds for divergent interests between them. The French are unable to abandon their self-image of grandeur and missionary independence even though it undermines their pan-European credentials and angers their neighbors.[37] The Greeks are still fighting a millennium-old mental war in Kosovo,

Macedonia and the rest of the Balkans to the amazement and irritation of other EU states.

The needs of states and their people for prestige, identity, and a moral mission are of course quite irrational, but they are nevertheless a fact of life in actual foreign policy making and no national politician can ignore such pressures completely. Even Hans Morgenthau, an advocate of power politics, emphasized the role of "national character" in shaping individual foreign policies of states. He asked:

Is it not an incontestable fact that Kant and Hegel are as typical of the philosophic tradition of Germany as Descartes and Voltaire are of the French mind, as Locke and Burke are of the political thought of Great Britain? And can it be denied that these philosophic differences are but expressions, on the highest level of abstraction and systematization, of fundamental intellectual and moral traits that reveal themselves on all levels of thought and action and that give each nation its unmistakable distinctiveness?... National character and national morale stand out both for their elusiveness from the point of view of rational prognosis and for their permanent and decisive influence upon the weight a nation is able to put into the scales of international politics.[38]

But if each country cultivates a distinct vision of itself and a different style and tradition, how can policies of EU states ever meet? How can one have a common policy for Europe if "irrational" cultural, historical, and psychological factors dominate policies of individual states? If identity and tradition are resistant to external pressures where is the space for all-European engineering? In fact, the post-Maastricht squabble indicated that the more integration pressure on particular states there is, the more there is cultural and psychological resistance to such pressure. It looks like the issues of identity, status and prestige have become the major obstacles on the road towards common foreign and security policies in Europe.

In sum, policies of individual EU states do not follow a clear pattern of divergence and convergence. Differences exist but they are not fundamental in terms of economic interest and security. Agreements are often reached but they tend to be short-lived and deal with minor if not irrelevant political questions. While EU countries seem increasingly concerned about and focused on Europe, different styles, traditions and self-images persist. Walter Laqueur's earlier point was that the countries of Europe suffer from "mental disorders."[39] This is probably too harsh, but cultural and psychological explanations are certainly needed to explain why members of the European Union, with their largely integrated economies and no military antagonisms, still maintain largely divergent foreign and security policies.

CONFUSING VISIONS OF EUROPE

If there is a problem to describe and understand national identities, there is an even greater problem to describe and understand a European identity. Yet the European Union can hardly have a coherent foreign and security policy without specifying where Europe ends and what Europe means. This shows the impossible task at present: Europe remains the most mystical and misused term in politics and history.[40]

Europe may well be, as Jean Jacques Rousseau put it: "an invisible nation," or as William Wallace put it two hundred years later: "a geographical expression with political significance and immense symbolic weight, but without clear definition or agreed boundaries."[41] Nevertheless one thing is certain, Europe exists and no "European" project can do without either real or even false European credentials. Jacques Delors, the President of the European Commission, understood this very well. In his 1991 Alastair Buchan Memorial Lecture devoted to common foreign and security policy, he stated bluntly: "Europe must want to be European."[42]

The questions "where does Europe end?" and "what does Europe mean?" are closely intertwined, especially in security terms. If Europe is about an independent power status with its own security policies and military capabilities the question arises: who are Europe's enemies and friends? Against whom does Europe need its own security framework? If, however, Europe is merely about economic and cultural matters the question arises: who is going to take care of Europe's protection? Does Europe still expect the US to provide it with a security umbrella, even though Europe tries to compete with America in economic terms and distances itself from it in cultural ones?

In political terms the issue looks equally tricky. The political slogan of the final phase of the Cold War was to make Europe "whole and free." Now it is difficult to maintain that the political construction of Europe should exclude former communist states. And if Eastern European countries are admitted what about Turkey, Morocco, and other Islamic states in the South? But as Edgard Pisani once observed: "Widening Europe indefinitely would destroy it, would stop it from becoming a strong reality in a selfish world, an all-powerful, all-conquering

West, and a global economy that serves big business, a world hostile to the genuine expression of the cultures and the political will of peoples."[43]

What "Europe" means in foreign and security terms is specified in the Treaty of Maastricht. The CFSP is to safeguard common values, develop and consolidate democracy, preserve peace, strengthen international security and the like. One cannot argue with such objectives but the question is open to what extent is Europe willing and able to carry out these goals? In recent years there has been a clear rise in Europe's ambitions: the EU was seen in such complex roles as a regional pacifier, global interventionist, mediator of conflicts, bridge between rich and poor, joint supervisor of the world economy, and even "a replacement for the USSR in the global balance of power."[44] Even the usually modest Douglas Hurd declared that the main task for the European Union is to "carry into the rest of our continent the security and prosperity which, with all our bickerings, we take for granted in the West."[45] And he added: "CFSP has no geographical limitations."[46]

Europe's current ambition to have an independent foreign and security policy reflects in part wishful thinking and in part necessity. There is an enormous gap between EU proclaimed aspirations and its actual capabilities. As Christopher Hill put it: "The Community [read the Union] does not have the resources or the political structure to be able to respond to the demands which the Commission and certain Member States have virtually invited through their bullishness over the pace of internal change."[47] To play the role of a regional pacifier or a global economic pilot Europe would need to become a complete international actor with supranational diplomatic powers and independent military capability. We do not know whether this is visible, and we doubt whether it is really needed. But can the Union avoid responsibility for its own backyard or act as a lame duck in the world of economic competition? What happens in Bosnia, Turkey, or the Baltic States has direct implications for Europe's own security. It is one thing to argue that hegemonic politics makes little sense among the most advanced industrialized countries, it is another to discount the danger of local conflicts flaring up on Europe's borders. Likewise Europe's global economic reach exposes it to political instability, economic protectionism and violence in the most remote parts of the world. There is some truth in saying that Europe cannot afford to be an economic giant and a political dwarf. If Europe wants to remain a "civilian power," it must determine for itself how to cope with the "uncivilized policies" of other actors.[48] And thus some hard choices about Europe's ambitions and capabilities would have to be made, which would have direct implications for Europe's political and cultural identity.

THE WEST, ATLANTICISM AND EURAMERICA

The question where Europe ends in political and security terms will depend on two basic factors: enlargement of the European Union and the shape of transatlantic relations.

Before the end of the Cold War, Europe was more about Atlantic rather than continental politics; Europe was so to speak: "a pillar of the Western system under the American leadership."[49] This notion of Europe clearly defied geography and history and it did great injustice to Europeans who found themselves under the Soviet grip. But Europe, which meant Western Europe organized in the European Community, was working closely with the United States and not with Eastern Europe in all areas of culture, economics, and politics. This does not mean that transatlantic links were problem free; consider General de Gaulle's rift with NATO or the Urengoi pipeline crisis. With the end of the Cold War, old problems began to vanish but new problems arose. Europe is too important for America to turn its back on it: this was the message of the previous chapter. However, the alliance must readjust to the new circumstances and this readjustment is not about to be painless.

If one tries to look beyond daily squabbles and political rhetoric, one must address at least three important questions: is Europe's ambition to act as an independent international actor compatible with US leadership? Does Europe need NATO to provide firm defense and security? And can "The West" survive as a political and cultural entity? The first question is about the future structure of power politics; the second about the major institutional pillar of transatlantic cooperation, and the third about the cultural and ideological underpinning of any workable partnership.[50] The answer to all three questions is, in principle, yes. In practice, however, things might turn out to be more complicated.

Europe's rise to independent power status has some advantages for the United States. As Jacques Delors argued: "The United States has nothing to gain from a politically impotent and economically subordinate Community... A European Europe intends to confirm its attachment to the Alliance and its objectives and to shoulder a larger part of the burden thanks to a common defense policy. This, surely, is what the Americans have always wanted."[51] But is it really what the Americans have always wanted? There is no doubt that the United States would like to share with Europe some burdens of its leadership. It is less clear whether it is also prepared to share the leadership itself. Time and again, Europeans accuse the United States of forcing unilateral policies on them. Consider, for instance, the United States' bullying on trade issues, spurning pleas by Europeans to take urgent measures to control global warming, ignoring European partners by imposing its view on NATO expansion, or undermining European efforts in Africa, Latin America, or the Middle East.[52]

However, the Union is not a totally "innocent" partner either. Europe's independent power status in the world of economics implies more competition, if not protectionism *vis-à-vis* the United States. And a politically united Europe is likely to be a more assertive diplomatic partner than a divided Europe. A new distribution of power and responsibility among transatlantic allies is therefore nothing but a troublesome process. The EU is unable fully to assume a regional, let alone global, leadership but in the process of extending its functions and tasks it may well be seen as America's rising rival. The potential cocktail of economic, political, and even security rivalries can seriously damage Europe's Atlantic profile.

Before the end of the Cold War, American links with Europe were primarily via NATO. NATO was not only about integration of defense forces to meet a common threat; it was a symbol of the Atlantic Europe with borders reaching from the German river Elbe to San Francisco and Vancouver. Now that the old threat is gone, together with the Iron Curtain along the river Elbe, NATO is in the throes of an identity crisis. Nobody wants to do away with NATO and its integrated forces, but it is no longer clear what NATO is for, where its commitments end, and how the new balance of burden and power sharing should look. Moreover, Europe has begun to search for its own independent role in security and defense and it is far from certain whether the Western European Union or Eurocorps can live in harmony with NATO. More detailed institutional dilemmas arising from the new situation will be dealt with in another chapter. But now it is important to draw one conclusion: the Atlantic notion of Europe will be an empty slogan without a purposeful and workable NATO.

Finally the question: does "The West" continue to exist as a transatlantic entity? Before the end of the Cold War, strategic self interest was but one pillar of Western partnership, other pillars were cultural identity and ideological affinity. Common history, culture, economic principles, and political values were all important in maintaining a unity of thoughts and deeds across the Atlantic.

The cultural identity of the West was vague but real. Europe was the main source of nearly all the first waves of immigration to America, Judeo-Christian religion was dominant on both continents, people and goods traveled freely over the Atlantic, history books referred to the same history, and there was mutual absorption of each other's music, literature, and mass media. Ideological links were based on a common hostility to communism, and common embracing of democracy, liberty, human rights, and a free market.

However, with the end of the Cold War ideology has declined in importance: there is no communism to hate, while democracy, human rights and capitalism are no longer "exclusively" Western values. There are now many semi-free, semi-capitalist, and semi-democratic countries that make black-and-white ideological judgments pointless if not silly. Most of them are young aspirants to the "Western club," countries such as Russia, Turkey, and Bulgaria. But the group of semi-democratic states also seems to include some founding members of the Western club; think about Italy, Belgium, or France with their corruption scandals, party clientelism, and parliamentary instability.[53]

With ideology in decline, is not culture the most durable foundation of the Western partnership? And if the fault lines between civilizations will be the battle lines of the future, is not Western cultural partnership condemned to survival? [54] The problem is that common cultural links do not automatically guarantee political solidarity, let alone security commitments involving human sacrifice. Moreover, the earlier scope and durability of transatlantic cultural links is not guaranteed either. Immigration from Europe to the "promised land" has been replaced by emigration from Latin and Asian countries. Religious identity has either been weakened by secularization or diluted by religious diversification: the Muslim population is growing in Europe and various small religious sects are spreading in the United States. Intellectual concepts of rationalism and individualism are still dominant on both sides of the Atlantic, but they are also under pressure from postmodernist relativism on the one hand, and ethnic or religious fundamentalism on the other. The EU's somewhat forced effort to acquire a distinct European cultural identity with clear anti-American undertones can hardly help the Atlantic links either.

All these developments prompted some observers to announce the collapse of the West and the end of the Atlantic partnership.[55] Such claims seem too simplistic. As Francis Fukuyama rightly argued, a

North Atlantic *gesellschaft* – meaning the legal, impersonal ties of modern societies – continues to exist, in the form of the NATO treaty and all the buildings and bureaucrats that embody it at Mons and Evere outside Brussels. However, more problematic is the continued existence of a North Atlantic *gemeinschaft*, meaning the moral community which began with the Anglo-American alliance during World War II and which endured during the prolonged struggles of the Cold War.[56] In other words, Europe will be unable to preserve its Atlantic reach and profile without cultivating its Western identity in the field of politics, ideology, and culture. *Gemeinschaft* is not about legal treaties and diplomatic window-dressing; it is about spontaneous social links, communal solidarity, and shared values. It is not clear whether Europe will be able to maintain such a relationship over the Atlantic. It is also not clear whether leading European governments and EU officials truly seek such a relationship.

Atlantic partnership based on merely legal rather than moral and cultural foundations is a matter for concern, but not a matter for panic. The alliance is not confronted with major external threats; and despite frequent disputes and irritations, Europe and America are not about to rely on either force or intimidation to solve their disagreements. Besides, political, cultural, and ideological differences across the Atlantic are not necessarily greater than those within Europe itself. In due course, the likelihood of ending up with only one continental Europe is not greater than the likelihood of ending up with a new East and new West.[57] One can also argue that a new identity across Europe and the Atlantic should emerge. As Charles A. Kupchan put it in 1996:

> Deeper European integration has lost not only its popular appeal, but its strategic purpose. Current schemes for NATO enlargement are equally fanciful and dangerous. The solution to the West's troubles is an Atlantic Union (AU) that would subsume both NATO and the European Union. The EU would abandon its federal aspirations and concentrate on the extension of its single market east to Central Europe and west to North America. NATO would become the new group's defense arm, but its biding commitments to collective defense of state borders would give way to more relaxed commitments to uphold collective security through peace enforcement, peacekeeping, and preventive diplomacy.[58]

Is this vision in line with the EU's aspirations?[59] We do not really know, because the Union is still unwilling (or unable) to define clearly its own ambitions and a framework for desired transatlantic cooperation.

DEFINING EUROPE'S BORDERS

Europe's relations with America are of fundamental strategic importance and directly affect Europe's political, economic, and defense
identity. But the United States is not about to end up within EU
borders. The same cannot be said about Europe's northern, southern,
and eastern flanks: countries such as Estonia, Poland, Cyprus, and
even Turkey may soon become EU members of some sort.[60] The
question "Where does Europe end?" is therefore directly linked to
the issue of EU enlargement. To act as an effective international actor
the Union needs clearly defined and durable borders. As William
Wallace rightly argued: "Political systems cannot operate without
boundaries, nor markets without rules enforced within their limits,
and boundaries necessarily exclude as well as include."[61]

Although the EC/EU has vast experience in handling several past
enlargements no clear aims, criteria, and geographic limits of enlargements were ever set.[62] Besides, it is uncertain to what extent future
enlargements are to be guided by the experience with the past ones. Is
the aim of enlargement economic: creating a vast free-trade area? Is it
political: preventing instability just across EU borders? Or maybe the
aim is cultural: bringing under one roof all "truly" European countries? One can hardly answer these questions without first determining
what the European Union itself is about. Is the Union primarily about
economics or politics or culture? The problem is that the Union's basic
purpose and profile are still being debated, re-articulated, and re-
adjusted.

Some priorities in the aims of enlargement are nevertheless needed if
only because various economic, political, and cultural aims are not
necessarily in harmony but in conflict. Economic aims envisage the
policy of financial profit, while political aims envisage the policy of
financial sacrifice. Economic aims argue for embracing stable and prosperous countries, while political aims argue for embracing weak and
unstable ones. Countries with strong European credentials in terms of
culture are not always the most attractive economic targets. Nor can one
guarantee that the list of culturally most "European" EU candidates
will overlap with the list of countries deserving EU's political embrace.

If the aims of future enlargement are to remain uncertain, what
about enlargement criteria? If culture is the criterion then Russia
surely ought to be included. But can Russia become an EU member
in economic and political terms?[63] Cultural criteria should not be
dismissed, however, because without cultural cohesion the whole

concept of a distinct European identity will be on sand. In fact, EU officials explicitly use cultural criteria in deterring EU aspirations of Turkey and the countries of the Maghreb.

Does this mean that the borders of the EU are to be determined by the borders between Christianity and Islam? And on the Eastern flank, are the borders of the EU to coincide with the borders between orthodox and non-orthodox Christianity? Can a country's choice for Rome or Byzantium several hundred years ago determine EU membership? Should a country be prevented from joining the EU because it had the historic misfortune to be swallowed up by the Ottoman rather than the Habsburg empire? The answer is: no! And yet, it is difficult to deny that such historic and cultural characteristics make it easier for some countries to catch up with the core of today's Europe. As Jacques Rupnik put it:

> When one looks at a prospective map based on the socioeconomic criteria (industrialization, urbanization, and communications) that identify the postcommunist regions most likely to "reconnect" with Western Europe, one is struck by its similarity to Europe in 1914. The "Habsburg factor" seems to be an important ingredient in assessing the chances of the democratic and market-oriented transition and of a successful "reconnection" with the European Union countries. Another historical query for the future concerns the extent of German influence in this process knowing that East Prussia used to stretch to Kaliningrad, alias Köningsberg... If the Baltic states are added to "Habsburg" Central Europe, we come closer to another dividing line in the "reconnection" process; the line between Western and Eastern Christendom. One should beware of historical or cultural determinism, but the correlations between the three maps are striking.[64]

Economic and political criteria of enlargement are no firmer than cultural ones. Should the level of growth be decisive or the size of the economic market? Should one watch inflation and the budget deficit or the progress of privatization? Is democratization or liberalization the most crucial political criterion? What is more detrimental to EU membership: (post)communism, nationalism or Islamic fundamentalism? And how should democratic progress be assessed: in terms of regular elections, media freedom, human rights, or vitality of political parties? Can one say that Slovakia is politically more ripe for EU membership than Romania? Does Bulgaria's economy deserve better EU treatment than the economy of Israel, Cyprus, or Morocco? It is one thing to strive for some clear-cut criteria of EU enlargement as a way out of the existing confusion, it is another thing to pretend that any such criteria could be lucid, firm, and just.

Geography also affects the policy of enlargement as various members of the Union have different links with the outside world and subsequently different interests in promoting some but not other directions of enlargement.[65] Greece has naturally more links with Cyprus than with Estonia; Spain has more in common with Morocco than with Romania; France is more dependent on developments in Algeria than in Slovakia; and for Austria, Hungary counts more than Lebanon. During the Cold War these regional links never ceased to be important, but the bi-polar competition imposed its own peculiar laws and constraints on regional encounters. With the demise of the Cold War, regionalism is back in fashion, not so much in economic policy, which is still preoccupied with the EU internal market, but in security policy. The immediate concern of EU countries is no longer a possible Soviet assault, but the potential cross-border consequences of refugee flows and exile communities supporting rival contenders. This urges states to take greater care of their own geographic courtyard with obvious implications for unity among EU states. The main division line within the Union runs between those primarily concerned with Eastern Europe and those primarily concerned with the *Méditerranée*. Of course, for some countries the above-mentioned dichotomy does not apply. Ireland is not very much affected by instability in either Eastern or Southern Europe: its prime concern is Britain and Northern Ireland. Portugal is more concerned about its former colonies in Africa and trade relations with Brazil than about developments in Tunisia or Poland.[66] Large countries such as Britain, Germany, and France can hardly look only at their own geographic corners. The Baltic sea and the Balkans form regional concerns on their own. Yet the major geographic dilemma facing the Union is about commitments *vis-à-vis* Eastern Europe and the Mediterranean.

The collapse of communism in Eastern Europe has forced the Union into a more active policy towards the region. The Union funded a large aid program aimed at supporting reforms in Eastern Europe and began signing the so-called "Association Agreements" with several Eastern European countries. The 1993 European Council in Copenhagen officially stated that negotiations about joining the Union by these countries can start no later than 1998.[67] It looked as if in the years to come, Eastern Europe would monopolize a large part of the Union's diplomatic energy and economic resources. If indeed there were to be another round of enlargement after incorporating the EFTA countries it would be in an eastward direction rather than southward one. Poland, Hungary, and the Czech Republic were the most obvious candidates at the time, but the Baltic states, Romania, Bulgaria, Slovakia, and Slovenia have also been seriously considered.

But then a dramatic rise in Islamic fundamentalism and severe economic crises in the Maghreb countries of North Africa have forced the Union to divert some energy and resources to the Mediterranean. Again some countries in the Union have been concerned with the situation in the South more than other EU members. France's Prime Minister, Edouard Balladur, called the civil war in Algeria his country's number one foreign policy priority, and the Spanish EU commissioner, Manuel Marin, insisted that the time had come for the EU to tilt its foreign policy more towards the Mediterranean rather than Eastern Europe. "The difference is that with the East, we are talking about future members of a prosperous and democratic club of European states", said Marin, "With the South, we are, at best, talking about associate states with open trading arrangements but who will never be part of the club. We need to do something more to rectify this imbalance."[68]

But what could the Union do in order to rectify the imbalance between its policy towards the East and the South? And how could the Union bridge the gap between those of its members that are either primarily concerned with the East or with the South? The Union coped with the East-South dilemma and the pressure for enlargement in a characteristic fashion: it focused on money rather than on more substantive aspects of regional politics, economics, security, and culture. In other words, the debate within the Union focused primarily on the issue of aid distribution to the two regions. The debate reached its climax during the 1995 European Council meeting in Cannes. The French and Spanish governments demanded a major shift in reallocation of resources between the East and the South, while Germany, Great Britain, Denmark, and The Netherlands wanted to stick to the 5:1 ratio adopted for the period of 1992–96. In the end, the ratio was changed from 5:1 to 5:3.5 for the following period which represented a significant reallocation of resources in favor of the Mediterranean. The resources for the Mediterranean (ECU 4,685m) were increased 22 percent while those for Eastern Europe rose only 8 percent. But here the balancing policy of the EU has been exhausted. A widely publicized Euro-Mediterranean Conference in Barcelona organized by the Spanish presidency in November 1995 produced few, if any, tangible results.[69] None of the more ambitious political and economic initiatives *vis-à-vis* the Mediterranean region such as a European Economic Space, Economic Bank for Reconstruction and Development for the Mediterranean, or Euro-Med Stability Pact have been adopted. Most notably, EU membership has not been seriously considered for any countries in the region except Malta and Cyprus.

All this raises painful questions about the Union's willingness and ability to stabilize its Southern backyard. Can aid without the prospect of full EU membership solely improve the Mediterranean situation? It also raises painful questions about the Union's differentiation policy of enlargement. Is not preferential treatment of Eastern Europe a matter of cultural preference? The Czechs, Hungarians, Romanians and even Albanians are European, the argument goes, while the Turks, Tunisians, and Moroccans are not. Did not the treaties of Maastricht and Rome insist that only "European" states can become EC/EU members?

Compare, for instance, some economic factors that make countries more or less "ripe" for admission to the Union. Algeria with its $2,060 GNP per capita in 1990 seemed economically more advanced than most Eastern European countries at the time.[70] Even Tunisia with its $1,420 per capita and Morocco with $950 look better than Romania with its $610 per capita in 1992.[71] The assumption is that Eastern Europe would catch up quicker with Western Europe than the Maghreb countries, but North Africans argue that this would largely happen due to the EU shift of investment and aid away from Maghreb to Eastern Europe. In other words, they fear that the current EU preoccupation with Eastern Europe condemns them to economic marginalization.[72]

Security arguments were also used in justifying the refusal to admit some Mediterranean countries to the EU. It has often been argued that Islamic fundamentalism has replaced communism as the main security threat to the West. However, this always has been disputed by the leading Western specialists in the region who point out that none of the current Muslim leaders in the Mediterranean entertains any ambition to dominate or conquer Europe through military force.[73] Although many Muslims sympathized with "holy" wars against Westerners instigated by Saddam Hussein and Colonel Gaddafi, their governments proved willing to side with the Western powers in order to strengthen their own positions. Just as in postcommunist Eastern Europe, the security problems emerging on Europe's southern flank have economic, demographic and political roots. And if radical

Muslim politics is getting the upper hand in some North African countries with damaging spill-over effects for Southern European countries, isn't this because of the EU's failure to embrace economic development and democracy there?[74]

And thus we are left with cultural arguments against southern enlargement that are vague, controversial and fiercely disputed by the Mediterranean states aspiring to EU membership.[75] After the December 1997 Luxembourg European Council decided to open accession negotiations with several Eastern European countries, but not with Turkey, prime minister Mesut Yilmaz angrily asserted that a "new cultural Berlin Wall" is being erected between Christian Europe and Muslim Turkey.[76] And King Hassan of Morocco added:

> On the cultural level the West and the Moslem world have contributed equally to world cultures. We are just as cultivated as the West, and we will never clash with it on the level of culture or of civilization... [But Europeans] think of themselves as the whites, the colonizers, while we are the former colonies. We are not full citizens... And so they look for allies more to the East, because there people are white,... because it's one big family. And they look across the Mediterranean and say: "Ah yes, it's true, there are those poor little people that we colonized..."[77]

All this is *not* to argue that Morocco or Turkey should become EU members sooner than Hungary or Poland, but to show Europe's dilemmas in searching for common ground in crafting its policy of enlargement. Of course, enlargement is not the only way of addressing instability on the Union's borders. There will always be politicians advocating a policy of insulation and containment.[78] Others will advocate half measures such as free-trade zones, association agreements or EU membership restricted to some selected areas: a semi-demi membership. Different measures will be applied towards different countries and probably with different degrees of success. The picture will become complex with no fixed borders of the Union at any given time. The Union will increasingly be acting in different circles and at different speeds and its links with the outside world will be diversified and never stable. Europe will be comprised of several overlapping subsystems without a clear distinction between the hard-core center and the periphery.

If such developments will indeed be the case, what about Europe's identity? Will there come a clash between countries' desire to belong to a hard-core Europe with all its confusing legal and political arrange-ments? Or maybe a fluid and loose framework would accommodate converging interests and sentiments in Europe. And can a common foreign and security policy get off the ground within a Union com-prised of political and geographic sub-systems?[79] If the meaning of Europe is ambiguous and its borders uncertain, can Europe act as an international actor?

NATIONAL VERSUS EUROPEAN IDENTITY

This chapter has tried to show that European states are not necessarily pursuing power and hegemony, but that their diverging policies stem from different historical experiences, geographic location, patterns of economic interdependence, and cultural links with the outside world. (The absence of any clear and broadly shared vision of Europe is also hampering common European efforts.) There is nothing sinister about the existence of such differences, but recent years have shown that they do lead to a dangerously chaotic situation in the field of security and foreign affairs. As Martin Wight put it: "just disorder does not exist," and one may add that chaos is also detrimental to the economic well-being of Europe.[80] As national interests and visions of Europe seriously diverge what can provide the necessary solidarity on the continent? The usual response suggests an institutional solution: unity of action and values can well be enhanced by the creation of a common supranational government. But the opposite is also true, namely that any common European government could not properly function without a certain degree of common purpose and shared values throughout the continent. Chapter 5 will study the institutional factor, here I will try to explore the cultural factor.

It is easy and often right to blame bad politics for fueling national resentments and pursuing parochial rather than pan-European object-ives. As stated earlier, national governmental elites are all too eager to utilize their monopoly over foreign and defense matters for the pur-pose of short-term electoral gains rather than common European endeavors. Yet governmental elites are only partly responsible for the fact that national rather than European loyalties prevail among the peoples on the continent.[81] Supremacy of national loyalties and ident-ities results from a complex interplay of ethnic, cultural, territorial, economic, legal, and political factors that are far beyond the control of the present-day governments.[82] Populist politicians exploit national sentiments, but it is hardly their fault that Europeans at large are more attracted to national than to European projects. It may no longer be true that people in the western part of the continent are prepared to fight and die for their nation rather than for Europe. Probably, most of them are willing to fight and die for neither.[83] Equally, it is risky to assert that people on the continent are happy about their political participation in nation states but unhappy about their participation in the European Union. Probably, most of them are happy with neither.[84] It is also unwise to claim that a nation state rather than a European state is best suited to provide security and economic well-being to individual citizens. In a world of modern technology and mass communication a nation state is probably less capable delivering the goods than larger multinational units. That said, one assertion seems certain: national identity remains a more potent form of collective identification than any other cultural, economic, or political ident-ities.[85] The European Union may be in principle better suited to cope with the challenges of the modern world, but it lacks the emotional sustenance, cultural affinity, and historical symbolism that makes people invest their trust and loyalties for any serious collective endeavor.[86] Today, as old certainties collapse and people are confused by all the rapid changes on the continent the question of identity has become central. People ask themselves: who are we, where do we belong, who are our enemies and friends, why and for whom should we sacrifice our lives and careers? They may distrust national pol-iticians, they may be skeptical about national crusades, but they have nothing firmer to identify themselves with in cultural terms than their nation. True, nationalism is a vague and mystical concept.[87] Moreover, nationalism is a transitory phenomenon which was born only a century or so ago and may already be in descent, at least in the western part of Europe.[88] Yet to date, all other forms of collective identity appear wan and artificial by comparison with national identities, for better or worse. As Benedict Anderson put it bluntly: "Nation-ness is the most universally legitimate value in the political life of our time."[89]

This is not to negate the importance of multiple collective ident-ities.[90] After all, I am a living example of such a complex identity: I am a Polish national, a Dutch citizen, and an Italian resident, and have spent much of my academic career in Great Britain. But such a com-plex multinational background is still an exception rather than the rule. Moreover, a multi-national background does not always produce cos-mopolitan, let alone "European" beliefs and values. And it is also hard to deny that (post)modern elites have usually fewer problems functioning with multiple identities than the public at large.[91] While it is good to insist that identity is not a zero-sum concept it is also important to keep in mind that a simple national identity remains the basic and most precious one for the majority of Europeans.

What does this persistent importance of national identity imply for the EU common foreign and security project? First, unless ordinary citizens are willing to transfer their loyalties and sentiments away from their nation states to a broader European unit the CFSP will be built on sand. This seems like a pretty obvious statement, but Cold War security analysts used to fuse people, government, and state into one image and present a picture of European politics merely consisting of interactions among nation states. Such simplistic reasoning must be abandoned as it is increasingly evident that intergovernmental efforts aimed at CFSP are not necessarily in tune with the public search for security and peace. As Ole Waever put it: "The struggle for Europe begins with a struggle inside each nation. The main question for the future of Europe, for stability and peaceful change, is now not directly the relations among the major powers, but the inner struggles over national identity/Europe projects in France, Germany and Russia."[92]

Secondly, cultural identity is an odd notion for diplomats and security experts who are preoccupied with interests and threats to the economic, political, and military sectors rather than with the cultural domain. However, it is increasingly evident that a lack of a strong grassroots pan-European cultural identification undermines otherwise useful and successful European initiatives. While it is probably an exaggeration to state that "modern man is not loyal to a monarch or a land or a faith, whatever he may say, but to culture,"[93] ignoring collective cultural identities has already produced a setback for the European project as manifested by the post-Maastricht political deadlock.

There are many ways to approach the identity crisis in present-day Europe. One can talk about a double dilemma of identity: the temporal dimension of continuity and change, and the spatial dimension of closure and overture.[94] The European Union offers a more optimal size for effective action in the foreign and security field, but cultural sentiments of belonging to smaller national units produce the identity crisis that prevents the Union from doing anything much of value. One can also talk about the identity crisis evoked by the fear of the ever-greater presence of aliens within national entities, through the freedom of migration within the Union, successive enlargement of the Union and waves of refugees. People fear the loss of territory, personality, and the power to control their own affairs.[95] Finally, one can also talk about the difficult choice between manufacturing artificial European myths and historical memories on the one hand, and on the other, relying on a memoryless scientific "culture" held together solely by political will and economic interests that are so often subject to change.[96]

The question of cultural identity is thus very complex and it is difficult to grasp its exact meaning for security and foreign affairs.[97] But how much can common foreign and security policy accomplish without the firm backing by the public in various corners of the continent? If the interests of various EU members are not identical, how can one expect the citizens of different states to express solidarity with each other and be ready to offer sacrifices at the altar of the CFSP? Such solidarity and sacrifice can possibly come about through strong cultural linkages across national borders. But it would not be easy to produce such linkages because collective identities tend to be "pervasive and persistent," to use Anthony D. Smith's words.[98] However, the Union has no other choice but to try to do just that.

The Union might be helped by the emergence of new unifying threats to Europe. In the absence of such threats it can rely on cultural and educational policies emphasizing a common European experience and shared symbols of identification. It can promote economic and social welfare programs facilitating upward mobility across the continent and diminishing economic resentments. It can provide charismatic leadership of the Union and increase openness of its decision making.[99] While it is crucial to respect national cultures and peripheral ambitions, there is also a need to expose and combat manifestations of xenophobia and national egoism.

Of course, there is no point in engineering love for a new European *patria* or in creating a European *supernation*. The aim is to encourage compatible loyalties from local to the European level and to strengthen multiple identities in concentric circles.[100] The aim is to enhance mutual respect and solidarity among various European nations, to create a family of cultures sharing similar tradition, ethics, law, economy, and parliamentary institutions.[101] This will not add up to become a distinct European culture that would replace national ones. But it could allow a stronger European culture to emerge next to national ones.

The Union can also try to compensate for the lack of common ethnic and cultural properties by building up something that Jürgen Habermas named a "European constitutional patriotism" based on participatory democracy and the republican concept of citizenship.[102] The idea is to search for an identity that is rooted in the *praxis* of European citizens actively exercising their civil rights rather than in a shared historical tradition, common language and other pre-political factors. But this would require foregoing the existing democratic deficit of the Union; a formidable task indeed, especially so far as foreign policy is concerned. But even if this strategy succeeds a total escape from culture is hardly possible. Constitutional patriotism cannot exist in opposition to existing cultures. Moreover, constitutional patriotism can only work in a culture imbued with the concept of political participation and freedom.[103]

In the final analysis it is not very clear what would be the exact impact of various cultural developments on common foreign policies. The marriage between security, diplomacy, and culture continues to look strange. However, there seems to be enough evidence to argue that divorcing the three might prove fatal for CFSP endeavors.

CONCLUSIONS

Different national policies are certainly behind the Union's failure to get common policies off the ground. However, I have argued that the degree of divergence among individual EU members should not be exaggerated. First of all, there are vast areas of convergence among them. National policies of EU states are increasingly geared towards Europe. The EU framework is used as a means to cope with ever growing global pressures and various types of local instabilities. Moreover, the EU framework has become a center of European foreign policy debates where national policies meet and part.

Secondly, divergent policies do not always imply divergent interests. Individual "national interests" are often presented as being eternal if not sacred, but in fact I have argued that they are usually vague and fluid. Moreover, what is presented as "national interest" is often cooked-up by a narrow group of unelected officials with little regard for any broader nationwide considerations or the principle of democratic representation. In a democratic body politic, a national interest is synonymous with public interest which should be openly debated and justified rather than presented as "given" and "correct."[104] If this is so, it is difficult to claim that national interests in Europe are divergent *a priori* and for good.

Thirdly, divergence is seldom a product of any sinister hegemonic ambitions but results from the simple fact that all EU members are different. They are also surrounded by a different type of international environment in terms of security, economics, and culture. In short, divergence in national policies does not necessarily imply conflict.

All this suggests that divergence in national policies can well be mitigated by skillful political engineering, legal arrangements, and procedural tricks. However, there is one serious complication: divergence in national policies within the Union is largely if not increasingly a function of different cultural identities and these are not easy targets for legal and political engineering.[105] The unprecedented scope and speed of changes that we are currently observing in Europe seem to reinforce the cultural identity factor. Amidst growing uncertainties, people stick to what they know: national identity is the most precious binding factor despite all its well-known weaknesses. Why should the people of Europe sacrifice their national identities for the sake of an abstract if not artificial body: the European Union? Why should governments in member states argue against national identity if this identity provides them with a scarce resource: legitimacy? And if national loyalties continue to persist is there any reason to believe that the national policies of member states can ever be squeezed onto one common line?

However, I would argue that the challenge for the Union is not so much to squeeze all different national identities, but to create a European one. This is a very daunting task because cultural loyalties, images, and identities are usually vague, fluid, and irrational; as such they can hardly be dealt with by legal treaties, institutional maneuvers, and military commands. This does not mean that identities are not subject to manipulation. But the Union cannot manipulate identities the way nationalist demagogues do, by mystifying history and propagating the politics of hatred and exclusion.[106]

That said, EU leaders are not virtually helpless in addressing the identity issue. After all, identity is not only about culture, but also about politics. In other words, politicians may have problems in trying to manipulate culture, but they should certainly be in a position to give the Union a more identifiable political profile. Most notably, the Union's leaders should be able to state clearly what the Union's basic aims are and which countries will soon become its members. This step would greatly enhance the identity of the European Union and its common foreign and security policy.

In view of persistent divergence of national interests, specifying and shaping the Union's profile is bound to be a conflict-ridden operation. Moreover, some flexibility is required for the Union to cope with the complexity of the modern world. But a faceless, enigmatic, and purposeless Union can hardly generate any genuine public support. A faceless, enigmatic, and purposeless Union is bound to generate bureaucratic inertia, contradictory policies, and more conflict. In short, shaping the identity of the Union is the key to making European politics work.

Which issues ought to be addressed first? And which choices ought to be made in terms of substance? Will any identity of the Union do? Or are we advocating a Union with a certain kind of profile? This chapter suggests three specific measures that would greatly enhance the identity of the Union.

First of all, we suggest specifying the Union's aims and functions. This is primarily a self-constraining operation. The Union has a vague and confusing image because it promises far too much. Certain ambitions, such as hard-core security and defense have to be set aside. As shown in the previous chapter, a civilian-power model would suit the Union well. Moreover, I will argue later in the book that a common defense policy is potentially a very sensitive issue both in terms of democratic representation and national sovereignty.

Secondly, I suggest specifying the Union's policy of enlargement. This is primarily about stating clearly what the Union's borders will look like in the foreseeable future and why.[107] If the Union wants to be a coherent cultural and political entity, it cannot expand endlessly without clear rules, aims and a timetable. This chapter argues, in particular, that neither economics nor culture are sufficient criteria for evaluating applications for EU membership; democracy should also be considered. This is because "constitutional patriotism" can help the Union enhance its identity in the absence of any strong cultural or economic "patriotisms."[108]

Thirdly, I suggest aiming at an open and outward-looking identity for the Union, rather than at a closed, protectionist, and inward-looking one. Identity is usually constructed in opposition to a significant "other": in order to know who "we" are, we need to know who "we" are not.[109] But this need not imply a policy of hostility and exclusion.[110] Defining the Union's borders is not the same as closing them. The Union should try to maintain and deepen its various links with the outside world and reject an introverted or Euro-centric approach. This applies, in particular, to relations with the United States. After all, Europe was able to grow and prosper largely because of its transatlantic links based on the notion of "Western" culture with its emphasis on liberal democracy, human rights, and free trade. The lack of any genuine defense identity also supports the maintenance of strong transatlantic links.[111]

The three steps suggested cannot solve all the problems confronting common policies, but can make these policies look more identifiable and purposeful. The aim is to dispose of the long tradition of cultivating a vague, ambivalent and all-absorbing vision of the Union. The complexity of the modern world may still require the Union to act in different circles and at different speeds. But the identity requirement should also be taken seriously. If the Union wants to embark on modern flexible ways of governing, it should also take care of its image. Citizens of the Union can hardly identify themselves with a Union whose aims and territory are not clearly defined. The challenge is to find a proper balance between stability and flexibility.

NOTES

1. There is a certain overlap between the pursuit of divergent national policies discussed in this chapter and hegemonic atavism indicated in the previous chapter. The difference is not in appearance but in motivation. Not all cases of national egoism are about an atavistic drive for power and hegemony. Divergent national policies usually stem from the different circumstances of individual countries and are, so to speak, a normal state of affairs.
2. William Pfaff, "Nations Can Resolve to Act, But Europe Isn't a Nation", *International Herald Tribune*, February 2, 1994.
3. Ole Waever, "Insecurity and Identity Unlimited", paper presented at the international conference *The European Disorder*, CERI, Paris, September 29–30, 1994, p. 2.
4. See Robert O. Keohane and Joseph S. Ney Jr., "Power and Interdependence Revisited", *International Organization*, Vol. 41, No. 4 (Autumn 1987), p. 730.
5. Walter Laqueur, *A Continent Astray. Europe, 1970–1978* (Oxford and New York: Oxford University Press, 1979), pp. 8–9.
6. Ibidem, p. 6. In 1996 a young Spanish girl, Maria Canal Fontcuberta, won first prize in the inaugural Schuman Essay Competition. Her essay describes the EU states from the viewpoint of St Benedict, celestial protector of Europe. As far as Benedict is concerned, the states are 15 squabbling brothers and sisters. As a loving grandfather figure, he is aware of the difficulty in bringing them together – Germany is "responsible and hard working", Britain fiercely independent, France and Austria are the intellectuals, while Mediterranean "kids" prefer to "spend their time paddling about at the beach". See Sam King,

"Saintly Vision Draws Path to – First Prize", *The European*, May 9–15, 1996, p. 3.

7. Joanne Wright, "France and European Security", *European Security*, Vol. 2, No. 1 (Spring 1993), pp. 39–40.

8. As reported in *The Economist*, March 22, 1997.

9. In 1994 the Constitutional Court made it possible for Germany to send its military forces abroad, but only after the consent of the Bundestag, and as part of a UN-legitimized multilateral action. Excerpts of the ruling are reprinted, e.g., in *Frankfurter Rundschau*, July 22, 1994, p. 16.

10. Douglas Hurd, "Old Foes but New Friends", *The Times*, October 28, 1994. (The article was based upon the Foreign Secretary's speech to the Franco-British Council). For a French endorsement of similar views see Jean-Louis Bourlanges, "Et si on disait oui aux Allemands?", *Le Monde*, September 29, 1994.

11. See Andrew Marshall and Richard Dowden, "Britain Eyes New Pact with Paris", *The Independent*, November 18, 1994. Also Anand Menon, "NATO the French Way – From Independence to Cooperation: France, NATO and European Security", *International Affairs*, Vol. 71, No. 1 (1995), pp. 19–34.

12. See, e.g., Charles Powell, "A Fundamental Incompatibility?", *The Spectator*, September 3, 1994, pp. 8–10.

13. Alan Clark, "Why We Need a Strategy, Not Platitudes", *The Times*, November 1, 1994. Clark's reading of history was not reassuring for any Franco-British post-Cold War entente either: "The Vichy government collaborated with the Nazis and was resolutely hostile to Britain until it became clear that the Axis was going to be defeated. It fought bitterly against us at Dakar and in Syria. In 1941, more British servicemen were killed by the French than by the Italians, and the antipathy was maintained by de Gaulle, who despite implied assurances to Macmillan vetoed our entry into the EEC in 1962."

14. Ibidem.

15. See Karl Kaiser and Pierre Lellouche, eds., *Le Couple franco-allemand et la défense de l'Europe* (Paris: IFRI, 1986). Also J. Gaffney and E. Kolinksy, eds., *Political Culture in France and Germany* (London: Routledge, 1990).

16. Stanley Hoffmann, "Europe's Identity Crisis Revisited", *Daedalus*, Vol. 123, No. 2 (Spring 1994), p. 8. See also Jean-Louis Bourlanges, op. cit. German misgivings about French policy are well expressed in Ingo van Kolboom, "Dialog mit Bauchgrimmen? Die Zukunft der deutsch-französischen Beziehungen", *Europa-Archiv*, Folge 9 (1994), pp. 259–60.

17. The terms "magnetic core, attraction, repulsion" were first used in Timothy Garton Ash, "The European Disunion", *Time*, September 19, 1994, p. 69. Helmut Kohl seems well aware of the danger of creating a "repulsive" image of the Franco-German alliance. See his interview in *Le Monde*, October 1, 1994.

18. The term "Mulhouse-dendertrein" refers to the decision by Helmut Kohl and François Mitterrand during their meeting on May 30, 1994 in Mulhouse, concerning their mutual support of the candidacy of

the Belgian Prime Minister, Jean-Luc Dehaene, for the post of President of the EU Commission. "Dendertrein" means a train that moves forward in a very insensitive way, smashing all obstacles in its path like a tank. See an interview with Ruud Lubbers in *NRC Handelsblad*, July 1, 1994.

19. It is still rather unclear whether the electoral defeat of the Conservative Party will change Great Britain's political course. Tony Blair announced that he intends to regain significant influence in the Union by adopting more constructive policies on certain issues. However, his tough stance during the negotiations in Amsterdam prompted some analysts to conclude that he was "throwing sand in the eyes" of his colleagues in other EU member states. (See Ewoud Nysingh, "Bijna liep Amsterdam top uit op fiasco," *De Volksskrant*, June 19, 1997. See also Robert Preston, "Blair's line: win friends and influence results," *Financial Times*, June 18, 1997.) In any case Great Britain under the leadership of Tony Blair will have to cope with some troubling empirical facts. As Christopher Hill pointed out, Germany is now more than three times as big again as Britain in terms of population, and approaching twice its size in terms of GDP. Moreover, since the mid-1980s Britain has been persistently flat-footed by a series of joint Franco-German diplomatic initiatives within the EPC/CFSP framework. See Christopher Hill, "United Kingdom. Sharpening Contradictions", in *The Actors in Europe's Foreign Policy*, Christopher Hill, ed. (London and New York: Routledge, 1996), pp. 78–80.

20. This was especially the case under the conservative governments of Margaret Thatcher and John Major. In fact, the 1997 electoral campaign of the Conservative Party tried to portray Tony Blair as a German puppet. One of the Conservative Party's electoral posters, for instance, presented a picture of a small Tony Blair sitting on the knees of an enormous Helmut Kohl.

21. For a detailed analysis of the Spanish policy within the EU see Esther Barbé, "Spain: Realist Integrationism", in *Synergy at Work: Spain and Portugal in European Foreign Policy*, Franco Algieri and Elfriede Regelsberger, eds. (Bonn: Europa Union Verlag, 1996), pp. 259–78. For an analysis of the Italian policy see, e.g., Gianni Bonvicini, "Regional Reassertion: The Dilemmas of Italy", in *The Actors in Europe's Foreign Policy*, Christopher Hill, ed. op. cit., pp. 90–109.

22. For a detailed analysis of the behavior of small countries within the EPC see Françoise de la Serre, "The Scope of National Adaptation to EPC", in *European Political Cooperation in the 1980s. A Common Foreign Policy for Western Europe?*, Alfred E. Pijpers, Elfriede Regelsberger and Wolfgang Wessels, eds. (Dordrecht: Martinus Nijhoff, 1988), pp. 203–5. For a more recent picture see Heinz Gärtner, "Small States and Concepts of European Security", *European Security*, Vol. 2, No. 2 (Summer 1993), pp. 188–99.

23. Frank Pfetsch, "Tensions in Sovereignty: Foreign Policies of EC Members Compared", in *European Foreign Policy. The EC and Changing Perspectives in Europe*, Walter Carlsnaes and Steve Smith, eds. (London: Sage, 1994), pp. 124–30.

24. Christopher Hill, "National Interests – The Insuperable Obstacles?", in *National Foreign Policies and European Political Cooperation*, Christopher Hill, ed. (London: George Allen & Unwin, 1983), p. 196. Although Hill's comments are about the EPC they can well apply to the EU in its current form.

25. See Elfriede Regelsberger, "European Political Cooperation", in *The New Europe. Politics, Government and Economy since 1945*, Jonathan Story, ed., (Oxford and Cambridge: Blackwell, 1993), pp. 270–90.

26. Knud Erik Jørgensen suggested that the immensely dense interplay between national and European levels of policy-making suggests the rise of a "Euro-polity in the field of foreign policy," which is very decentralized, socialized, multi-layered and has policy outputs at different levels. See Knud Erik Jørgensen, "Modern European Diplomacy: A Research Agenda" *Discussion Papers*, (Leicester: Centre for the study of Diplomacy, 1997) pp. 8–9.

27. Alfred E. Pijpers, "The Twelve Out-of-Area: a Civilian Power in an Uncivil World?" op. cit., p. 160. It would be worth exploring whether the Europeans maintained unity by adhering firmly to some clear international principles, but at the price of not really engaging in constructive dialogue with the parties. To have done the latter might have risked exposing cracks in the European line.

28. Rt Hon. David Howell MP, "Seizing the Initiative in Europe", *Reformer. The Journal of Debate within the Conservative Party*, February 1994, p. 17.

29. Christopher Hill, for instance, observed that Margaret Thatcher may have been frustrated by the FCO (the Foreign and Commonwealth Office) and its predilection for European cooperation, but even she realized that the FCO officials are very able in making the EPC/EC system work in Britain's interests. See Christopher Hill, "United Kingdom. Sharpening Contradictions," op. cit., pp. 74–5.

30. See also *Duitsland als Partner*, Advies Raad Vrede en Veiligheid, (Advisory Council on Peace and Security) The Hague, March 1994, and M.C. Brands, "Vanuit de luwte in de drup. Noodzaak van een beweeglijker Nederlands buitenlands beleid", *Internationale Spectator*, Vol. 42, No. 1 (January 1993), pp. 6–12.

31. The shift in Swedish and Finnish policy is well explained in Ole Waever, "Nordic Nostalgia: Northern Europe after the Cold War", *International Affairs*, Vol. 68, No. 1 (1992), pp. 77–102.

32. Knud Erik Jørgensen, "Modern European Diplomacy: A Research Agenda" (op. cit.), p. 8.

33. See, e.g., Keith R. Legg and James F. Morrison, *Politics and the International System: An Introduction* (New York: Harper and Row, 1971), pp. 140–50.

34. William Wallace, "British Foreign Policy after the Cold War", *International Affairs*, Vol. 68, No. 3 (1992), p. 440.

35. Quoted in F.S. Northedge, ed., *The Foreign Policies of the Powers* (London: Faber and Faber, 1968), p. 12.

36. See Ole Waever, "Nordic Nostalgia: Northern Europe after the Cold War", *International Affairs*, Vol. 68, No. 1 (1992), p. 77. For a more comprehensive analysis of the Nordic countries see Lee Miles, ed., *The*

European Union and the Nordic Countries (London and New York: Routledge, 1996), p. 310.

37. See Gilles Martinet, *Le réveil des nationalismes français* (Paris: Éditions du Seuil, 1994), pp. 15–37.

38. Hans J. Morgenthau, *Politics Among Nations* (New York: Alfred A. Knopf, 1960), pp. 125–6. Morgenthau's reasoning is echoed in numerous present day statements. As the former British Minister of Defense, Alan Clark, described the policy attitudes of Britain and France: "One is devious, nationalistic and single-minded, the other is hesitant, ingratiating and inconsistent." See Alan Clark, "Why We Need a Strategy, not Platitudes", *The Times*, November 1, 1994.

39. Walter Laqueur, *A Continent Astray*, op. cit., p. 8.

40. In this section the term Europe is also open-ended, but to talk merely about the EU as having been formally shaped in the short period between the Maastricht Treaty and the Amsterdam Draft Treaty would be pointless if not misleading. There is simply no way to use the term Europe in any specific and satisfactory manner. For a more systematic effort to define Europe in foreign and security terms see Edward Mortimer, "European Security after the Cold War", *Adelphi Paper* No. 271 (1992), pp. 5–6.

41. Jean Jacques Rousseau, *Oeuvres complètes*, Vol. 10 (Brussels: Th. Lejeune, 1827), p. 172, and William Wallace, *The Transformation of Western Europe* (London: Pinter Publishers for The Royal Institute of International Relations, 1990), p. 7.

42. Jacques Delors, "European Integration and Security," *Survival*, Vol. 33, No. 2 (March/April 1991), p. 104.

43. Edgard Pisani, "Europe: Unity and Diversity", *Contemporary European Affairs*, Vol. 4, No. 2–3 (1991), p. 151.

44. See Christopher Hill, "The Capability-Expectations Gap, or Conceptualizing Europe's International Role", *Journal of Common Market Studies*, Vol. 31, No. 3 (September 1993), pp. 312–15.

45. Douglas Hurd, "Foreign and Security Policy", *International Affairs*, Vol. 70, No. 3 (July 1994), p. 423. See also speech by Hans van den Broek, Member of the European Commission, "The Common Foreign and Security Policy of the European Union – an Initial Assessment", Clingendael Institute, The Hague, May 24, 1994, pp. 2–4.

46. Ibidem. A good example of the EU global ambitions is provided by the Communication from the Commission to the Council entitled *Towards A New Asia Strategy*, especially chapter III: "The European Union's New Political Approach Towards Asia", Commission of the European Communities, Brussels, July 13, 1994, pp. 7–12.

47. Christopher Hill, "The Capability-Expectations Gap", op. cit., p. 315.

48. The term "civilian power" was introduced by François Duchène in the early 1970s. See, e.g., François Duchène, "The European Community and the Uncertainties of Interdependence," in *A Nation Writ Large? Foreign-Policy Problems Before the European Community*, Max Kohnstamm and Wolfgang Hager, eds. (London: Macmillan, 1973), pp. 19–20, or François Duchène, "Europe's Role in World Peace," in *Europe Tomorrow: Sixteen Europeans Look Ahead*, Richard Mayne, ed.

(London: Fontana/Collins, 1972), pp. 32–47. EC record of coping with an "uncivilized world" has been analyzed in Alfred E. Pijpers, *The Vicissitudes of European Political Cooperation. Towards a Realist Interpretation of the EC's Collective Diplomacy* (Leiden: University of Leiden, 1990), pp. 171–91.

49. See William Wallace, "From Twelve to Twenty-Four? The Challenges to the EC Posed by the Revolution in Eastern Europe", in *Towards Greater Europe? A Continent Without an Iron Curtain*, Colin Crouch and David Marquand, eds (Oxford: Blackwell Publishers, 1992), p. 34.

50. Before the end of the Cold War it was rather foolish to talk about Europe's independent global role: the United States was the undisputed leader of the entire "free world." With the Iron Curtain running across the old continent "Western" rather than "European" loyalties prevailed: in economic, political, and cultural terms New York or even Seattle had more in common with "Europe proper" than St Petersburg (then still Leningrad) or even Budapest. And there was never any competition to NATO's primacy in the field of security and defense. All this is not that simple at present. See, e.g., Frans Alting von Geusau, *De som der delen. Europa voor en na de omwenteling* (Amsterdam: Meulenhoff, 1991), pp. 50–4.

51. Jacques Delors, "European Integration and Security", op. cit., pp. 105 and 109.

52. See, e.g., Anneke van Dok-van Weele, "US Should Quit Bossing Its Friends," *International Herald Tribune*, July 1, 1997. The writer is The Netherlands' minister for foreign trade.

53. As an editorial of *The Economist* put it in the Autumn of 1996: "Belgians are learning that, like some other Europeans, they also have a flawed democracy. It is plain that Belgium's judiciary has indeed been subject to political patronage and manipulation, and that the country's politicians, if not its entire political class, have presided over a rotten system. If all this sounds familiar, it is because it echoes of Italy, not Africa or Central America. (...) In Italy and France, as in Belgium, it took an independent magistrate to start revealing the enormous fraud being perpetrated on the people by politicians." See "Belgium's Shame", *The Economist*, October 26, 1996, p. 17.

54. As Samuel P. Huntington argued: "The fundamental source of conflict in this new world will not be primarily ideological or primarily economic. The great divisions among humankind and the dominating source of conflict will be cultural. The clash of civilizations will dominate global politics ... the paramount axis of world politics will be the relations between "the West and the Rest." See Samuel P. Huntington, "The Clash of Civilizations?" *Foreign Affairs*, Vol. 72, No. 3 (Summer 1993), pp. 22 and 48.

55. See Owen Harries, "The Collapse of 'The West'", *Foreign Affairs*, Vol. 72, No. 4 (September/October 1993), pp. 41–53.

56. Francis Fukuyama, "For the Atlantic Allies Today, a Fraying of the Sense of Moral Community", *International Herald Tribune*, June 6, 1994.

57. See Chrisoph Bertram, "Let's Be Clear: Not One Europe but a New West and a New East", *International Herald Tribune*, July 12, 1994.

58. Charles A. Kupchan, "Reviving the West", *Foreign Affairs*, Vol. 75, No. 3 (May/June 1996), pp. 92–3.

59. In 1990 William Wallace still argued that *Euramerica* was and still is a mythical concept. See William Wallace, *The Transformation of Western Europe* (London: Pinter, 1990), p. 11.

60. Turkey was already an EC associate member in 1964 and in the 1990s "association agreements" were under negotiation with Israel, Tunisia and Morocco. By 1997 ten Central and Eastern European states officially applied to join the EU: Bulgaria, the Czech Republic, Estonia, Hungary, Latvia, Lithuania, Poland, Romania, Slovakia and Slovenia. Cyprus also wants to join, and Malta may reconsider its current hesitation to join the Union under a different government. The issue of membership for other than Slovenia successor states in former Yugoslavia and some of the CIS countries may also be likely to arise. However, when the 1997 European Council in Luxembourg decided to put Turkey in a category different from and less adventageous than that of other countries that have applied to join the EU, its government threatened to withdraw its application to the Union.

61. William Wallace, *The Transformation of Western Europe*, op. cit., p. 105.

62. The Treaty of Rome vaguely states that any European state may apply to become a member of the European Community (Art. 237). The same phrase was repeated in the Treaty of Maastricht. For a detailed analysis of the enlargement question see Anna Michalski and Helen Wallace, *The European Community: The Challenge of Enlargement*, European Programme Special Paper (London: Royal Institute of International Affairs, 1992).

63. One may add the question: does the EU really want to become a Pacific actor with its Eastern outpost in Vladivostok?

64. Jacques Rupnik, "Europe's New Frontiers: Remapping Europe", *Daedalus*, Vol. 123, No. 3 (Spring 1994), pp. 92–3.

65. A return of geography is heralded by David Hoonson in *Geography and National Identity*, David Hoonson, ed. (Oxford: Blackwell, 1994), p. 2.

66. Portugal's defense structure built in the 1970s is largely designed for the purpose of fighting wars in Africa. To this day Portugal contributes military advisers and logistic support to several African countries. Brazil is the fourth direct investor in Portugal, and 25,000 Brazilians work in Portugal. See Herminio Santos, "The Portuguese National Security Policy", in *Southern European Security in the 1990s*, Roberto Aliboni, ed. (London: Pinter, 1992), pp. 86–98. Also José de Silva Lopes, ed., *Portugal and EC Membership Evaluated* (London: Pinter, 1992), pp. 95–6.

67. Negotiations about accession to the Union could not start earlier than after the conclusion of the 1996–97 Intergovernmental Conference which wanted to make sure that EU institutions were fit for any further enlargement. The Copenhagen Council also set out the conditions that the applying countries should meet before being admitted:

  – stability of institutions guaranteeing democracy, the rule of law, human rights and respect for and protection of minorities

       – the existence of a functioning market economy as well as the capacity to cope with competitive pressure and market forces within the Union
       – the candidate's ability to take on the obligations of membership including adherence to the aims of political, economic and monetary Union.

       See "European Council of Copenhagen 21–22 June 1993, Conclusions of the Presidency", *Agence Europe*, No. 1844/45, June 24, 1993, or "The Europe Agreements and Beyond: A Strategy to Prepare the Countries of Central and Eastern Europe for Accession", Communication from the Commission to the Council, COM (94) 320 final, Brussels, July 13, 1994. For a more in-depth analysis of the eastward enlargement see Heather Grabbe and Kirsty Hughes, *Eastward Enlargement of the European Union* (London: The Royal Institute of International Affairs, 1997), pp. 1–59.

68.   Manuel Marin quoted in William Drozdiak, "Perils on 2 Flanks Challenge EU Unity", *International Herald Tribune*, January 6, 1995.

69.   In Barcelona 15 EU ministers met with their 12 Mediterranean partners from the countries that had signed agreements with the Union: Algeria, Cyprus, Egypt, Israel, Jordan, Lebanon, Malta, Morocco, Syria, Tunisia, Turkey and the Palestinian Authority. For an in-depth analysis of the Barcelona Conference see Esther Barbé, "The Barcelona Conference: Launching Pad of a Process", *Mediterranean Politics*, Vol. 1, No. 1 (Summer 1996), pp. 25–42.

70.   According to the same indicators, Turkey with its $1,630 per capita in 1990 looks weaker than, e.g., Hungary with its $3,446 per capita in 1992, but better than other Eastern European countries. Libya, on the other hand, with its $5,310 GNP per capita in 1990 is well ahead of any country in Eastern Europe. See Alfred Tovias, "The Mediterranean Economy," in *Europe and the Mediterranean*, Peter Ludlow, ed. (London: Macmillan, 1994), p. 8. See also "A Survey of Eastern Europe," *The Economist*, March 13, 1993, p. 18.

71.   How they compare: the population of the Mediterranean countries (Algeria, Cyprus, Egypt, Israel, Jordan, Lebanon, Malta, Morocco, Syria, Tunisia, and Turkey) in 1993 was 204 million and is estimated to grow to 297 million by 2010. The population of East European countries (Albania, Bulgaria, Czech Republic, Estonia, Hungary, Latvia, Lithuania, Poland, Romania, Slovakia, and Slovenia) in 1993 was 109 million, and is projected to grow to 116 million by 2010. In 1993, the GDP in the Mediterranean countries was $365 billion, and GDP per head was $1,746. The 1993 GDP of East Europe was $224 billion, while GDP per head was $2,057. Source: *The Economist*, September 2, 1995 (p. 28).

72.   See Margaret Blunden, "Security on Europe's Southern Flank", *Survival*, Vol. 36, No. 2 (Summer 1994), p. 137. Also Paul Balta, "En Méditerranée, une coopération semée d'embûches", *Le Monde Diplomatique*, October 1994, p. 23.

73.   See Edward Mortimer, "European Security After the Cold War", *Adelphi Paper* No. 271 (1992), pp. 36–7, Álvaro de Vasconcelos, "The Shaping of a Subregional Identity," in *Southern European Security in the*

1990s, Roberto Albioni, ed. (London: Pinter, 1992), p. 26, and Claire Spencer, "The Maghreb in the 1990s", *Adelphi Paper* No. 274 (1993), pp. 57–8.

74. See an interview with President Mubarak of Egypt in *The Times*, November 18, 1994, (by Christopher Walker, "Mubarak warns of Islamic threat to Europe"). One should also keep in mind that the 6 million emigrants within the European Union from the Maghreb make it difficult for the Union to embark on a policy of military or ideological confrontation with the Muslim world.

75. Cultural arguments against EU enlargement southwards are widespread even in a Mediterranean country like France. For instance, in a French opinion poll conducted in 1990, 60 percent of respondents associated Islam with violence, while 71 percent associated it with fanaticism. Figures reproduced in *Magreb Magazine*, October 1992.

76. As quoted in *The Economist*, December 20, 1997, p. 30.

77. An interview with King Hassan in *Financial Times*, October 28, 1994, (by Edward Mortimer and Francis Ghiles, "The discreet intermediary").

78. The policy of containment of local conflicts on Europe's Eastern or Southern flanks can only be partially effective at best. For instance, the refugee flow might remain manageable, but it would nevertheless add further to existing migration problems. The exiled communities will stir up trouble either by turning their anger on their host countries or by siding with opposition homeland contenders. Various national and international bureaucracies would be preoccupied with the conflict, and would be unable to attend to other important affairs. Banks would worry about bad debts, and trade and investment firms about losing business. There would also be the media coverage of conflicts exercising political pressure for doing something more than only practicing containment.

79. See Philippe de Schoutheete, "The European Community and Its Sub-Systems", in *The Dynamics of European Integration* , William Wallace, ed. (London: Pinter, 1990), pp. 106–24.

80. Martin Wight, *Power Politics* (Harmondsworth: Penguin, 1986), second edition, pp. 212–13.

81. Nor are governmental elites responsible for the fact that geography is now imposing diverging political agendas on individual EU members. Germany's preoccupation with Eastern Europe is dictated by the need to manage instability on its borders rather than by a sinister design to create a Teutonic power bloc in the North-East of Europe. The same rationale applies to Greece's behavior in the Balkans or France's behavior in the Maghreb region. Governmental elites could be less vague about the future borders of the European Union, but these borders are being shaped not merely by decisions in London, Paris and Brussels. Can one say where the borders of Russia will be in ten years time, for instance?

82. See Philip Everts and Richard Sinnott, "Conclusion: European Publics and the Legitimacy of Internationalized Governance", in *Public Opinion and the Internationalization of Governance*, Oskar Niedermayer and Richard Sinnott, eds. (Oxford: Oxford University Press, 1995), pp. 441–5.

83.   In the 1981 European survey on values, it was asked: "Are you willing to fight for your country?" and an average of 40 percent said that they were not. These averages did not change significantly when the survey was repeated in 1990–91. See Mattei Dogan, "Comparing the Decline of Nationalisms in Western Europe: the Generational Dynamic", *International Social Science Journal*, Vol. XLV, No. 2 (May 1993), p. 185.

84.   According to a 1994 public opinion survey, in all EU member states satisfaction with the functioning of European democracy was indeed low (48 percent dissatisfied, 40 percent satisfied), but not lower than satisfaction with the way the national democracies work (on average 53 percent dissatisfied, and 43 percent satisfied). See European Commission, *Eurobarometer: Opinion in the European Union*, No. 41, Brussels, July 1994, pp. 1–3.

85.   This point is well argued in Louis L. Snyder, *The New Nationalism* (Ithaca, NY: Cornell University Press, 1968), pp. 323 and 357–73. For a thesis that the heyday of nation-building is over, being superseded by the imperatives of the global economy see Eric J. Hobsbawm, "Nationalism in the Late Twentieth Century", in *Nations and Nationalism since 1780: Programme, Myth, Reality*, Eric J. Hobsbawn, ed. (Cambridge: Cambridge University Press, 1990), pp. 163–84.

86.   The interplay of political culture, values, attitudes and images of the world are well analyzed in Richard Muir and Ronan Paddison, *Politics, Geography and Behaviour* (London and New York: Methuen, 1981), pp. 22–50.

87.   Although James Mayall rightly argued: "From a sociological or historical standpoint, there are clearly many kinds of nationalism, but the national idea itself is not unclear. It holds that the world is (or should be) divided into nations and that the nation is the only proper basis for a sovereign state and the ultimate source of governmental authority." See James Mayall, *Nationalism and International Society* (Cambridge: Cambridge University Press, 1990), p. 2. That said, one should keep in mind that nations can have moving boundaries and unclear identity as well.

88.   Ernest Gellner identified four different manners in which nationalism manifested itself in various parts of Europe: the time zones of Europe. See Ernest Gellner, *Conditions of Liberty. Civil Society and Its Rivals* (London: Hamish Hamilton, 1994), pp. 113–18. See also Hugh Seton-Watson, *Nations and States. An Enquiry into the Origins of Nations and the Politics of Nationalism* (London: Methuen, 1977), pp. 463–5.

89.   Benedict Anderson, *Imagined Communities. Reflections on the Origin and Spread of Nationalism* (London: Verso, 1991), p. 3.

90.   For a detailed analysis of multiple identities see Anthony D. Smith, *National Identity* (London: Penguin Books, 1990), pp. 3–8.

91.   Charles Taylor went even further to argue that we are now increasingly confronted with a conflict between those who accept a complex identity and those who stick to a simple one. See Charles Taylor, "Democratic exclusion (and its remedies?)" A paper presented at the international conference on "Democratic Politics: Agenda of the Future," organized by the Institute for Human Sciences, Vienna, June 11–14, 1997, unpublished draft, pp. 1–17.

92. Ole Waever, "Insecurity and Identity Unlimited", paper presented at a conference by CERI in Paris, September 29–30 1994, p. 27. The linkage between societal changes and international relations was well grasped by E.H. Carr some fifty years ago. Analyzing the shift from enlightened absolutism to romantic nationalism, Carr wrote: "International relations were henceforth to be governed not by the personal interests, ambitions and emotions of the monarch, but by the collective interests, ambitions and emotions of the nation." E.H. Carr, *Nationalism and After* (London: Macmillan, 1945), p. 8.

93. Ernest Gellner, *Nations and Nationalism* (Oxford: Blackwell, 1983), p. 86.

94. See Pierre Hassner quoted in *The New Europe: Politics, Government and Economy since 1995*, Jonathan Story, ed. (Oxford: Blackwell, 1993), p. 494.

95. See Josep Llobera, "The Role of the State and the Nation in Europe", in *European Identity and the Search for Legitimacy*, Soledad Garcia, ed. (London: Pinter, 1993), p. 77.

96. See Anthony D. Smith, "National Identity and the Idea of European Unity", *International Affairs*, Vol. 68, No. 1 (1992), p. 74.

97. For a recent and excellent effort to link the issue of identity and security see: Paul Taylor, *The European Union in the 1990s*, (Oxford: Oxford University Press, 1996), pp. 165–77.

98. Anthony D. Smith, op. cit., p. 59.

99. For a detailed set of policies for nation-building see William Bloom, *Personal Identity, National Identity and International Relations* (Cambridge: Cambridge University Press, 1990), pp. 142–50.

100. This is well argued by Soledad Garcia and Helen Wallace in Soledad Garcia, ed., *European Identity*, op. cit., "Conclusion", p. 172.

101. The concept of the European family of cultures is elaborated in Anthony D. Smith, "National Identity and the Idea of European Unity", op. cit., pp. 67–74. See also Lord Gladwyn, *The European Idea* (London: New English Library, 1967).

102. Jürgen Habermas, "Citizenship and National Identity: Some Reflections on the Future of Europe", *Praxis International*, Vol. 12, No. 1 (April 1992), p. 12.

103. This was well argued by Charles Taylor, "The Liberal-Communitarian Debate", in *Liberalism and the Moral Life*, Nancy Rosenblum, ed. (Cambridge, MA: Harvard University Press, 1989), p. 178.

104. See especially Friedrich Kratochwil, "On the Notion of 'Interest' in International Relations", *International Organization*, Vol. 36, No. 1 (Winter 1982), pp. 1–30.

105. National interests and national identities may well be interconnected, but they are basically about different things. Identities are about subjective feelings of belonging, be they individual or collective. Interests are basically normative and claim to be objective rather than subjective. For more on the problem of definitions see: Yosef Lapid, "Culture's Ship: Returns and Departures in International Relations Theory," in *The Return of Culture and Identity in International Relations Theory*, Yosef Lapid, ed. (Boulder: Lynne Rienner, 1995), pp. 6–9; and Friedrich

Kratochwil, "On the Notion of 'Interest' in International Relations," op. cit., pp. 1–30.

106. A gentler version of such a policy is presented by Elisabeth Bakke. As she put it: "In order to spread a European identity, the European Union, with some qualifications, would have to use methods of a nationalist movement, a movement from below, in order to convince the members of the alleged "nation", the Europeans, that they are really Europeans, and not Germans or Italians or Danes. In order to mobilize them for the European cause, the European "awakeners" must invent or discover a shared history by selecting the parts of European history that suit this aim, and by idealizing the European cultural manifestations. In order to succeed, the elite needs to be able to return to a "living past," one people can recognize as theirs." See Elisabeth Bakke, "Towards a European Identity?", *Arena Working Papers* No. 10 (April 1995), pp. 21–2.

107. The salience of territory is decreasing in terms of power politics: that was the message in the previous chapter. This does not mean, however, that territory is losing its importance in terms of identity. I will return to the complex issue of boundaries and territory in the book's conclusions. For a more in-depth analysis of the problem see, e.g., John Gerard Ruggie, "Territory and Beyond: Problematizing Modernity in International Relations," *International Organization*, Vol. 47, No. 1 (Winter 1993), pp. 171–4 or Friedrich Kratochwil, "Of Systems, Boundaries and Territoriality: An Inquiry into the Formation of the State System," *World Politics*, Vol. 34, No. 1 (October 1986), pp. 27–52.

108. And thus the borders of the Union should be the borders between democracy and autocracy in Europe and not primarily between poverty and affluence or between different religions and civilizations. If Belarus, Albania, or Morocco have little chance of becoming members of the Union it is not only because they are either poor or non-Christian, but because they are undemocratic. In short, successful foreign policy within the Union requires that all member states be fully democratic.

109. See Ole Waever, "European Security Identities", *Journal of Common Market Studies*, Vol. 34, No. 1 (March 1996), p. 127.

110. As Gerard Delanty forcefully argues: "Identities take on a pathological form when they are constructed against a category of otherness. Instead of identity being defined by a sense of belongingness and solidarity arising out of shared life-worlds, it becomes focused on opposition to an Other: the 'We' is defined not by reference to a framework of shared experiences, common goals and a collective horizon, but by the negation of the Other. Identification takes place through the imposition of otherness in the formation of a binary typology of 'Us' and 'Them.' The purity and stability of the 'We' is guaranteed first in the naming, then in the demonization and, finally, in the cleansing of otherness." See Gerard Delanty, *Inventing Europe. Idea, Identity, Reality*. (London: Macmillan, 1995), p. 5.

111. This is not to imply that the Union should act as a lame duck in its relations with Washington, but to reject a caricatured description of transatlantic relations as guided merely by a zero-sum game if not a head-on competition.

3 Paradigm lost and conceptual confusion

It is easy to blame divergent national traditions and conflicting interests for the current state of Euro-paralysis. But if unity was the order of the day within the European Union would the Union know what it is aiming at in international affairs? What principles and values are guiding its policy? Where is it going in terms of military and diplomatic commitments? In short, can a foreign and security policy of the Union get off the ground if Europe does not know what kind of order it intends to have, how to achieve it, and at what price?

Initially, things looked pretty clear: Europe "whole and free" was proclaimed to be the West's aim. In a sense, this aim has been reached very quickly. The rapid collapse of the Soviet empire produced an end to Europe's division, especially to the division of Germany, and communist dictatorships fell one by one throughout Eastern Europe. Moreover, Moscow abandoned its offensive military doctrine and agreed on significant reductions in its nuclear and conventional forces. The Cold War was over and the West had won. The victors' celebration was short-lived, however, as it became painfully clear that successive debates about the future of European security produced nothing but a plethora of vague plans, instant disagreements, and confusion. In the meantime the vicious war in the Balkans has shaken European self-confidence, Russia has leveled to the ground vast parts of Chechnya, and former communists began their re-entry into power all over Eastern Europe.

The Cold War security system in Europe was unjust, but it was fairly stable. The Soviet threat was imminent, but it was neutralized by a sound nuclear deterrence posture and the unambiguous "first strike" doctrine. Military budgets were high, but generals knew what was needed for a clearly-defined scenario of a possible conflict. The collapse of the Soviet empire produced what the West had always wanted, but it also produced an entirely new Europe in which old diplomatic and security concepts look obsolete and new ones have yet to be created. Western Europe has lost its major enemy, but it also lost the sextant by which its ship has been guided for the last five decades. The new era in Europe's history has called for a new thinking about security and international affairs. However, new ideas are in short supply, and clearly inadequate for coping with new challenges confronting the old continent. And thus the initial euphoria has been replaced by bitterness, fear, and confusion. Brave visions of the new pan-European security architecture created in the aftermath of the Cold War soon proved misconceived and hopelessly optimistic in their schedules and anticipated accomplishments. Long-proclaimed principles and values have been repeatedly compromised in day-to-day practices. New threats or risks to Europe's security were seen as real but vague, and it was highly unclear what type of solutions would prove suitable in addressing these threats. Several years after the fall of the Berlin Wall security specialists still talk about the "strategic arthritis," "psychosomatic immobilism" and "intellectual impotence" of Europe and the Western world.[1] The European Union has lost its sense of direction, its leaders look cynical and powerless, and its people seem confused and uninterested.

In this chapter I will try to address the origins and nature of the conceptual confusion that has affected the Union's ability to foster a credible and effective foreign and security policy. I will argue that the dramatic and unexpected collapse of the bi-polar system is largely responsible for this confusion. However, the problem is not likely to disappear as the pace of events slows. The entire hierarchy of interests and values guiding Western security thinking is now being re-examined, if not openly questioned. Several basic principles of international relations are now considered either irrelevant or in conflict with each other. There is confusion about both the aims and means of European foreign policy. Even the basic logic of modern rational thinking about security and international affairs is now under fire from an ever-growing stratum of intellectual dissidents. Security experts and politicians are again struggling with questions that have seemed relatively easy for the last fifty years. Is security a function of developments in the field of arms control, military alliances, and weapons technology, or is it related to economic growth, domestic stability, and leadership change? Are the basic notions of "rational choice," "national interest," or "system stability" adequate for describing relations between states in Europe? Can a collective security system ever work? Does European integration offer a better prospect for stability and peace? Is stability or change Europe's most desired objective? Today, there are no longer straight and convincing answers to such questions and hence confusion prevails.

After reviewing the initial problems in coping with the post-Cold War transformation this chapter will analyze three basic conceptual dilemmas facing Europe's politicians and experts. They concern: (1) *challenges* to Europe's security, (2) *solutions* aimed at addressing these challenges, and (3) basic modes of *rationality* guiding Western foreign policy behavior. This functional analysis will be illustrated by examples from three different policy areas: military intervention, nuclear non-proliferation, and the Union's eastward enlargement.

Our search for a way out of the current confusion will lead us to Kant's concept of a "common commonwealth," stressing the import-ance of civil society in a given international setting.[2] Our conclusion will be that without the emergence of a truly European civil society, the Union will find it difficult to accommodate the conflicting values of its unlike-minded citizens. Procedural and institutional solutions merely provide a partial escape from intellectual challenges facing Europe at present. With the end of the Cold War, Europe has lost an interna-tional system that served as an ordering principle of relations between states and did not gain an international civil society with common values and culture which would reduce incentives to use force on the continent. A new order can hardly emerge out of the present chaos unless the foundations of a European civil society are firmly in place.

THE MADNESS OF UNLIMITED CHOICE

Since World War II the "menu for choice" in European politics was gradually expanding due to a steady economic, technological, and cultural progress on the continent.[3] Yet the Cold War bi-polar rivalry imposed on European actors some well-known constraints which prev-ented them from "testing" all possible courses available on the polit-ical menu. Raymond Aron named this phenomenon "a slowing down of history": the military balance between Great Powers tends towards the maintenance of the status quo, with all its absurdities.[4] But in the short period between 1989 and 1991, these artificial constraints of the Cold War bi-polarity suddenly disappeared and European actors began facing an enormous sea of opportunities. Liberation of Central and Eastern Europe, diplomatic concord between Russia and NATO countries, major disarmament agreements, all these developments, previously inconceivable, became possible. Small states could, from then on, choose their own path between membership in an alliance, regional defense cooperation, and neutrality. Large states became free to intervene or to refrain from intervening. Places labeled "strategic" in the Cold War period could now be ignored. What only weapons could previously achieve was now frequently available through dial-ogue and economic cooperation. As never before one could choose between power and morality, between the pursuit of military might and the pursuit of economic prosperity, between national, regional, and global interests and values.

New visions and brave rhetoric instantly followed. "Nothing will stop us, everything is possible, Berlin is free!" declared President Clinton.[5] And the Italian Foreign Minister proclaimed "a new chapter in polit-ical engineering, one that gives rise to a new organization of Europe."[6] Security experts, for their part, competed in promoting new architec-tural designs for Europe and models of the new order that would ensure stability if not perpetual peace on the continent.[7] But all these visions and brave talk came to nothing as the feeling of unlimited choice proved very much illusory.[8] First, problems emerged in the structure of the European system: the elimination of Cold War con-straints meant the destruction of the old balance, hierarchy, and stab-ility. And thus, for instance, some local warlords figured out that they could now use violence indiscriminately in order to enhance their petty ambitions without any serious punishment from either the major powers or the international community. Secondly, problems emerged in terms of laws and procedures: the new unconstrained environment required new rules and routines, and there were no ready-made blue-prints. Most notably, the international community found it extremely difficult to create rules of coping with civil wars and ethnic killing.[9] Thirdly, problems emerged in terms of policy formulation and imple-mentation: the end of the Cold War produced a general ethical and intellectual disorientation that obstructed any swift decision making. It proved quite impossible to make sense of the choices facing European policy-makers without some sort of moral compass and strategic pur-pose which were now buried under the rubble of the Berlin Wall. And thus, after a few years it became increasingly evident that the Union had serious problems in coping with the cascading change that, iron-ically, it had always hoped for.

Change is always difficult to handle. As Ralf Dahrendorf put it: "The trouble with change in human affairs is that it is so hard to pin down. It happens all the time. But while it happens it eludes our grasp, and once we feel able to come to grips with it, it has become past history."[10] The trouble with the post-Cold War type of change was that it was a complex mixture of novelty and continuity, that it was dramatic and chaotic, comprehensive and multi-dimensional, and above all it was totally unexpected. Some changes had been evolving for a long time unnoticed. Others had been unable to develop properly. The erosion of the nation state, the growth of economic interdependence, the assertion of liberal ideology, all these processes have been going on in Europe for many years only to be fully appreciated in the post-Cold War era and then fused with the melting pot of daily events. Other changes were novel but related to similar historical developments. For instance, the fall of the Soviet empire was unprecedented, but it also fits well into the post-1945 trend of decolonization.[11] Similarly, the novel phenomenon of decommunization was intertwined with an ancient phenomenon of modernization.[12] Long-term technological change has been mixed up with short-term changes in public perceptions. Change affected not only states but also ordinary people, threatening their values, their identity, their social structure. There was so much change that the term itself became inflated and it was difficult to distinguish between a superficial change and a deep international breakthrough. As Ole Waever argued: "There is good reason to be careful not to proclaim a radical transformation every time one sees change."[13] Change was for good and for bad, creating massive opportunities, but also many threats. And there was also a cumulative effect of change as developments in one country or in one small field produced a domino effect in various fields throughout the entire region. For instance, the Hungarian government's decision to allow East German refugees to cross its border with the West prompted a chain of political and economic reactions all over Europe.

To grasp that kind of change was practically impossible, and yet it was also necessary because as Alastair Buchan once said:

> For a framework or a chart we must have: events move too fast, too many countries are affected, public opinion is too articulate, to enable us to rest content with the improvisation of a few political leaders, the more so since this is not an age that will be remembered for its towering leadership.[14]

In principle, the task of elaborating a conceptual framework for the post-Cold War transformation was assigned to scholars in international relations and strategic studies analysts. However, they seemed to perform their job very poorly: most of them failed to imagine, let alone predict, the fall of the Berlin Wall, were unable to go beyond the rigidity of self-imposed disciplinary boundaries, stuck to their increasingly irrelevant ideological prejudices, and proved unable to liberate themselves from largely outdated theories and methodologies.[15] The discipline of international relations has been accused of being "reactionary, theoretically naive, male based, gender insensitive and generally ill-equipped even to start thinking about the problems of contemporary world politics in any more than superficial way."[16] Strategic studies analysts were seen as having "very little grasp of the forces which were moving and shaping international politics;" and as such not even deserving of "compassion and pity."[17]

Such criticism was only partly justified. After all, there is no strategic blueprint for dealing with major historical events such as the fall of the Berlin Wall, disintegration of the Soviet Union, and the end to bi-polar rivalry. Strategists and theorists have often promised more than they could deliver but journalists or politicians were hardly doing the conceptual work any better. True, academics failed to predict the current change and they are still having problems in explaining it in a widely-acceptable manner. But they have identified major moral and strategic dilemmas facing Europe in these turbulent years. This by itself is helpful in finding a way out of the current conceptual confusion.

AMBIGUOUS CHALLENGES, RISKS, AND THREATS

During the Cold War there were many challenges, and risks but the key word was threat. It came from the Soviet Union, it was military in nature and its target was the entire NATO area (NATO as an ultimate security guardian of its member states and people). Now that this threat is gone, challenges and risks are more prominent on the European security agenda.[18] But what kind of challenges exactly, for whom and from where? There is no clear European answer to these questions.

According to Jacques Delors challenges range from poverty and underdevelopment to environmental degradation, demographic pressures, and substantial geopolitical changes.[19] Risks include actual and potential instability in Eastern Europe, the Mediterranean, and the Middle East. The dangers presented by the spread of weapons of mass destruction, extreme nationalism, religious fundamentalism, massive, uncontrolled migration, and terrorism must also be taken into account, according to Delors.[20] The list is long and comprehensive, and Delors openly admits: "Anything could happen in the present situation."[21]

The first serious problem with this long list of risks and challenges is that it lacks any clear-cut priorities. If anything can happen, how can the Union try to prevent it? Investing in preparations for every kind of imaginable scenario is uneconomical, if not senseless. Those who prepare for everything may well end up accomplishing nothing.[22]

Some European politicians seem to follow the opposite reasoning and simply do nothing to cope with the current risks on the continent. This is also because the above list of risks and challenges is not credible enough. How can we know that certain risks will transform themselves into threats calling for the countervailing deployment of military forces? Over-sensitivity and scaremongering can be self-defeating if not dangerous. Moreover, terms such as instability, religious fundamentalism or nationalism are rather vague when translated into the language of security and international relations. If presidential tanks in Moscow pound the building of the Russian parliament, what should the Union do exactly in the military and diplomatic field? Is religious fundamentalism the source of instability in Islamic states, or is it underdevelopment, inequality, and poverty? The cultural, political, and economic background in various countries also differs, and is thus likely to produce different results. Consider, for instance, the very different backgrounds of nationalistic fervor in Croatia, Estonia, and Silesia. Can one say that they all raise the same security concern?

There is also a problem with the question: risks for whom and from where? Geography, history, and cultural links make some countries particularly exposed to instabilities in some regions. For instance, France is obviously more exposed to developments in the Maghreb than, say, Austria or Denmark, and thus cherishes and promotes different threat perceptions than other states. Yet this question can be seen in a different light if we ask: are we concerned with the security of European states or of people; only in Europe or everywhere? As Ken Booth and Peter Vale argued, states are not the only consumers of security, alternatives include "individual human beings, nations, ethnic and kinship groups and, potentially, the whole global community of humankind."[23]

The sources of risks are also unclear. Are risks coming from certain regimes or from certain civilizations? In the age of high-tech, interdependence, and mass communication can we credibly point to specific geographic areas around Europe as most likely sources of concern? Or maybe major risks and challenges are simply coming from within us, from our ineffective system of government, from our moral ambivalence and cultural indifference, from what François Heisbourg called the "collective equivalent of a nervous breakdown" that prevents any constructive policy and provides a feeding ground for politicians such as Jean-Marie Le Pen?[24]

Finally, the very nature of challenges and risks is confusing and vague. The distinction between risks and threats is based on the assumption that threats entail the existence of an armed capability at the service of unfriendly states. Risks, on the other hand, usually entail non-military or quasi-military developments that can be managed by "soft" rather than "hard" security measures. But economic, environmental, or cultural risks are so widely ranged that it is difficult to distinguish between legitimate and illegitimate developments, to localize the area of concern, or to establish clear relations between "soft-core" risks and "hard-core" threats. Of course, assessing military threats is never easy either.[25] It is also hard to deny the security consequences of various economic, environmental, societal, and cultural developments. But saying that "economics and security are two sides of the same coin" is not very helpful in drafting concrete tasks for European diplomats and military men.[26] Nor is it helpful to proclaim a clash of civilizations without identifying real threats, or embark on an environmental crusade that merely focuses on Europe rather than on the entire world.

Vague and unspecified security risks provide little more than signposts for European policy makers and they are also ripe for manipulation. For instance, Eastern European steel producers have been accused of "environmental dumping" and of endangering "job security" within the European Union, but one is inclined to believe that protectionism rather than genuine security concerns prompted the accusation. The Islamic fundamentalism in the Maghreb region has been identified as a major security challenge despite the fact that no country across the Mediterranean threatens the territorial integrity of the European Union and in view of the colonial legacy and the recent history of Western intervention in Maghreb the opposite point could be made more convincingly. Besides, putting all Islamic and North African states under one heading is also highly misleading, just as it is inappropriate to talk about one Eastern Europe and a universal post-communist risk syndrome.

At the bottom of this confusing debate is the concept of security. The Helsinki Final Act of 1975 tried to suggest that security has many domestic, societal, and economic facets and therefore cannot be reduced to external and basically military matters. But this broad meaning of security was never endorsed by Western security experts.[27] For them security referred to the relationship between states and was concerned with such issues as sovereignty, alliance, interstate negotiations, strategic deterrence, military balance, and conventional and nuclear battlefields. Such a narrow concept of security was inadequate already in the Cold War years and is even more inadequate in the post-Cold War years.[28] Yet it is one thing to identify various non-military facets of security and point to multiple domestic and international "consumers" of security, quite another to comprehend and operationalize the problem in policy terms. Costas M. Constantinou grasped the latter dilemma as no one else when analyzing Western efforts in the Balkans:

> If the Yugoslav crisis has taught us a lesson it is that attempts to maintain international or regional security and avoid another Balkan crisis mingle with attempts to restore national or state security (the identity of which constantly changes), which in turn mingle with attempts to enhance the security of ethnic or religious groups, which in turn mingle with attempts to secure individuals caught in the middle of all these (and for whom all these identities make no sense, such as mixed marriages or atheist Muslims), which in turn mingle with attempts to secure the place and safety of UN troops on the ground, which even mingle with attempts to secure European cultural heritage (Dubrovnik) or historical copyrights (Macedonia), and which lastly mingle with attempts to secure a face for the West...[29]

Constantinou asserts that we hardly know what we are supposed to secure in ex-Yugoslavia, let alone how we are to go about doing it. But a similar assertion also applies to other troubling regions in Europe. In short, the Union does not really know what the greatest dangers are, for whom, why, and when.

CONFUSING STRATEGIES

Since risks and challenges to Europe are ambiguous and vague it is difficult for the Union to craft any strategies for combating them. Strategy must anticipate events, not only respond to them. Defense planning should be concerned with the most likely course of events, it should neither be based on blind optimism nor on war-game nightmares. Strategies divorced from any political and geographical context are, as Michael Howard put it, "pointless and devoid of sense."[30] But, of course, something ought to be done to cope with the complex situation of today. Faced with a plethora of novel developments, strategic experts rely on some basic assumptions about the nature of international relations and they often look back at history in search of solutions to the current developments. Their arguments fall into three distinct categories which can be called Hobbesian, Grotian, and Kantian.[31]

The Hobbesian school of thought is primarily concerned with the collapse of the bi-polar Cold War system in Europe, with all its stability and predictability. Terms such as power – understood in crude military terms – sovereignty, and national interest are central in its rationale. International relations is about a relentless security competition, it is argued, with the possibility of war always in the background. Alliances among like-minded governments are the favored vehicle for aggregating power and enhancing national interests but the dominating logic of security competition imposes severe limits on the utility of any form of international cooperation. Humanitarian concerns, domestic order, and economic interdependence are regarded as marginal, if not irrelevant, strategic questions. International law and institutions are merely instruments of manipulation in the power game among major states.

According to the Hobbesian school of thought, the major task for today is maintaining order and stability amidst disintegrating tendencies in Europe and elsewhere. This should be done by the balance of power politics and by bandwagoning against trouble-making countries such as Russia, Iraq, Serbia, and if needed even against some EU members such as Germany or Greece. As Josef Joffe recently observed: "Short of empire, a primary power must choose between balancing à la Britain and bandwagoning à la Bismarck... The purpose is to deny other powers both the motive and the opportunity for confrontation..."[32] NATO is seen as the most suitable tool of maintaining balance and stability on the continent, even though some French or Spanish followers of Hobbesian thinking would prefer the Union to do the balancing. In a conflict situation, such as the one in the Balkans, the prime objective is to prevent major power competition rather than trying to solve things on the ground or search for "just" and humanitarian solutions.

The strength of Hobbesian thinking is in its emphasis on the dangers emerging from the current change in the international structure, with all the uncertainties about who threatens who, about who will oppose who, and about who will gain or lose from the actions of other states.[33] Today, the European security system is in flux, with the spheres of influence being increasingly less sharply defined than in the past decades and with the re-nationalization of defense postures proceeding apace. But the structure argument is not very clear: A transition to what? A multi-polar or uni-polar structure, or to a sort of uni-multipolar structure that is neither bi-polar nor truly uni-polar?[34] And what difference would it make for Europe's security if the end destination is a uni-polar, multi-polar or uni-multipolar structure? Hobbesian thinking is also right in emphasizing the ever-present danger of war on the European continent. However, its preoccupation with the inter-state type of conflict ignores the origins, dynamics, and importance of civil wars and ethnic conflicts in the present-day Europe. Hobbesians, in particular, are unable to establish the causal link between ethnic nationalist sentiment and interstate violence.[35] In a similar fashion, the Hobbesian school of thought provides few guidelines for dealing with important economic, political, and humanitarian problems within states, which are after all the most evident source of instability in several European countries and states bordering Europe. Moreover, relations between members of the European Union as such can no longer be understood in terms of bandwagoning, relentless security competition, and self interest. In fact, one can no longer be certain that these terms continue to apply to relations between Eastern and Western Europe or between Western Europe and the Maghreb.

The Grotian approach rests on enhancing European integration and institution building. Institutions guarantee multilateral involvement, rely on established decision-making procedures, and provide important linkages between various economic, military, and political fields. Integration worked well to reduce ethnic conflicts and national rivalries within the European Union and could also have a healing effect in Eastern Europe and Maghreb.[36] The EU integration proved to be effective in reducing economic discrepancies between rich and poor countries, introducing many common laws and administrative procedures, and creating a comprehensive system of international consultation and cooperation that allowed states to abandon the balance-of-power rationale. As Jacques Delors argued: "The European Community [read: Union] has a special responsibility not only because of its importance as a pole of stability and prosperity, but also because it has an armory of instruments to deal with the most pressing problems in the East and in the South. Never has the link between economic stability and security been so obvious."[37]

Moreover, the EU is not alone in providing order and security on the continent. By now there are at least 15 multilateral groupings involved in shaping Europe's collective destiny. The multi-layered set of supposedly complementary, mutually-reinforcing, and interlocking institutions should provide a flexible system for dealing with the various problems facing the continent. The institutional structure, Grotians argue, offers the most effective and legitimate channels for reconciling conflicting national interests.[38] Integration shifts states' loyalties, expectations, and activities towards the center, where institutions possess or demand jurisdiction over the pre-existing national states. A new security regime in Europe based on a series of commonly agreed upon norms, principles and decision-making procedures should be able to provide enough incentives for states to cooperate instead of indulging in relentless security competition and conflict.[39]

But are not institutions essentially manipulative instruments in the hands of mighty European states or, as Evans and Wilson put it; "arenas for acting out power relationships"?[40] Was not preoccupation with institutions for the last few years a means by which the leading states could avoid individual responsibility by passing the buck to a multinational body? Were not all the various institutions inter-blocking rather than inter-locking? Would not cooperation among European states work better without a labyrinth of bureaucratic institutions? Are institutions responsible for integration in Western Europe or is it the pacifying role played by the US? Are states constrained by international law even when it does not suit their national interests? Are post-Cold War international institutions in such good shape that they can make Eastern Europe function like Western Europe within a couple of decades? And what about the European Union's role in Bosnia? Did it live up to Grotian pledges? Did any other institution except the "Hobbesian" NATO do its job in Bosnia any better? Surely, this is a list of rather rhetorical questions, but they indicate that it is rather risky to put too much trust in institutions *per se*.[41]

Grotians are right in looking beyond power struggles and military questions, but the beneficial role of international institutions, international laws, and integration should not be taken for granted in the current situation. As the history of the Cold War clearly shows, institutions, laws and integration work best in a stable international environment and among like-minded democratic states. This brings us closer to the Kantian type of argument.

The Kantian approach rests on enhancing common perceptions of politics, economics, and human rights. When people cherish common ideals and political values, when they recognize a similar catalogue of citizen's rights and duties, when they are guided by a shared communal spirit, then the chance for a violent conflict in Europe is minimal, it is argued. Power, laws, and institutions are therefore less important than a common culture based on peace and trade, compromise and co-operation, interdependence of mutual interests and interpenetration of divergent societies. Kantians try, in Pierre Hassner's words, "to overcome the conflicts of states neither by suppressing their plurality nor by trying to convince them to adopt other rules of behavior, but by shifting the ground of their rivalry through social, technological, cultural or even anthropological change, uncovered by the philosophy of history."[42]

The notion of a democratic peace is especially popular among present-day Kantians.[43] Democratic states not only share the culture, perceptions, and practices that permit compromise and the peaceful resolution of conflicts, but they also assume that other democracies subscribe to similar methods of regulating disagreements and thus do not view each other as zero-sum threats. As Michael W. Doyle argued, democracies, "which rest on consent, presume foreign republics to be also consensual, just and therefore deserving of accommodation."[44] If a "democratic ethos" and a "liberal conscience" based on peaceful competition, persuasion, and compromise will spread into the eastern part of the continent, a truly pan-European collective security system could then emerge.[45]

Developments of the late 1980s and early 1990s strongly reinforced Kantian arguments. After all, the Cold War came to an end more as a result of democratic trends in Eastern Europe than as a result of any spectacular successes in managing the military competition between NATO and the Warsaw Pact. Yet the road from a repressive to a democratic form of government proved to be pretty bumpy and has already led to ethnic and political violence in a number of cases. Recent years have also shown how difficult it is for the EU to engineer democratic change in societies with a long history of autocracy (e.g. Russia) or widespread religious fundamentalism (e.g. Algeria). And can one expect an assertion of truly democratic culture in the unstable security environment of today? What if the democratic project fails in some countries? Should they be embraced or contained? Does not the Union still need some harsh military precautions to prevent a possible outbreak of violence on the continent? And if the Union tries to promote Kantian ideals of freedom, democracy, and community should it not open its borders to immigrants from other countries and allow its poor neighbors to obtain EU membership? Would such a policy export stability to Eastern Europe and Maghreb or would it rather import instability into the European Union?

The debate between Hobbesians, Grotians, and Kantians is thus very inconclusive and obviously contributes to the existing conceptual disarray. All schools of thought work on different theoretical assumptions and argue on different levels of analysis.[46] They also have a different hierarchy of concerns: Hobbesians are primarily concerned about the fortunes of individual nation states, Grotians about the fortunes of the community of states in Europe, and Kantians about the fortunes of a broad community of people: the cosmopolitan polity to use Kant's own words. Besides, all schools of thought are better at suggesting the overall long-term strategy for the European Union than at drafting practical daily policies. On the practical level all the various strategies are often fused and presented as one comprehensive, coherent, and workable policy program. Governments and EU officials try to avoid tight identification with any single school of strategic thought. They prefer to assume complementarity of various strategies and pursue a policy à la carte, constantly switching political gears, from worthy Grotian schemes to tacky Hobbesian manipulation. The result is even greater chaos because Hobbesian, Grotian, and Kantian strategies are often in conflict with each other and cannot be pursued simultaneously.[47] And thus the policy-making process within the European Union tends to resemble a famous passage from T.S. Eliot: "Time yet for a hundred indecisions/And for a hundred visions and revisions,/Before taking of a toast and tea."[48]

COMPETING RATIONALITIES

Although Hobbesian, Grotian, and Kantian strategies are often in conflict, they reflect one common tradition of modern rational thinking. However, this tradition is today being challenged by the re-emergence of the pre-modern romantic type of thinking on the one hand, and the post-modern relativist type of thinking on the other hand.[49] This challenge is partly a response to the rigidities of modernist assumptions guiding Cold War policies. The end of the Cold War exposed the "irrationality" of some supposedly "rational" solutions to international politics and demanded a new way of approaching European politics. The death of communism, if not socialism altogether, as the major alternative to capitalism and liberalism also stimulated a search for new intellectual approaches and it is therefore not surprising that many long-standing, anti-establishment dissenters are now to be found among either romantics or post-modernists.[50]

While it would still be premature to proclaim a fatal crisis of rational politics it is important to emphasize the influence of antimodernist intellectual dissent on governments and public opinion in Europe. To the extent that this dissent concerns foreign and security issues it further contributes to the existing conceptual confusion discussed here, with obvious implications for the functioning of the European Union.

The Cold War was an era of triumphant modernism. We lived in a Europe of "national interest" and *"realpolitik."* Governments trusted the power of "reason" and relied on "conscious" political choices. They could tell what was speculation and wishful-thinking and what was "objective" if not "absolute" truth. They believed in "progress" and "enlightened" institutional engineering. They embarked on "rational planning" of "ideal" social orders. They based their policies on "scientific" predictions, even when they concerned foreign and security issues.[51]

The logic of nuclear deterrence that guided Western strategic thinking would be empty without accepting the principle of "rigorous reasoning." The quest for a military balance would be folly had Westerners not believed in "objective evidence." Agonizing superpower competition would be unsustainable unless one knew what represented the real "truth" in politics. And the whole concept of national security interest would look ridiculous if based on short-lived public moods rather than on quantitative and thus "objective" economic and military equations.

Modernism triumphed not only in the West but also in the eastern part of the continent. After all, Marxism with its claim to discovery of the scientific truth and objective class interests, with its absolute trust in social engineering and obsession with quantitative rather than qualitative progress was a super-version of modernism.

Of course, there were always voices criticizing the most arrogant versions of modernism that ignored moral and human dimensions of international politics and looked at Europe in egotistical and technocratic terms. But they were always being silenced by the imminence of the Soviet threat that left little space for either "relativism" or "moralism" in security thinking. For instance, "moralist" arguments for elevating human rights to the top of the East-West agenda have always had to give way to "positivistic" arguments that such a policy would endanger peace on the continent.

The challenge to modernist *realpolitik* came in the 1980s from a tiny group of Eastern European dissidents. They defied the balance of power rationale and began a struggle which, in the eyes of modernist experts, was highly utopian if not dangerous. Dissidents talked about national pride rather than national interest, they talked about human rights and human dignity rather than about economic or military equations, objective truth was for them a function of morality rather than rationality, peace in Europe was about justice and not deterrence. As Václav Havel argued in a clearly anti-modernist manner:

> The existential revolution should provide hope of a moral reconstitution of society, which means a radical renewal of the relationship of human beings to what I have called the 'human order,' which no political order can replace... The issue is the rehabilitation of values like trust, openness, responsibility, solidarity, love... Any accumulation of power whatsoever (one of the characteristics of automatism) should be profoundly alien to it... Yes, 'anti-political politics' is possible. Politics 'from below'. Politics of man, not of the apparatus. Politics growing from the heart, not from a thesis... Does not the perspective of a better future depend on something like an international community of the shaken which, ignoring state boundaries, political systems, and power blocs, standing outside the high game of traditional politics, will seek to make a real political force out of a phenomenon so ridiculed by the technicians of power – the phenomenon of human conscience?... Modern rationalism and modern science, developed within our natural world, now systematically leave it behind, deny it, degradate and defame it – and, of course, at the same time colonize it.[52]

Dissidents' rhetoric and their belief system resembled 19th century romanticism with its enthusiasm for passion, imagination, and improvization, with its mysticism, symbolism, and messianism, with its heroism and readiness to sacrifice. And of course, there was also the idea of the chosen nation: "the nation on the rack, all anguish, all spirit, all idea, a pure principle."[53]

The romantic creed was condemned to failure, but to the great surprise of modernist experts the Soviet system has indeed collapsed and romantics, such as Václav Havel, assumed power in Eastern European states. Had they listened to "rational" arguments of security experts, they would probably have remained in prison and their countries under the Soviet yoke for many more years. But in fact the romantic anti-modernist rhetoric combined with symbolic campaigns of non-violence contributed to, if not produced, the historic breakthrough in Europe. Needless to say, non-violent actions, such as forming a human chain across the Baltic countries, lighting candles in Dresden, signing petitions and charters in Prague, and mass gatherings in churches of Warsaw and Timisoara, did not belong to the standard repertoire of modernist security experts. If such campaigns were endorsed by these experts it was because they could weaken the Soviet system, but not dismantle it altogether. Modernists not only ignored the possibility of a major change; they actually found the prospect of such change frightening.[54] But the romantics were proved right and the modernists were proved wrong, and from then on the modernist model of rationality has had to compete with the pre-modern rationality of romantics.

Since the end of the Cold War, romanticism has evolved in various forms in different parts of Europe. Its most vivid and disturbing manifestation has been seen in the Balkan countries where it promotes the idea of a chosen nation, religious brotherhood, and violent insurrection. In Western Europe, romanticism is linked with the rhetoric of political emancipation.[55] Its proponents argue that traditional security thinking, focusing on statist elites, military power, and the preservation of the status quo, ignored the most important moral and human aspects of security. In place of modernist values, a more secure foundation for security is the pursuit of emancipation, since it encourages a focus on people, justice, and change. As Ken Booth forcefully argued:

> Against the destructive and dismal rationality of Westphalia, Machiavelli and Clausewitz, which has shaped the statist outlook of this and earlier centuries .. we need to fashion the axioms of a new rationality for the next century. . . . Emancipation and security are two sides of the same coin. Emancipation, not power and order, produces true security. . . . What is needed must have moral at its center because the fundamental questions of how we might and can live together, concerns values, not instrumental rationality. . . . War obviously remains a scourge, a fascination, and an area for study and control; but why not hunger, or oppression?[56]

It should also be stressed that modernism is also fiercely contested by Islamic countries in the Middle East and Maghreb as well as by Asian countries with a historic tradition of Hinduism and Confucianism.[57] This has profound consequences for the security of the European Union. Not that a clash of rationalities, or as Samuel P. Huntington put it, a clash of civilizations, would necessarily lead to war.[58] But because contending views on what is legitimate, possible, and worth fighting for can seriously hamper communication and security dialogue between the Union and these regions.[59]

While the current romantic mode of thinking is largely of non-Western origin, post-modernism is very much a Western invention with little prospect of becoming an export product to the non-Western world. In this case, the modernist rationale is questioned not because it lacks spiritual and moral depth, but because it is too rigid and arbitrary to cope with an increasingly complex international environment. According to post-modernists there is no single and absolute truth, as there is no single and clear national interest. There is a variety of perspectives on European politics and hardly any "objective" pattern of inter-state relations. Rational thinking about security is replaced by the ability to respond to always fluid and conflicting pressures. Principles are useless in the post-modernist rationale since anything goes that can be negotiated and sold to the European electorate. The factual world is replaced by the world of media where facts are re-modeled in order to satisfy the principle of entertainment. Reality is thus replaced by "hyper-reality". International politics is primarily about images, pluralism, skepticism, and relativism. Fragmentation, indeterminacy, and intense distrust of any universal visions and concepts are the hallmarks of post-modernist thought.[60] All moral claims, traditional institutions, underlying rules and laws are ridiculed and rejected. As Richard K. Ashley put it:

> International community can only be seen as a never completed product of multiple historical practices, a still contested product of struggle to impose interpretation upon interpretation. In its form, it can only be understood as a network of historically fabricated practical understandings, precedents, skills, and procedures that define competent international subjectivity...Nothing is finally stable. There are no constants, no fixed meanings, no secure grounds, no profound secrets, no final structure or limits of history...[no] notion of universal truths or deep identities.[61]

According to post-modern thinkers, existing theories of international relations aspiring to represent objective knowledge are nothing but a set of rhetorical statements employed for the purpose of manipulation and power. For as Michael Foucault argued, power and knowledge are inextricably linked. To claim knowledge is to claim power.[62] However, one should study the existing theories of international relations, not because they tell us how things are, but because of what the theories tell us about themselves. In this context, language is also very important because it reflects changes in our view of Europe and international relations. As Markus Fisher put it: "social reality is

constituted by intersubjective consciousness based on language."[63]
The key to achieving a post-modern international system is to alter
state identity radically by transforming the way states think about
themselves, talk about themselves, and then transform their mutual
relationships.

In conclusion, with the end of the Cold War the monopoly of
modernist thinking has been seriously eroded: European politics is
now influenced by three different types of "rationality." Of course,
the division between romantics, modernists, and post-modernists is not
clear-cut. Romantic thinking often overlaps with the Kantian modernist tradition. Hobbesian modernists can switch from one interpretation
to another in a truly post-modern fashion. Moreover, deviations from
modernism are seldom openly acknowledged, especially within foreign
and security policy circles: diplomats and soldiers are not eager to
admit any "irrational" predilections. So far, post-modernism is openly
preached in dissenting academic circles only, while even the most
idealistic action groups do not like to call themselves "romantic."
One should also keep in mind that the competitors of modernist
thinking are fundamentally divided: post-modernism is seen by romantics as a form of nihilism, while post-modernists view romanticism as
misleading and oppressive. But the challenge to modernist thinking is
fairly evident in the political and intellectual discourse of today. Post-
modern relativism and romantic messianism clearly add new dimensions to old quarrels between Hobbesians, Grotians, and Kantians.
Modernism may still have the upper hand in the foreign and security
field, but various forms of "irrational" or "non-rational" thinking run
parallel to "rational" modernist thinking and at times mix with it or
even superimpose it. In such a situation one can forget about any
unambiguous and coherent strategy such as that which guided Europe
during the Cold War years. Instead we are confronted with a plethora
of strategic signposts, all pointing in different directions and making
the art of drafting foreign policies a nightmare. The end result is an
"anything-goes" policy that shifts from one position to another.[64]

DRAFTING SPECIFIC POLICIES: THREE CASES

Of course, one can argue that policy-making in the Union is not about
wobbling between Hobbes and Kant but about addressing a set of
specific challenges. The job of EU officials is to fix problems as they
arise, not to deliberate about post-modernism. Yet, even a very brief

look at practical problems confronting EU policy-making shows how difficult it is to separate conceptual dilemmas from daily policies. After all, policy is about making choices but these are not easy without any moral, ideological, or strategic paradigms. The cases chosen illustrate the complexity of making practical choices in three different areas of foreign and security policy: (1) military intervention, (2) enlargement of the Union, and (3) non-proliferation. The purpose is not to engage in a detailed empirical analysis, but to show the paralyzing division of views that exist not only between but also within various schools of thought, and independent from all individual national preferences.

The issue of peace-enforcing military intervention has been present on the EU agenda since the Gulf War, but it was the tragedy in the Balkans that made this issue central in all European foreign policy deliberations. Questions like; "whether?" "why?" "how?" and "when?" to intervene in the Balkan War have been asked time and again since 1991, but no satisfactory answer has ever been given by the Union's politicians. They were, to use James Gow's words, "like losing gamblers, constantly hoping that diplomacy and non-violent pressures would be enough, or like rabbits frozen in the glare of Bosnian head-lamps, afraid to jump."[65] When a decisive peace-enforcing operation was undertaken in August 1995 it was NATO, led by the United States, which took the initiative. The EU for its part was always painfully indecisive and torn by a series of conceptual and practical dilemmas. EU officials and politicians simply did not know whether military intervention, it was argued, would be the most appropriate and sufficiently-justified means of policy in the Balkans. Justification was offered in terms of national interest: EU members can never effectively insulate themselves from the horrors in the Balkans and prevent violence from spreading. But the same notion of national interest warned against being dragged into a bloody and chaotic war as long as there was no direct military threat to EU members. Refugee flows, economic dislocations, and the breakdown of the regional order, however bad, can somehow be managed, but intervention might create problems that could get out of control as individual EU members will start to side with their own protégés, terrorism among expatriate Balkan groups will erupt within the Union itself, and EU troops will begin to suffer combat casualties on a great scale. And thus Hobbesian realists clashed with each other about the value of national interest involved, and the justification for the military intervention in hard-core security terms.

Grotians and Kantians appeared to be in a similar conceptual disarray. On the one hand, non-intervention carried with it high costs for the Grotians, including persistent violation of international norms, the loss of credibility of major international institutions, and an end to hopes for the creation of any credible collective security system. But on the other hand, intervention might even further discredit existing institutions. Legal grounds for intervention were ambivalent at best, and it was difficult to imagine any collective security system working in the Balkans, with or without EU military involvement. Some Kantians justified intervention on moral grounds, but others argued that intervention would bring about more rather than less human suffering. It was also debated whether achieving moral aims in the Balkans justifies the use of "immoral" violent means. Is killing the best way to prevent further killing? Besides, drawing moral lines in the Balkan imbroglio was a risky business anyway. Some Kantians lamented that non-intervention undermined the concept of multi-national societies, others argued that intervention would end up splitting Bosnia and the rest of the Balkans into separate ethnic states.

These controversies concerned not only justifying intervention but also the practicality of such a step as it was feared that the injection of an international military force would involve enormous costs but prove largely ineffective, if not counter-productive altogether. Few believed that a decisive "in-and-out" military operation would be possible in the Balkan circumstances and halfway responses with ambiguous and unpredictable cost-benefit equations were open to question and endless debate. To put it differently, while the horrors of the Balkan War eased Western reluctance to use military intervention there was no simultaneous willingness to underwrite such intervention in either blood or treasure.[66] Moreover, a peace-enforcing operation could undermine other important missions carried out by the Union. As one observer succinctly put it: "It is a lesson which the EU will have to learn: humanitarian aid, peace-keeping and peace-enforcement, each have their legitimate and positive uses, but combining them at the same time and in the same place may lead to disastrous paralysis."[67] And there was always the difficult question "what next?" after a possibly successful peace-enforcing intervention. Is the Union willing to sign an expensive "maintenance contract" in the Balkans after completing the emergency "repair service"?[68] And if so, for how long?

The issue of peace-enforcing military intervention in the Balkans has also revealed differences in substance and style between romantics, modernists, and post-modernists. Romantics usually argued in favor of intervention not only on moral grounds, but also to underline the principles of "brotherhood" and "solidarity" with the oppressed Bosnian nation. Romantics criticized the modernist position exemplified, for instance, by successive EU envoys that looked at the correlation of forces on the ground in Bosnia and tried to suggest a "realist" solution which would bring "irrational" violence to an end, terminate "unnecessary" human suffering and reflect the balance of power between Pale and Sarajevo in the proposed division of disputed land. Romantics would refuse such a deal as "unjust," "inhuman," and "power-centered," and instead would opt for a "liberating" military intervention. The post-modern position was exemplified by those EU politicians who did not stick to any clear rules or principles but were constantly shifting positions depending on public opinion moods, media evaluation, interdepartmental squabbles, inter-alliance negotiations, and permanent soul-searching interpretations and reinterpretations.

The result of the above mentioned deliberations is well known: a series of indecisions, procrastinations and poorly timed, inconsistent and uncoordinated measures that undermined the credibility of the Union time and again. Despite the apparent success of the deployment of NATO forces in 1995 most questions about the utility of a military intervention are still unanswered, and there is no reason to believe that the EU as such would be any wiser when dealing with another ethnic conflict in Europe or elsewhere. Some in the Union seem to believe that bombing local warlords proved to be the optimal solution for dealing with ethnic conflicts and civil wars in Europe. Others, have become skeptical about the utility and rationale of any outside military intervention in such a complex conflict like the one in the Balkans. Consider for instance, the current reluctance of the Dutch to participate in similar operations after its trauma in Srebrenica, where the Dutch battalion handed over to the Serbs several thousand Muslims, who faced certain death. Revelations about the atrocities committed by Belgian and Italian soldiers during their missions in Somalia only strengthened anti-interventionist arguments in Europe.

The very different issue of EU enlargement did not involve agonizing decisions about the use of military force, but it also proved to be very complicated and divisive.[69] In principle, there is much consensus about the wisdom of integrating several Eastern European Countries. Enlargement is expected to have a stabilizing if not pacifying effect on them, and thus it should help to prevent another Bosnia in the center of the continent. Moreover, some EU countries are more directly exposed to Central European problems than others, and the lack of a coordinated Western effort may induce them to resort to controversial unilateral actions. Germany, in particular, cannot turn a blind eye towards Central European problems, and failure to recognize this fact may produce a serious split within the EU and NATO. And finally, any Western design for security cooperation with Eastern Europe should first prove its feasibility in the countries with the most advanced democracy and market economy. If chaos and brutality prevail in Central European politics, there are few chances for stability in the rest of the post-communist world. But here clarity and consensus end, while confusion and squabbling begin. Some disagreements are linked to specific national interests arising from different geographic and historical perspectives within the European Union. But most clashes are of a general conceptual nature and have little to do with a selfish interpretation of national interests.

First of all, the scope of enlargement and criteria for admission are being questioned. Why should only some Eastern European countries be taken in and not others? Which admission criteria are the most important: economic, political, or cultural? If enlargement is about economics should one look at inflation, privatization or the level of growth? If enlargement is about peace and security should the Union concentrate on most stable or most unstable Eastern European countries? General considerations aside, what about some tough cases such as Russia? Can Europe exist in cultural terms if it excludes the country of Tchaikovsky and Dostoyevsky? Or what about Slovakia, with its authoritarian prime minister, but high economic growth, sensitive geopolitical position, and close cultural links with all of Central Europe including Germany and Austria?[70]

Moreover, the different aims behind enlargement call for different institutional solutions. If security in Central Europe is the greatest Western concern, then membership in NATO and WEU should come before membership in the European Union. But is not economics the best means for addressing instability in the post-communist region? In other words, are not the roots of present conflicts in Central Europe mainly economic and should they not be treated accordingly? If yes, what is the best economic solution: integration, trade, or aid? Or maybe economic growth in Central and Eastern Europe requires first of all a secure international environment? Will membership in the Union provide such an environment? Will membership in NATO for the Visegrad three stabilize or destabilize the situation, especially considering Russian disapproval?

Finally, the costs of enlargement are being debated.[71] The 1997 "Agenda 2000" program of the European Commission envisages an "enlargement package" of no less than ECU 75 billion: "A veritable Marshall Plan for the countries of Central and Eastern Europe," as President Jacques Santer described it.[72] But are the necessary resources available? Will the Commission's proposal be accepted by powerful farm lobbies across the Union as well as by the countries benefiting from structural aid, such as Greece, Spain, and Portugal?[73] After all, in 1990–91 the German government committed no less than $200 billion to the small area of the former GDR. Does this mean that further eastward enlargement of the EU would involve comparable financial sacrifices? Would not eastward enlargement ruin several Western European industries such as mining, textiles, or steel? And what about the costs in terms of the EU internal decision-making structure? Must the Union forget about deepening when it embarks on the project of widening? Can one provide guarantees that enlargement will actually enhance rather than jeopardize stability within and outside the Union?

The obvious difficulty of coping with these questions has made it impossible for the Union to commit itself fully to the idea of enlargement for several years already. While the idea has been accepted in principle by all EU members and the list of five countries to open entrance negotiations in 1998 has been drawn up, double-talk, wobbling, and indecision are still the order of the day as EU member states try to come up with a practical policy against the backdrop of conceptual disarray. Although Agenda 2000 provides a very long list of entrance criteria, no attempt was made to weight them and no system of judging each of them was suggested. The road to EU membership for individual applicant countries is thus rife with hurdles, and with neither signposts indicating the required direction nor instructions indicating which hurdles to jump over first. In the meantime, debates between various schools of thought in the Union proceed apace. Hobbesians are obsessed with the power vacuum in Central and Eastern Europe, Grotians look at enlargement from the institutional perspective, while Kantians talk about enlargement of the existing zone of peace based on democracy, and open markets. For romantics, enlargement is about trust, emancipation, and human dignity, not about power, order, and institutional engineering, as modernists would have it. Post-modernists have usually no strong feelings about enlargement, but they probably view it like anything else: an exercise in manufacturing international images and hyper-realities.

EU policy against the spread of nuclear weapons is of a different nature than either military intervention or enlargement. Its scope is global, its implications are of a purely strategic nature, and its tools involve a broad range of diplomatic, economic, and military measures. While always important, the policy of non-proliferation has been elevated to the top of the EU foreign and security agenda only with the demise of the Cold War.[74] But again, a series of daunting conceptual ambiguities have prevented EU from crafting a credible, coherent, and effective policy.[75] As in the two previous cases, the exact nature of the threat has been at the center of the argument. Nuclear weapons are clearly dangerous, but the question is: why should the use of nuclear weapons be more likely in a post-Cold War era than in the Cold War era? Today, as never before, nuclear weapons threaten to make the costs of war immense for everybody, including fanatical theocracies in the Middle East and undemocratic empires in Asia. Why should a nuclear Korea behave less responsibly in the 1990s than a nuclear China in the 1960s? Now indeed the world is more complex if not dangerously messier than before 1989, but is it not true that nuclear weapons actually reduce the danger of miscalculation because states do not have to make guesses about who is stronger and what the balance of power is? And if we worry about accidental explosions in an unstable post-Cold War environment of Europe should we not rather concentrate on civilian nuclear plants such as Chernobyl rather than spending money and energy on non-proliferation? In fact, for the entire Cold War period EU governments fiercely argued that nuclear weapons were stabilizing, so why should these weapons lose their stabilizing characteristics with the end of the Cold War? And if so, does this also apply to the nuclear arsenals of France and the United Kingdom?

As in the two previous cases, the search for the most suitable strategy also evokes controversies and shows distinct traces of Hobbesian, Grotian, and Kantian thinking, not to mention the usual dissent of post-modernists and romantics.[76] Should the EU pursue a policy of denial or of encouragement *vis-à-vis* potential proliferators? Should it aim at security against or at security within? Should it address the demand-side or the supply-side of weapons proliferation? Does a global or a regional approach to proliferation work better? Should the Union rely on military, economic or diplomatic means in promoting non-proliferation? And one should immediately add that neither diplomatic efforts (especially NPT), economic means (export controls) nor military means (counter-proliferation) can prevent proliferation by themselves, while the simultaneous use of all three or even two of them causes practical difficulties.

For instance, the diplomatic arrangement behind the NPT is that all states adhering to the non-proliferation regime receive in return guarantees of their right to develop nuclear energy for peaceful purposes. However, technology used for civilian purposes can often be used for defense purposes as well. Western countries have therefore created an export control system aimed at preventing the flow of certain technologies to certain countries even if they claim to use the imports for peaceful purposes only.[77] This is exactly what the 1995 NPT Review Conference was quarreling about, with Iran leading the anti-Western campaign against export control practices. But should the international community allow Iran to import any items it wants? Should the EU ignore export restrictions imposed on Iran by the United States? And should export controls towards Russia be maintained, reduced, or abolished? Is not preventing nuclear technology from leaving Russia more important than allowing it to go in? And how can one expect a clear and effective non-proliferation policy if it is carried out within no less than five distinct institutional regimes?

All this is not to minimize the danger of nuclear weapons nor is it to claim that there is nothing good about the current non-proliferation policy, but to show the complexity of the problems faced by EU foreign policy-makers; problems that often lead to paralysis. In fact, all three cases discussed here show that one does not need to assume the re-emergence of hegemonic power struggles in order to explain the existing paralysis in foreign and security fields. Nor does one need to believe in a paralyzing clash of national interests among individual states in Europe. The three cases give enough grounds for believing that ad-hocary, zigzags, and paralysis are caused by problems in comprehending current change and adapting to it. The European Union is faced with new and largely unknown challenges, international institutions are undergoing major restructuring, and new political arrangements are slow to emerge under ever-changing circumstances. Coping with this process requires the existence of a coherent and widely-shared conceptual framework. But this is exactly what is lacking in present-day Europe. Various schools of thought about security and international relations compete with each other causing conceptual confusion and political chaos. How can the Union get out of this vicious circle?

BEYOND CONCEPTUAL CONSENSUS

The argument so far has hardly been constructive. It has pointed at conceptual gaps but has not provided a solution for bridging them. It has raised numerous questions, and left them unanswered. The problem is, however, that all solutions for overcoming the existing conceptual confusion seem terribly ambitious and yet largely inadequate. One such solution would emphasize the role of norms and values in reconstructing a coherent European view of the outside world. Common values could provide a sense of direction, a concentration of energy, an instinctive recognition of friends and enemies that is lacking in the Union's current endeavors. But can one envisage a catalogue of norms and values that would be equally endorsed and shared by all the different governments in Europe? How can a highly pluralistic environment of different nations, cultures, religions, and ideologies subscribe to one code of morality and behavior? Concern about the "spiritual emptiness," "permissive cornucopia," "irrational escapism," and "moral relativism" of present-day Europe may well be justified.[78] However, there are clear limits to the Union's ability to create, let alone impose, a common ethical predicament upon its liberal, sophisticated, and affluent citizens.

Some kind of a normative consensus is, of course, possible but it can hardly go beyond such vague generalities as the attachment to civic liberties, peace and social justice, tolerance, human rights, and the rule of law.[79] Can one design any specific European policy on the basis of such general values? Would one know what the Union should do in Bosnia when guided by its Judeo-Christian tradition? There is little operational utility in saying that the contemporary European idea "gives full expression to diversity, choice and quality," or to proclaim that Europe is both about "unity and diversity" at the same time.[80]

Procedural solutions represent another possible way of overcoming the current conceptual confusion. If compromise about norms and values is impractical or unwise, what about a compromise in terms of decision-making procedures? The major advantage of procedural solutions is that they are about technicalities rather than substance. Procedures help to arrive at common decisions while avoiding endless moral and ideological squabbles. But the major strength of procedural solutions is also their major weakness. Governments tend to ignore or manipulate the agreed procedures when their application runs against values that are dear to them. Even if governments are able to strike procedural deals there is little hope that the policies originating from such deals would ever attract genuine support of public opinion: procedural solutions are seldom appealing in either moral or emotional terms. And a procedural consensus on specific policies does not guarantee effective policies because procedures can only help to arrive at decisions without saying what is empirically wrong and right.

Another way of overcoming the current conceptual confusion is to emphasize the role of civil society in Europe. The civil society solution does not search for consensus in either normative or procedural terms, but instead relies on spontaneous alliances among various social movements within and across the national borders of the European Union. In fact, consensus is viewed as unrealistic if not undesirable in a pluralistic modern European setting. As Nicholas Rescher argued:

> Consensus is not a criterion of truth
> is not a standard of value
> is not an index of moral or ethical appropriateness
> is not a requisite for co-operation
> is not a communal imperative for a just social order
> is not, in and of itself, an appropriate ideal...
> Consensus is no more than one positive factor that has to be weighed on the scale along with many others."[81]

The appeal of the civil society solution lies in its attempt to get closer to the people of Europe, with their cross-cutting multiple identities and interests in concentric circles. The solution does not ignore national states and the European Union, but it emphasizes the role of various sub-and trans-state associations reflecting personal preferences in terms of interests and values. The civil society solution does not try to indoctrinate people; nor does it ask them to ignore important ideological or moral questions and instead concentrate on technical procedures. It tries to enhance people's competence in dealing with each other and with the surrounding pluralistic environment. It tries to view international politics as a process of learning, learning from mistakes and successes, learning through variety and selection, learning by absorbing new ideas rather than trying to suppress them.[82] Trust is the greatest benefit emanating from the civil society system. As Robert Putnam argued: "Voluntary cooperation (like rotating credit associations) depends on social capital. Norms of generalized reciprocity and networks of civic engagement encourage social trust and cooperation because they reduce incentives to defect, reduce uncertainty, and provide models for future cooperation."[83]

However, the civil society solution has also some obvious weaknesses. For instance, its advocates have never made it clear how much voluntary grassroots cooperation is required for the civil society solution to work. And if people do not join associations of their choice en masse, should other forms of cooperation be allowed to prevail? Moreover, the civil society solution ignores the question of power, order, and hierarchy in international affairs. Would not stronger associations try to impose their will on weaker ones? Can a civil society system do without a superior authority to manage cooperation and conflicts? As Michael Walzer, one of the most outspoken advocates of the civil society concepts, has admitted: "There is no escape from power and coercion, no possibility of choosing, like old anarchists, civil society alone. [The state] both frames civil society and occupies space within it. It fixes the boundary conditions and the basic rules of all association members to think about a common good, beyond their own conceptions of the good life. Here is the paradox of the civil society argument."[84] But would an international community of independent states substitute for a community of sub- and trans-state associations? Is the former more visible than the latter in the present-day Europe? And will not the insistence on unconstrained pluralism in either conceptual or institutional terms result in more rather than less chaos on the continent?

These questions are not merely about the confusing picture of international affairs. They concern the very essence of public choice in a modern democracy. The next chapter will address this question head on. It will try to establish how public policies can be made and sustained in the complex, pluralistic and often selfish social environment of present-day Europe.

CONCLUSIONS

The EU has problems in crafting a common foreign policy not necessarily because each European state pretends to know better what to do, but because states usually *do not know what to do* under the ever-changing circumstances of today. This is the major finding of this chapter. European states and their politicians are currently presented with an unusually wide set of choices. However, they have lost their sense of strategic purpose, which would help them to make these choices in a coherent and comprehensible manner. They are unable to identify basic foreign and security risks, let alone craft suitable responses to address them. While the old dispute between Hobbesian, Grotian, and Kantian approaches to international politics is still unresolved, the assertion of romantic and post-modern types of thinking undermines the very foundation of modern rational thinking about international affairs. On top of that, there are ancient problems of coping with change which this time around is truly spectacular in terms of scope and pace. History may slow down in the next couple of years, injecting a greater sense of stability and predictability in policy analysis and planning. However, the complex nature of the conceptual confusion discussed on these pages suggests that the simplistic intellectual clarity of the Cold War years is gone for good. The CFSP crafters will have to rise to this challenge.

How is conceptual confusion to be dealt with? How are we to proceed amidst enormous complexity, diversity, and change? What should we look at when trying to formulate a new conceptual framework for European foreign policy? This chapter has suggested looking at normative, procedural, and civil society factors. All three suggestions are linked to the issues that are emerging as truly central to our effort to explain Euro-paralysis: identity, democracy, and legitimacy. The normative solution is basically about identity, the procedural solution about democracy, and the civil society one about bridging the gap between individuals and the community.

Although there is vast proliferation if not inflation of values and norms, it is still impossible to construct the notions of public interest and common good in Europe without referring to certain values that are binding the people of Europe together. This is not a call for a new ideological discourse or moralistic crusades. Nor is it suggested that certain values be labeled as exclusively European rather than Western or human in more universal terms. It is a call to de-emphasize the notions of power and interest, and instead recognize the importance of trust, solidarity, responsibility, and openness. It is a call to oppose extreme manifestations of cynicism and relativism that lead to an "anything goes" approach in foreign affairs. In short, the EU foreign policy cannot do without a moral compass. Such a compass would probably ask us to follow different norms and values than those promoted in the Cold War period. New norms and values will emphasize plurality and liberty. They will be less concerned with universal duties, eternal truths and strategic imponderability.

It is also clear from what we said in this chapter that the EU foreign policy cannot only be about "exciting" normative substance, but also about "boring" rules and procedures. The question of "how to arrive at policies?" is as important as the question "what is the value of these policies?" Moreover, foreign policy will increasingly be about creating and multiplying certain rules of behavior and working out procedural routines. However, the attitude to rules and procedures must also change. Rules and procedures in foreign policy should be more about shaping interactions and enhancing joint learning rather than about crude application of rewards and punishments. Rules and procedures should help us to "garden" a complex European process rather than to "engineer" a single European "masterplan" or "strategy."[85] They should be more about coordinating multiple players in a complex setting of mutual interdependence than about hierarchy and authority for making decisions and choosing the instruments. They should be about guiding and steering rather than about controlling.

But the most important element in the Union's future foreign policy will be upgrading the civil society factor. This needs to reflect a growing plurality of views among Europeans and to overcome the inflexibility and rigidity of existing institutions. As Jean-Marie Guéhenno rightly argues, the Union's foreign policies should be in "constant search of polity!"[86] In other words, the primary role of the CFSP ought to be definition and creation of a genuine European "community" linked by similar interests and values. The first indispensable step in achieving this goal would be a diffusion of authority and power in foreign policy. The second step would be to enhance channels of communication between the officialdom at the top and the grassroots societal bottom. The third step would be to draw up solutions that would give EU citizens a greater say in the creation and implementation of common foreign policies. Foreign policies are too important to be left in the hands of Eurocrats.

This is not an easy task, but the Union should try to find ways of "decentralizing" and "socializing" foreign policies. "Small" decisions at the local level should be able to proceed rather than follow "big" decisions at the top EU level. Such an attitude would imply a different role for the Union. The Union will basically coordinate and mediate between various parochial interests rather than provide leadership on its own. It will guide states and their citizens in a coherent and predictable manner rather than tell them which policy is "right" or "wrong." Its aim would be to provide a forum for expressing grassroots initiatives without allowing chaos and wild competition. Its aim would be to treat foreign affairs as a kind of "social work" and not as a means in imperial power politics.[87] Without a social dimension, the CFSP will fail to attract the loyalty of European citizens. It will remain a plaything for nationalists and bureaucrats which can hardly enjoy legitimacy either in cultural or civic (democratic) terms.

All three suggestions are closely intertwined. For instance, trust is stronger if the initiative comes not from the top, but from the bottom of the polity. Trust is also stronger when embedded in a set of internalized rules and procedures. Moreover, it is important to emphasize the change of concepts that should guide foreign policies. The key concepts in our argument have not been power, interest, and authority, but communication, participation, trust, learning, and transparency.

This is not a set of policy recommendations that is easily digestible by the community of diplomats and security analysts. The argument is abstract, if not philosophical. Moreover, it is easier to imagine a diffusion of power and down-graded procedures when dealing with foreign trade, border controls or cultural exchanges, than with hard-core security issues. But the aim of this chapter was not to come forward with a specific set of policies, let alone a new catalogue of international dogmas. Its aim was to show the intellectual complexity of European politics and to identify some general ways of coping with this complexity. As we try to comprehend, articulate, and address new problems in a new Europe, the major challenge is to adjust our mental framework with the help of different concepts and terminology. The challenge is to search for common (but constantly moving) ground among increasingly diverging views and beliefs. The way suggested to cope with foreign policy conceptual problems is clearly Kantian, and I endorse the modernist quest for rationality, provided that it does not end up in arrogance.

NOTES

1. See the successive issues of the IISS *Strategic Survey* published in 1994 and 1995, p. 5 in both cases. (The 1994 edition was published in London by Brassey's, and the 1995 edition in Oxford by Oxford University Press.)
2. A modern equivalent of a similar argument can be found in Karl W. Deutsch, S.A. Burell et al., *Political Community and the North Atlantic Area* (Princeton, NJ: Princeton University Press, 1957), p. 5.
3. Bruce Russett and Harvey Starr introduced the term "menu for choice" in international politics. In their words "The key to the menu analogy is to understand that the opportunities of international actors are

constrained in various ways and that these constraints affect the willingness of decision makers to act." See Bruce Russett and Harvey Starr, *World Politics. The Menu for Choice* (New York: W.H. Freeman and Co., 1992), fourth edition, p. 24.

4. Raymond Aron, *On War* (London: Secker & Warburg, 1958), p. 80. However, Aron also insisted that the slowing down of history is not "immobilism" and in a very prophetic manner stated: "Germany, and even Europe as a whole, may some day become reunited without resort to arms or *a fortiori*, atomic weapons. Europe is only temporarily, not indefinitely, a continent ruled by machines instead of men." (p. 93).

5. President Clinton quoted in *The European*, July 15–21, 1994.

6. Gianni De Michelis, "Reaching Out to the East", *Foreign Policy*, No. 79 (Summer 1990), p. 49.

7. "Free from the constraints of the old order, Europe's political responsibilities begin with the calculation of the uncalculable" declared two leading German experts. See Werner Weidenfeld and Josef Janning, "Europe in Tomorrow's World", in *Global Responsibilities: Europe in Tomorow's World. Strategies and Options for the Future of Europe*, Werner Weidenfeld and Josef Janning, eds. (Gütersloh: Bertelsmann Foundation Publishers, 1991), p. 218.

8. In 1995, a man responsible for a "Europe vision" within the Union, put it bluntly: "Europe does not need visionaries." See an interview with Carlos Westendorp, Spanish Secretary of State for European Affairs in charge of preparing the 1996 intergovernmental conference of the Union, in *NRC Handelsblad*, September 22, 1995.

9. See R. Lefeber, M. Fitzmaurice and E.W. Vierdag, eds, *The Changing Political Structure of Europe. Aspects of International Law* (Dordrecht: Martinus Nijhoff, 1991).

10. Ralf Dahrendorf, "The Europeanization of Europe", in *A Widening Atlantic? Domestic Change and Foreign Policy*, A.J. Pierre, ed. (New York: Council on Foreign Relations, 1986), p. 5. For a comprehensive analysis of change in international relations see, e.g., K.J. Holsti, *Change in the International System. Essays on the Theory and Practice of International Relations*, (Aldershot: Edward Elgar, 1991), especially pp. 3–23.

11. See Lawrence Freedman, "Order and Disorder in the New World", *Foreign Affairs*, Vol. 71, No. 1 (1992), p. 22.

12. See Samuel P. Huntington, *Political Order in Changing Societies* (New Haven: Yale University Press, 1968), pp. 192–262.

13. Ole Waever, "Identity, Integration and Security. Solving the Sovereignty Puzzle in EU Studies", *Journal of International Affairs*, Vol. 48, No. 2 (Winter 1995), p. 390.

14. Alastair Buchan, *The End of the Postwar Era* (London: Weidenfeld and Nicolson, 1974), p. 313.

15. International relations and strategic studies specialists were not the only ones who came under fire in the 1990s. For a fundamental critique of professional economists see, for instance Alfred L. Malabre Jr., *Lost Prophets* (Cambridge, MA: Harvard Business School Press, 1993).

16. Marysia Zalewski, "Well, What Is the Feminist Perspective on Bosnia", *International Affairs*, Vol. 71, No. 2 (1995), p. 340.

17. Lawrence Freedman, "Strategic Studies and the New Europe", *Adelphi Paper* No. 284 (1994), p. 15.

18. For a comprehensive analysis of insecurity sources in Europe see Edward Mortimer, "European Security after the Cold War", *Adelphi Paper* No. 271 (1992), pp. 6–18.

19. Jacques Delors, "Europe's Ambitions", *Foreign Policy*, No. 80 (Fall 1990), p. 14.

20. See Jacques Delors, "European Unification and European Security", *Adelphi Paper* No. 284 (1994), p. 4. See also Willy Claes's address to the 40th General Assembly of NATO, The Hague, October 28, 1994.

21. Jacques Delors, "European Unification and European Security", op.cit.

22. Hans Binnendijk and Patrick Clawson suggested that "the best way to plan in a world with unknown enemies is to identify the sorts of tasks that the military will be called upon to do, not to guess about the specifics of where and whom the military will be asked to fight." However, one may add: easier said than done, gentlemen! See Hans Binnendijk and Patrick Clawson, "New Strategic Priorities", *The Washington Quarterly*, Vol. 18, No. 2 (1995), p. 123.

23. Ken Booth and Peter Vale, "Security in Southern Africa: After Apartheid, Beyond Realism", *International Affairs*, Vol. 71, No. 2 (1995), p. 294. See also "Redefining Security: The Human Dimension", Human Development Report 1994 by the United Nations Development Program, reprinted in *Current History*, May 1995, p. 236.

24. François Heisbourg, "The Future of the Atlantic Alliance: Whither NATO, Whether NATO?", in *US Security in an Uncertain Era*, Brad Roberts, ed. (Cambridge, MA and London: MIT Press, 1993), p. 104.

25. One should keep in mind various ambiguities involved in all sorts of threat assessment. Threat is always conditional, potential and hypothetical. Information about eventual causes of war and conflict is often opaque and incomplete. One can hardly say whether a considered scenario of conflict represents a realistic assessment or is a product of military psychopathology. Threat perceptions, after all, concern the future, and there can be no reliable information about the future. See Klaus Knorr, *Threat Perception in Historical Dimensions of National Security Problems* (Lawrence: University of Kansas Press, 1976), p. 84.

26. Jacques Delors, "European Unification and European Security", op. cit., p. 11. For a comprehensive analysis of economic security see Vincent Cable, "What is International Economic Security?", *International Affairs*, Vol. 71, No. 2 (1995), pp. 305–24.

27. Notable exceptions include, in particular, Barry Buzan, *People, States and Fear: The National Security Problem in International Relations* (Hemel Hempstead: Harvest Wheatsheaf, 1983), first edition, especially pp. 26–8.

28. One can argue that the Soviet military threat disappeared more because of domestic developments in the East than because of any spectacular successes in managing the military rivalry between the Warsaw Pact and NATO. As a Polish politician put it in 1990: "It is true that the Soviet empire is collapsing. And it is true that democracy is now re-emerging in

Eastern Europe. But this is neither the result of the strength of the military alliances nor the result of any political strategies. It is first of all the result of the efforts of societies, of Gdansk workers, of farmers, intellectuals and students." See Bronislaw Geremek, "Western World Lacks Real Response", *Atlantisch Perspectief*, Vol. 14, No. 2 (1990), p. 14.

29. Costas M. Constantinou, "NATO's Caps: European Security and the Future of the North Atlantic Alliance", *Alternatives*, Vol. 20 (1995), p. 160.

30. Michael Howard, *The Causes of Wars and Other Essays* (London: Temple Smith, 1983), second edition, p. 141.

31. This typology reflects three major currents in the theory of international relations presented in the 1991 Martin Wight Memorial Lecture at Chatham House. See Adam Roberts, "A New Age in International Relations," *International Affairs*, Vol. 67, No. 3 (July 1991), p. 512. Wight himself wrote about the realist, the rationalist and the revolutionarist tradition in international theory. See also K.J. Holsti, *The Dividing Discipline: Hegemony and Diversity in International Theory* (Boston: Unwin Hyman, 1985), pp. 26–7. In the United States the (neo)realist-(neo)liberal dichotomy is usually employed.

32. Josef Joffe, "'Bismarck' or 'Britain'?", *International Security*, Vol. 19, No. 4 (Spring 1995), pp. 116–17.

33. For a detailed analysis of such dangers see Kenneth Waltz, *Theory of International Politics* (Reading, MA: Addison-Wesley, 1979), p. 165.

34. See Charles Krauthammer, "The Unipolar Moment", in *Rethinking American Security: Beyond Cold War to New World Order*, Graham Allison and Gregory Treverton, eds. (New York: W.W. Norton, 1992), pp. 295–306.

35. This is well argued in V.P. Gagnon, Jr. "Ethnic Nationalism and International Conflict", *International Security*, Vol. 19, No. 3 (Winter 1994/95), pp. 130–66.

36. The peaceful way in which the Cold War ended also bears witness to the pacifying effects of institutional integration. For instance, contrary to Hobbesian predictions, the Soviet Union posed no obstacles to German unification, betting, in John Gerard Ruggie's words, "that a united Germany firmly embedded in a broader Western institutional matrix would pose far less of a security threat than a neutral Germany tugged in different directions in the center of Europe." See John Gerard Ruggie, "Multilateralism: the Anatomy of an Institution", *International Organization*, Vol. 46, No. 3 (Summer 1992), p. 562.

37. Jacques Delors, "European Unification and European Security", op. cit., p. 11.

38. See Jack Snyder, "Averting Anarchy in the New Europe", *International Security*, Vol. 14, No. 4 (Spring 1990), p. 15.

39. See Joachim Krause and Peter Schmidt, "The Evolving New European Architecture-Concepts, Problems and Pitfalls", *The Washington Quarterly*, Vol. 13, No. 4 (Autumn 1990), pp. 79–92 and Alfred van Staden, "De Veiligheid van Europa in theoretisch Perspectief", *Transactie*, Vol. 19, No. 3 (September 1990), pp. 199–213.

40. See Tony Evans and Peter Wilson, "Regime Theory and the English School of International Relations", *Millenium*, Vol. 21, No. 3 (Winter 1992), p. 330.

41. For a comprehensive critique of liberal institutionalism see especially John J. Mearsheimer, "The False Promise of International Institutions", *International Security*, Vol. 19, No. 3 (Winter 1994–95), pp. 5–49.

42. Pierre Hassner, "Beyond the Three Traditions: the Philosophy of War and Peace in Historical Perspective", *International Affairs*, Vol. 70, No. 4 (1994), p. 744.

43. See especially Bruce Russett, *Grasping the Democratic Peace: Principles for a Post-Cold War World* (Princeton: Princeton University Press, 1993), pp. 31ff. For a European tint on the same argument see, e.g., Ernst-Otto Czempiel, "Governance and Democratization", in *Governance Without Government: Order and Change in World Politics*, James N. Rosenau and Ernst-Otto Czempiel, eds. (Cambridge: Cambridge University Press, 1992), pp. 250–71.

44. Michael W. Doyle, "Kant, Liberal Legacies, and Foreign Affairs" (Part I), *Philosophy and Public Affairs*, Vol. 12, No. 3 (Summer 1983), p. 230. Doyle also argues that the predisposition of democratic states to regard other democracies favorably is reinforced by mutually beneficial economic ties between them.

45. The term "liberal conscience" is used by Michael Howard in *War and the Liberal Conscience* (New Brunswick, NJ: Rutgers University Press, 1986), second edition, while the term "democratic ethos" is used by Zeev Maoz and Bruce Russett in "Normative and Structural Causes of Democratic Peace", *American Political Science Review*, Vol. 87, No. 3 (September 1993), pp. 624–38.

46. See J. David Singer, "The Level-of-Analysis Problem in International Relations", in *The International System: Theoretical Essays*, Klaus Knorr and Sidney Verba, eds. (Princeton: Princeton University Press, 1961), pp. 77–92.

47. As Quincy Wright observed many years ago: "A government cannot at the same time behave according to the Machiavellian [read Hobbesian] assumptions of the balance of power and the Wilsonian [read Grotian] assumptions of international organization." See Quincy Wright, *A Study of War* (Chicago: University of Chicago Press, 1942), Vol. 2, p. 781.

48. T.S. Eliot, "The Love Song of J. Alfred Prufrock", in *The Waste Land and Other Poems* (New York: Harvest, 1930).

49. The terms romantic and post-modern could, of course, be supplemented by other terms used in the literature such as utopian or revolutionary instead of romantic and critical, post-structural, and reflectivist in the case of post-modern. For an historical overview of various types of similar typologies and terms see, e.g., Jeffrey C. Alexander, "Modern, Anti, Post, Neo", *The New Left Review*, No. 210 (March/April 1995), pp. 63–105.

50. At the same time, some former anti-establishment dissenters such as Victor Nee or Donald L. Horowitz are now to be found within the mainstream liberal-conservative current.

51. For a critical evaluation of scientific claims of international relations theory see John Lewis Gaddis, "International Relations Theory and the

End of Cold War", *International Security*, Vol. 17, No. 3 (Winter 1992/93), pp. 5–58.

52. Václav Havel, *Living in Truth* (London: Faber and Faber, 1990), pp. 118, 138–9, and 156–7. See also Václav Havel, "A Call for Sacrifice. The Co-Responsibility of the West", *Foreign Affairs*, Vol. 73, No. 2 (March/April 1994), pp. 2–7.

53. J.L. Talmon, *Political Messianism. The Romantic Phase* (London: Secker & Warburg, 1960), p. 268. See also Andrzej Walicki, *Filozofia a Mesjanizm* (Warsaw: Panstwowy Instytut Wydawniczy, 1970), especially pp. 46–52.

54. For instance, a leading authority in the theory of international relations, Robert Gilpin, argued that although "peaceful adjustment of the systemic disequilibrium is possible, the principal mechanism of change through history has been war, or what we shall call hegemonic war." See Robert Gilpin, *War and Change in World Politics* (New York: Cambridge University Press, 1981), p. 15.

55. See, e.g., Christian Reus-Smit, "Realist and Resistance Utopias: Community, Security and Political Action in the New Europe", *Millenium*, Vol. 21, No. 1 (Spring 1992), especially pp. 14–28. Also Mary Kaldor, Gerard Holden and Richard Falk, ed. *The New Detente: Rethinking East-West Relations* (London: Verso, 1989) or Egbert Jahn, *Europe, Eastern Europe, and Central Europe* (PRIF Report 1, 1989).

56. Ken Booth, "Human Wrongs and International Relations", *International Security*, Vol. 71, No. 1 (1995), pp. 110, 119 and 125, and Ken Booth, "Security and Emancipation", *Review of International Studies*, Vol. 17, No. 4 (October 1991), p. 319.

57. This has to do with a recent traditionalist revival in the non-Western culture. See Richard A. Falk, "Culture, Modernism, Postmodernism: A Challenge to International Relations", in *Culture and International Relations*, Jongsuk Chay, ed. (New York and London: Praeger, 1990), pp. 274–6.

58. Samuel P. Huntington, "The Clash of Civilizations?", *Foreign Affairs*, Vol. 72, No. 3 (Summer 1993), pp. 22–49.

59. See Alastair Iain Johnson, "Thinking About Strategic Culture", *International Security*, Vol. 19, No. 4 (Spring 1995), pp. 32–64.

60. See David Harvey, *The Condition of Postmodernity* (Cambridge, MA and Oxford: Blackwell, 1990), p. 9. As far as the post-modern approach to international relations is concerned see especially James Der Derian and Michael Shapiro, eds. *International/Intertextual Relations: Postmodern Readings of World Politics* (Lexington, MA: Lexington, 1989).

61. Richard K. Ashley, "The Geopolitics of Geopolitical Space: Toward a Critical Social Theory of International Politics", *Alternatives*, Vol. XII (1987), pp. 408–11.

62. Michael Foucault, *Power/Knowledge: Selected Interviews and Other Writings, 1972–1977* (New York: Pantheon, 1980).

63. Markus Fisher, "Feudal Europe, 800–1300: Communal Discourse and Conflictual Practices", *International Organization*, Vol. 46, No. 2 (Spring 1992), p. 430.

64. This is well argued in Josef Joffe, "Deutsche Aussenpolitik-Postmodern", *International Politik*, Vol. 50, No. 1 (January 1995), pp. 43–5.

65. James Gow, "Nervous Bunnies – The International Community and the Yugoslav War of Dissolution", in *Military Intervention in European Conflicts*, Lawrence Freedman, ed. (Oxford: Blackwell, 1994), p. 33.

66. See, e.g., Barry M. Blechman, "The Intervention Dilemma," *The Washington Quarterly*, Vol. 18, No. 3 (Summer 1995), p. 65.

67. Pierre Hassner, "The European Union and the Balkans," in *Challenges in the East*, Pierre Hassner Jacques Repnic, and Michel Tatu, et.al. eds. Netherlands Scientific Council for Government Policy, Preliminary and Background Studies (The Hague: Sdu Uitgeverij, 1995), p. 40.

68. Here, I use Lawrence Freedman's terminology, in "Strategic Studies and the New Europe", *Adelphi Paper* No. 284 (January 1994), p. 23.

69. For historical background of the current debate see Peter van Ham, *The EC, Eastern Europe and European Unity. Discord, Collaboration and Integration Since 1947* (London: Pinter, 1993). See also the Commission documents: "Europe and the Challenge of Enlargement," *EC Bulletin Supplement 3/92; Towards a Closer Association with the Countries of Central and Eastern Europe*, SEC (92) 2301 final, December 2, 1992 and SEC (93) 648 final.

70. I analyze these problems in more detail in "Policies without strategy: the EU's record in Eastern Europe," in: *Paradoxes of European Foreign Policy*, Jan Zielonka, ed. (London: Kluwer Law International, 1998), forthcoming. See also Heather Grabbe and Kirsty Hughes, *Eastward Enlargement of the European Union* (London: The Royal Institute of International Affairs, 1997).

71. See Thiemo W. Eser and Martin Hallet, "Der mögliche Beitrag der EG-Regionalpolitik bei einer Ost-Erweiterung der EG: Hilfe oder Hindernis?", *Osteuropa Wirtschaft*, Vol. 38, No. 3 (1993), pp. 195–217.

72. Intervention de M. Jacques Santer, Président de la Commission européenne devant le Parlement européen, Agenda 2000, Strasbourg, July 16, 1997, internet source: http://europa.eu.int/commm/agenda2000/eapid/ 9716fr.htm.

73. The opposition to the Agenda 2000 proposal outlining the enlargement budget has been signaled in: Lionel Barber, "EU alert over new members," *Financial Times*, July 15, 1997.

74. See Harald Müller, "West European Cooperation on Nuclear Proliferation", in *Toward Political Union. Planning a Common Foreign and Security Policy in the European Community*, Reinhardt Rummel, ed. (Baden-Baden: Nomos, 1992), pp. 191–210.

75. Major conceptual controversies are identified in Scott D. Sagan and Kenneth N. Waltz, *The Spread of Nuclear Weapons. A Debate* (London: W.W. Norton Co., 1995). See also Martin van Creveld, *Nuclear Proliferation and the Future of Conflict* (New York and Oxford: The Free Press and Macmillan, 1993).

76. Romantics would refuse to endorse the concept of nuclear deterrence as a manifestation of modern rationalism degrading man and the natural world, while post-modernists would refuse to view nuclear weapons in absolute terms for the purpose of either deterrence or destruction.

77. See Harald Müller, "The Export Controls Debate in the 'New' European Community", *Arms Control Today*, Vol. 3, No. 2 (March 1993), pp. 10–13.

78. See Zbigniew Brzezinski, *Out of Control. Global Turmoil on the Eve of the 21st Century* (New York: Maxwell Macmillan, 1993), pp. 64–74.

79. The Paris Charter of CSCE is a good illustration of an effort to create a normative framework for the whole of Europe. As we know, however, the set of norms and values expressed in the Charter has often been ignored by various international actors. See European Communities Commission – Secretariat General, "Charter of Paris for a New Europe – Summit Meeting of the Conference for Security and Cooperation in Europe, Paris, November 19–21 1990", published in *Bulletin of the European Communities*, Year 23, No. 11 (1990), pp. 126–40.

80. See European Communities, Economic and Social Committee of the EC (session of September 1992), "Opinion on the 'Citizen's Europe'", in OCJ C313 of 30.11.1992, p. 34.

81. Nicholas Rescher, *Pluralism: Against the Demand for Consensus* (Oxford: Clarendon Press, 1993), p. 199.

82. Herman van Gunsteren, who encouraged me to look into the civil society solution in coping with the conceptual confusion of today, pointed out that in the classroom the point of citizen education is not to provide a unity of values and meanings to be secured once and for all, but to acquire competence in dealing with difference in such a way that consensus is the outcome. See Herman van Gunsteren, *Organizing Plurality. Citizenship in post-1989 Democracies*, (manuscript in progress).

83. Robert Putnam, *Making Democracy Work: Civic Traditions in Modern Italy* (Princeton: Princeton University Press, 1993), p. 177.

84. Michael Walzer, "The Concept of Civil Society", in *Toward a Global Civil Society* Michael Walzer, ed., (Providence and Oxford: Berghahn Books, 1995), pp. 21 and 23.

85. The distinction between "gardening" and "engineering" comes from the works of March and Olsen. This section is also influenced by the work of Beate Kohler-Koch and Karl-Heinz Ladeur. See, e.g., Beate Kohler-Koch, "The Strength of Weakness: The Transformation of Governance in the EU", and Johan P. Olsen, "Europeanization and Nation-State Dynamics", in *The Future of the Nation State. Essays on Cultural Pluralism and Political Integration*, Sverker Gustavsson and Leif Lewin, eds. (London: Routledge, 1996), pp. 169–210 and 245–85.

86. See Jean-Marie Guéhenno, "Foreign Policy in Search of a Polity," in *Paradoxes of European Foreign Policy*, Jan Zielonka, ed. (London: Kluwer Law International, 1998), forthcoming.

87. The terms were borrowed from Michael Mandelbaum, who as a matter of fact criticized if not caricatured President Clinton's way of treating foreign policy as social work. In his words, "Applying the standards of Mother Theresa to US foreign policy is an expensive proposition." See Michael Mandelbaum, "Foreign Policy as Social Work," *Foreign Affairs*, Vol. 75, No. 1 (January/February 1996), p. 18.

4 The crisis of modern democracy

The assumption that *Euro-paralysis* in the foreign and security field stems solely from international developments may well be wrong.[1] In fact, this chapter will try to show that the roots of the problem may also be found in domestic developments. The argument is not merely about the obvious linkage between domestic and international issues.[2] It is also about judgment criteria and some essential cause-effect equations. If politicians ignore solidarity calls within their own domestic borders, can one expect them to act less selfishly across these borders? If people do not trust their own national governments, why should they endorse a European government with its still-nascent forms of representation? If European nation states fail to pass the efficiency test can the Union, composed of 15 such inefficient states, do any better?[3] Common policies within the Union are not made in a social, political, and cultural vacuum. Those policies are part of a complex democratic process sweeping across the entire continent. If Europe's democracy is in trouble, then diplomatic, military, and any other policies within the Union can hardly work. In short, democratic paralysis implies paralysis in the foreign and security field. This chapter will try to assess the credibility of this claim.

Another major issue examined here is the question of democratic control over foreign and security policies. Are democratic policies compatible with the efficient running of foreign and security affairs? And should we strive to make common foreign and security policies more democratic? A general crisis of democracy would obviously affect all different policy fields, including foreign affairs and security. But is that good or bad news for foreign affairs establishments? After all, democracy and diplomacy, not to mention a combination of democracy and defense, have been strange bed fellows throughout modern history. Why should one assume that foreign and security policy can be run in the same democratic manner as domestic policy? Why should one hope that more democracy would produce more sound policies in the field of foreign affairs? Why should one argue that we need more democratic scrutiny over the CFSP than over the foreign policies of individual member states?

I will start by analyzing claims about the crisis of modern democracy. Since these claims are catchy but dangerously vague, I will look at three specific aspects of the alleged crisis, all closely interrelated. First, I will look at the alleged crisis of representation manifesting itself in declining political participation, erosion of public trust in democratic institutions, falling membership of established parties, increased electoral volatility, support for extremist and anti-democratic politics, and mounting scandals and corruption within governmental circles. Needless to say, the common foreign and security policy of the Union can hardly be expected to get off the ground if handled by illegitimate institutions and discredited statesmen.

Secondly, I will look at the crisis in democratic culture manifesting itself in the collapse of collective solidarity and ethics. In an atmosphere of growing public cynicism, privatism, nihilism, hedonism, and greed any common foreign and security policy can be little more than an empty slogan. People are simply not prepared to bear any, even short-term, individual burdens for the sake of long-term collective gains. For a common foreign and security policy of the Union to work, a certain level of public trust, moral purpose, and collective responsibility is clearly needed.

Thirdly, I will look at the democratic efficiency crisis. Democracy in Europe is functioning primarily at the level of nation states. However, nation states are increasingly confronted with powerful transnational pressures that make it difficult, if not impossible, for them to function in a prompt and efficient manner. Larger units such as the European Union could possibly cope better with all these global pressures, but the capacity of citizens to control the government would obviously suffer when exercised at the Union rather than the nation state level.

This democracy versus efficiency dilemma is especially acute in the foreign and security field, which gives us an opportunity to move to another important matter: democracy and foreign policy. If the individual nation states of Europe have lost the capacity to provide a credible national defense, is the Union best suited to do the job? And if Europe's diplomacy has the greatest punch when exercised in a multilateral framework, should this framework be made more democratic?

My conclusions will point to a profound transformation rather than crisis of democracy within the European Union. Democracy is not immune to all the economic, societal, and cultural changes that constantly evolve in Europe and in the wider world. Some of these changes are not so new and have already been well thought through: the breakdown of traditional classes and community ties, the weakening of churches and secularization, the expanding bureaucracy and etatization of life, the rise of mass communication, the media revolution, the increased complexity of social and political issues, and the intensifying international interdependence. Other changes are new and as yet poorly comprehended: the collapse of the communist system, the structural unemployment crisis, the internet revolution, the technological advances in strategic defenses, the economic power of the Asian Tigers, the rise of post-modern relativism, and the growing ecological crisis. Democracy tries to adapt to all these changes with foreign and security issues forming a part of this adaptive endeavor.

The good news is that democracy seems to cope with the change better than any known undemocratic system. The bad news is that in the process of change democracy may well degenerate beyond recognition. Left largely without competition, democracy may become a procedural exercise deprived of any political substance, historical memory, and ethical purpose. It will become a part of media entertainment rather than a tool of people's power. It will become a ceremonial cover-up for very complex global operations that are largely unaccounted for if not secret. By the same token, democracy will stop performing its legitimizing and representative functions and we would have to live with a system that is largely false, deficient, unpredictable, and disoriented.

In my view, this danger is as yet not extremely pressing, but if it materializes it will have damaging implications for common foreign and security policy. In the long run, foreign policies can hardly work without being seen as legitimate, and such legitimacy cannot be gained without applying sound democratic mechanisms. It is obvious that foreign and security policies need to be effective, and that some forms of democratic control may well undermine such effectiveness. However, foreign policies do need to reflect a broader public purpose and those in charge of foreign policies do need to enjoy a strong representative mandate. In a highly pluralistic and complex European setting any workable policies cannot merely reflect the interests and ideas of a small group of unelected officials in charge of diplomacy and defense.

THE CRISIS OF REPRESENTATION

Democracy is primarily about procedures and institutions of representation. As Joseph A. Schumpeter put it, democracy is a "set of institutional arrangements for arriving at political decisions in which individuals acquire the power to decide by means of a competitive struggle for the people's vote."[4] This system is now under threat as citizens' participation in the electoral process is said to be declining, nonconventional politics or even anti-politics is gaining the upper hand, and governmental institutions can no longer enjoy public trust and confidence. The apparent weakness of mainstream political parties is particularly troubling, as these are parties that are supposed to provide a crucial bridge between the state and its citizens, basically through the process of communication, mediation, and mobilization – reaching its peak on election day.

Warnings about a forthcoming crisis of representation have been with us for some time, but they intensified dramatically in the 1990s. Jean-Marie Guéhenno entitled his best-selling book *La fin de la démocratie* and Hans-Georg Betz forcefully argued:

> During the past decade politics in Western Europe has increasingly come to be dominated by a climate of resentment and alienation. A majority of citizens no longer trust political institutions that they consider to be largely self-centered and self-serving, unresponsive to the ideas and wishes of the average person, and incapable of adopting viable solutions for society's most pressing problems. As the public's confidence in the established political parties, the political class, and some of the most important social and political institutions has steadily eroded, a growing number of voters have chosen either to turn their backs on politics altogether or to use the ballot as a means of protest.[5]

These arguments have been backed by some frightening statistics. For instance, according to some opinion polls, 90 percent of those sampled in Great Britain believed that politicians are not to be trusted and will not admit their mistakes, while in Germany almost two-thirds expressed an opinion that politicians are essentially corrupt.[6] In countries such as Austria, France, Germany, and Belgium extreme right-wing parties have been enjoying spectacular electoral gains. In Italy the Forza Italia movement defeated long-established political parties and took over the government. The number of political corruption scandals sky-rocketed not only in southern but also some northern European countries, such as Sweden and Belgium. Since 1992 more than 5,000 businessmen and politicians have been arrested in Milan alone![7] In France, five former ministers, and two former party leaders have been charged or sentenced in connection with scandals within the course of one single year.[8]

At the same time, fewer and fewer people have been registered at the ballot box, and the volatility of voting has increased. For instance, the Dutch parliamentary elections of 1994 witnessed an all-time low turnout and all-time high volatility: 34 of 150 parliamentary seats changed hands.[9] Moreover, the proportion of citizens who are members of political parties has fallen dramatically. For instance, in the 1960s more than 1 in 5 of the Danish electorate held a party card; in the 1990s, the figure is only 1 in 20. In the United Kingdom the proportion of electors who were party members used to be 1 in 10; now it is just 1 in 50, and falling.[10]

As yet, however, distrust of politicians does not show signs of undermining people's trust in democracy as a system or in its basic institutions such as parliaments. Between 1976 and 1991 the proportion of European citizens satisfied with the way democracy works in their country was 57 percent – ranging from a minimum of 49 percent in the autumn 1980 to a maximum of 59 percent in the autumn of 1989.[11] (Public support for the civil service and parliaments was also stable.) True, in 1994 as much as 53 percent of EU citizens were dissatisfied with their own country's democracy, and only 43 percent were satisfied.[12] However, these statistics have been greatly influenced by a widespread dissatisfaction with democracy in three Mediterranean countries: Italy, Greece, and Spain. In Italy only 19 percent of citizens were satisfied with their own country's democracy. In countries such as Denmark, Ireland, The Netherlands, Portugal, Belgium, Germany, UK and Luxembourg the proportion of those "satisfied" was higher than those "dissatisfied." In Denmark no less than 78 percent of citizens were satisfied with democracy in their country, and only 21 percent were dissatisfied.

Cartelization of political parties

Optimists and pessimists would read these statistics in different ways. However, it is hard to deny the existence of some serious troubles in the workings of Europe's representation system, even if the word "crisis" might seem exaggerated. What went wrong? Which institutional factors undermine the functioning of democracy at present? Two developments are particularly significant: the cartelization of political parties and the increasing role of television in the democratic process.

The problem with the parties is that they are drifting away from the people and getting closer and closer to the state. Parties are indeed losing members, but they are not losing their grip on the government.

Parties now have more power and more resources than ever before, but they are becoming increasingly isolated from their electorates and out of touch with the concerns of ordinary people. As Peter Mair put it:

> While the *partyness of society* is declining, the *partyness of the state* is increasing. The traditional parties are *not* in decline, but [they] are actually getting stronger by shifting towards an increasing penetration of, and reliance on, the state, a process which sits in marked contrast to that of earlier generations, when they rooted themselves in civil society, and drew on civil society for their resources...If there is indeed a gulf between society and politics, it is at least partly due to the behavior of the political class itself, which, over time has become more and more self-sufficient, and, hence, more and more remote. In doing so, it has helped to create a vacuum in representative politics.[13]

The growing wealth of political parties is the most striking manifestation of their enhanced position within the state. After all, the money comes usually from the state and not from the ever-shrinking contributions of party members.[14] In addition to the state's financial help, political parties in Europe are now basically relying on state-regulated channels of communication, they use state facilities in order to staff and support their own falling organization, and they reward their supporters and activists with the state's privileges and resources. By the same token, European parties are increasingly merging with the state and are abandoning their intermediate position between the state and the electorate.

Obviously, such a situation has a detrimental impact on the functioning of democratic representation. First of all, the interaction between mainstream parties and the state makes it difficult for the parties to distance themselves from the policy failures of the state.[15] In the domestic arena, there is hardly anyone else to be blamed. However, as I later argue, the ability of modern states to "deliver" is increasingly under strain and the risk is that the failure of the party-state will soon be seen as the failure of democracy as such. There is already statistical evidence showing that "performance" and "delivery" criteria are increasingly applied by European citizens when judging democracy as a system.[16]

In addition, the abandonment of the intermediate position between the state and the electorate creates a political vacuum that is already being exploited by extreme and often anti-democratic organizations.

Less dangerous, but also detrimental to democratic representation is the ability of various lobbyists and single-issue interest groups to exploit the existing vacuum for their partisan, if not selfish aims. Moreover, lobbyists and single-issue groups often try to avoid the parliamentary arena and seek direct contacts with either the public or the state.[17]

Cartelization of mainstream political parties also facilitates corruption and political patronage. Easy access to state resources makes it tempting to use them in order to reward political supporters, and in extreme cases to enhance private wealth. Besides, parties' access to state resources implies that there is plenty of money around, which by itself facilitates corruption. Moreover, as the costs of politics rise and the party-state relationship becomes increasingly intertwined, democratic control of such party-state finance is becoming very difficult. And there is always a suspicion that major parties within parliaments are reluctant to seek greater transparency in financial operations between the state and themselves.

Finally, the merging of major parties with the state implies serious communication problems. By losing their roots in civil society and shifting towards the state, parties are no longer able to communicate with their electorates through traditional grassroots channels and thus are increasingly dependent on television and other media as a means of communication. Of course, parties had no option but to make use of the new communication technology. The problem is that in the process of losing grassroots activists and ordinary members and turning for support to the state, parties have found themselves totally dependent on television in their efforts to communicate with the electorate. This leads us to the next major problem with the functioning of representative democracy at present.

Teledemocracy

Representative democracy used to be about elections every four years or so and parliaments were the place to conduct political discourse. But now television has become the main arena of public debate and politicians are hunting for voters every day by appearing and arguing on the evening news. In 1995, 75 percent of European citizens sampled said they watched the news on television "every day."[18]

Television brings politics directly into people's homes and it is also good at exposing wrong doings in politics. But the price for these advantages of television is very high because television is more about image than substance, more entertainment than values, more emotions than strategic thinking. Media-dominated politics have led to a style of governing that is more reactive than reflective. It has created the illusion of "people power" but offered the people little knowledge. It has encouraged a politics of sensation and enhanced a lowest-common-dominator culture.[19]

Television feeds citizens a shallow and selective diet of information and it often generates political events rather than simply reporting them. Television cannot but simplify complex political issues. In a report 60 to 80 seconds long, television is unable to provide any context or background, it can only provide a brief headline. Moreover, television has great problems in dealing with ambiguity, for as David Webster rightly argued: "it has trained its viewers to expect constant simplification, stipulation and hype, and the simple resolution of human dilemmas."[20]

The politicians and experts interviewed on television are carefully maneuvered to fit the white-and-black dichotomy of a soap-opera type conflict. They are not supposed to complicate things, they are to provide popular amusement.[21] Opinions of ordinary people appearing on the screen are presented as *vox populi*, but are in fact preselected if not manufactured by news makers. Besides, "ordinary people" interviewed on television do not represent anybody but themselves, and they usually have no fixed opinion on the questions asked; consequently they often express opinions presented by television on the previous day.

Television stirs up problems but seldom comes up with solutions. It tends to exaggerate and dramatize reported stories, but then forgets about them and moves on to other issues. The TV public, continually confronted with a plethora of unsolvable problems that come and go without conclusions, becomes confused, detached, and frustrated. As Giovanni Sartori forcefully argued:

> The people of the media age truly are 'media fabricated' people... [But] the television-fed public is, by all counts, a highly disinformed and ill-informed public. Television does reach larger audiences; but its visual messages, its newscasting, provide the semblance, not the substance of information... The priorities of television are the scoop, the shoot (a good image), and the ratings (the largest possible audience). And these are bound to be wrong priorities, priorities that are both overblown and wrongly ordered... Video-politics produces increasing affect-mobilized participation under conditions of

decreasing and impoverished information. And if this is the case, surely 'doing politics' (good politics) is in trouble.[22]

Television politics also stimulates something that Alain Minc called *la sondomanie* (the mania of polling).[23] The polls are supposed to reflect the views of the electorate, but in fact they usually reflect the views of the television politics itself. It is the television that largely shapes public opinion and then reports the results of public opinion polls describing them as representative and authentic. But polls are often misleading if not fundamentally incorrect.[24] First, poll findings are highly manipulative; much depends on which questions are asked and how. Secondly, statistical data are often opinions gathered from people who have no opinion (until the interviewer forced them into expressing one). Thirdly, the intensity with which an opinion is held is seldom probed by the media-serving pollsters, as if opinions are never subject to change.

Despite the obvious deficiencies of poll-taking, *la sondomanie* has become a legitimate phenomenon in all Western European democracies. Polls are seen as objective and reliable sources of information, constantly forcing politicians to respond to them. The results of such a response can easily be predicted: a zigzag set of usually wrong decisions leading to chaos and subsequently to paralysis.

Taken together, the poll mania and television politics provide the mechanism of democratic representation with at least three serious challenges. First, the television oligarchy is basically unaccountable.[25] The problem lies not so much in the lack of parliamentary control over television, as in the lack of any "responsibility" criteria that can be applied to television broadcasting. Television claims to report the news, not to solve problems, even if some of these problems are clearly fabricated by the media.

Secondly, opinion polls and television have produced an obsession with image at the expense of political substance. Politicians have turned to relying on sound bites and pictures rather than arguments, effectively substituting the power of television for the power of their own reasoning.[26] Politicians are now surrounded by pollsters and public relations specialists who have little interest in either the political producer or consumer, even less so in the final product. They are solely concerned with the poll results and the image, both closely interrelated. Even parliaments, which used to be a platform for an informed and rational debate, are now bowing to the ultimate telos of television which is entertainment.[27]

Finally, the polls and television have blurred the distinction between serious and trivial politics. Sometimes they even confuse reality with fiction, especially if the actual world does not fit the world of the polls and media. Alain Minc believes that the polls have become so nationally legitimized that when the results differ from those which had been predicted, it is the election that is wrong and the societal body, that did not respect the findings of the polls, is presented as very frivolous. Giovanni Sartori castigates the "poll-terror" and "video-power" as based on mere rumors, false statistics, and the blowing-up of trivia, and prompted by the "here and now" of thousands of little homelands; all having little if anything to do with reality.

But, of course, a return to the pre-television era is out of the question just as it is difficult to imagine politics without opinion polls. If so, governments' futures are not to be decided merely by parliaments and the electorate. The media, pollsters, and image-makers will also have their share of influence. As political parties desert their electorates even further, we may witness a shift from representative democracy to direct democracy in Europe. Direct democracy would make parliaments, parties, and elections less important because most big decisions would be taken by referendum. Television and polling would gain importance because the struggle for the citizen's vote would become permanent.

Is such a vision indeed in the making? At present, it is very difficult to judge. It is even more difficult to imagine the implications of direct democracy for the conduct of foreign and security affairs. For some time to come we will probably have more of the same, which means that we will have a democratic system that is less about representation and more about entertainment. We will have to tolerate parties that are closer to the state than to their own electorates. And we will have to rely on image-makers and poll-takers rather than the usual ideologues and grassroots activists. Such a system does not guarantee the smooth functioning of democratic institutions and procedures that were created for the old-fashioned system with central roles assigned to grassroots parties, elections, and working rather than entertaining parliaments. Moreover, it is difficult to imagine how trust and legitimacy can be regained if politicians are responding to the demands of pollsters and image-makers that are in flux and at odds with electoral promises, group loyalties, and procedural arrangements.

In short, the representation system will be under constant strain affecting various policy sectors, including foreign and security affairs.

Even those who are reluctant to mix democracy with international politics would probably admit that diplomats would rather cope with assertive parliaments than television newsmen. Not to mention the comfort that a foreign and security policy can enjoy when operating within a representation system that is predictable, worthy, and legitimate. I will return to this question somewhat later.

THE CRISIS OF THE DEMOCRATIC CULTURE

Democracy may well be about procedures and institutional questions, but all procedures and institutions operate within a civil society of some kind.[28] If Europe's society is undergoing change, democracy must change accordingly. Democracy's failure to cope with new attitudes and modes of behavior may result in a serious crisis.[29] If the current change implies that community, stability, and collectivism are replaced by individualism, consumerism, and hedonistic self-interest, then obviously democracy within the Union cannot remain immune to such a change.[30] If the current change implies that Europe's citizens become largely immoral, cynical, and aim merely at short-term individual gains, then one should re-examine the ability of democratic institutions to cope with the new situation. Jacques Thomassen grasped the problem very well by asking:

> What can we say about a democracy in which individual liberty prevails to the extent that the role of the government and institutionalized politics is increasingly questioned, where a pluralist process of decision-making leaves little room for an impartial interpretation of the general interest, where political participation seems to be directed to individual and private ends at the expense of the recognition and pursuit of the public good?[31]

There are good reasons to think that the on-going change in social attitudes and behavior may put democracy under severe strain. First of all, democracy tends to work better in a consensual rather than majoritarian fashion.[32] One can argue that a certain level of trust and cooperation is indispensable for democratic institutions and procedures to work. One may even go further and insist that Europe's post-Second World War democratic success is the product of a certain moral orientation that was geared towards the generation of collective rather than individual goods. If the current societal change in Europe involves a rise of instrumental and expressive orientations that do away with the existing collective solidarities and stimulate individual self-ishness, then any consociational, consensus, or Madisonian democratic ideal will stand no chance within a future European Union.

Even if one is happy with a majoritarian rather than consensual model of democracy it is still debatable whether this model can cope with a change that buries the notion of consensus, solidarity and moral purpose altogether. After all, one needs a certain level of consensus to make sure that rational and non-violent decision making takes place and that its outcomes are accepted even by the disadvantaged. In other words, for the majoritarian democracy to work, minorities ought to abide by the rules of the game. However, the aggressive pro-life campaigns and controversies around the issue of affirmative action indicate that minorities are increasingly reluctant to play the major-itarian democratic game.

If democracy is in trouble because of the on-going changes in social attitudes, values, and behavior, the impact on foreign policies can be enormous. Foreign and security policies have traditionally been run in a consensual, multi-partisan fashion. Does the current societal change imply that any future foreign and security policy can no longer be built on a broad public consensus? Does this mean that decisions about alliances, treaties, war and peace will be subject to the usual partisan squabbles as is the case with domestic questions? More problems could be expected if the assertive stance of certain minorities were to prevent majoritarian democracy from working. Imagine that French or Spanish farmers were to refuse to comply with the EU's policy of eastward enlargement. And what if various Muslim, Christian, and Orthodox groups within the Union were to run their own "foreign" policies *vis-à-vis* individual Balkan states?

Effective foreign policy might fall victim to domestic political squa-bbles, but also to inertia, indifference, and the lack of a common vision. Can the Union's policy of development aid be financed without a certain degree of public compassion and solidarity with the Third World? If foreign policy is not about morality and justice, should Europe's soldiers risk their lives in tracing war criminals in Rwanda or Bosnia? Clearly there is a need for some sort of collective respons-ibility, solidarity, and moral purpose within EU member states and among them for a common foreign and security policy to work. In other words, the smooth functioning of foreign and security policies of the Union requires the existence of something that might be called a democratic ethos or culture. The question is: can we proclaim this culture to be dead?

Careful studies on the subject indeed show a major change in social attitudes and behavior which dampens hopes for the maintenance of the long-standing democratic culture, based on communal links, religion, patriotism, and mainstream morality.[33] However, this does not necessarily mean that the present-day culture precludes democracy altogether and completely paralyzes democratic governments.

One of the most striking features of contemporary European society is its dispersion, diversity, and divergence. Recent years have witnessed a remarkable trend towards a more fragmented, heterogeneous, and pluralistic culture. Independence and self-fulfillment are stressed in all sociological inquiries.[34] People in Europe are more inclined to design their own set of values and choose political orientations à la carte.[35] As a consequence, governments are confronted with increasingly dispersed and conflicting demands that can hardly be accommodated by one broad political platform or pulled together by a single ideology. Fragmentation makes it difficult for any leadership to emerge and unite people under a common purpose. Remarkably, however, diversity along national lines becomes more eclectic, especially among the young population. And as Mattei Dogan put it: "There is a striking cross-national similarity between the intra-national diversities: there are more similarities between two bourgeois, one French and the other British, than between a British middle-class person and a British manual worker, or between a French lawyer and a French farmer."[36]

However, these new commonalities do not necessarily lead to new cross-national solidarities, because of the strong individualism, if not selfishness, of European citizens. Self-centered and calculating Europeans seem no longer to focus on national or cross-national community or on any general public interest; they primarily focus on "me" and "mine." When asked "in what kind of society are we living?", 88 percent of young English respondents replied: "In a society in which everyone is for himself."[37] The unbridled pursuit of self-fulfillment and personal gain not only undermines collective loyalties, community life, and citizenship, but leads to social disintegration, isolation, and atomization with detrimental consequences for democracy itself.

The emergence of a very instrumental, as opposed to moral or legalistic, orientation of Europe's citizens is another striking feature.[38] Citizens carefully calculate all costs and benefits of personal investment in the public sphere. They are no longer bound by tradition, trust or loyalty, but are guided by calculation of individual interests. Democratic authorities can no longer count on the unconditional support of their citizens, but must engage in a constant "give and take." Appeals to patriotism, communal solidarity, or public duty hardly work. Minority groups and individual citizens impose their parochial agendas on governments and demand ever more entitlements. The result is not only a social overstretch, but also a volatile, unpredictable, and instrumental form of mass politics, with little attachment to places, organizations, or political principles.

This is combined with the desire for immediate gratification from one's own actions and a quest for consumption, leisure, and hedonistic pleasure that cannot be satisfied by a democratic routine, consisting of elections, law making, and administration of public affairs. One result is a growing escapism and negativism on the part of those disillusioned with the "dull" goods produced by democratic governments. Another result is intensification of protest politics directed against democratic governments. Both attitudes are based on negativism in the sense that they are not aimed at building, integrating, or accommodating but at destroying, excluding, and isolating.

On top of that comes a change in moral attitudes. Values are no longer taken for granted, but have become dependent on the individual's judgment. Morality as prescribed by tradition, state institutions, or religious denominations is losing ground. There is a tendency to evade sensitive moral questions by imposing technical solutions on them, or even to ignore moral challenges altogether. As the old moral order is no longer widely accepted, moral relativism spreads leading in turn to ethical confusion, if not ambivalence.[39]

The above evaluation of the current cultural trends seems quite depressing. However, not all the evidence put forward represents bad news for the functioning of democratic governments in Europe. Fragmentation and dispersion means that the situation is more complex than in the past, but it is not necessarily worse. On the one hand, there are indeed people who are passive and cynical. On the other hand, however, there are also people who are active if not passionate about social and political issues. There is a rise in xenophobic and anti-liberal groups, but there is also an increased role for groups that promote pluralism, cosmopolitanism and international cooperation. Fragmentation does indeed put governments under a broad set of dispersed pressures, but such pressures may well be easier to handle than strong localized pressure caused by a single political, economic or ideological factor. The instrumental orientation of EU citizens might be more conducive to democracy than a misguided moral fundamentalism. Self-interest might be a better platform to unite people than such vague and often misused concepts as class solidarity or the brotherhood of nations. The rise of post-materialist and post-modern values is not merely about hedonism, but also about creativity, quality of life and emancipation. And there is little evidence for what Ignacio Ramonet termed *Agonie de la morale*.[40] Moral agony should not be confused with moral change. The latter is indeed taking place with the institutional morality dominated by religion fading away. But as the data from the European Values Study show, people do not become amoral, but rather their morality is increasingly based on personal convictions and considerations.[41] The notion that an ethos of "anything goes" prevails in contemporary Europe is hardly based on any hard-core evidence.

No doubt, democracies within the Union have to adapt to the ongoing change. They have to perform efficiently in order to enjoy popular backing rather than merely count on tradition, ideology, and charismatic leadership as a source of citizens' cooperation. They have to seek compromises and trade-offs with their electorates on a daily basis rather than merely rely on intra-party political pacts or artificial fronts of national unity. They have to allow individuals to decide more things for themselves rather than rely on a big patronizing government. And they have to learn to accommodate dispersed and fragmented demands while maintaining a coherent set of strategic goals and a clear sense of political direction.

No doubt, extreme selfishness, negativism, escapism, and hedonism ought to be combatted. But the proper way to do this is by providing incentives and engaging in a dialogue rather than embarking on moral crusades. After all, it is not the job of a democratic government to decree what is morally right and wrong. Besides, the ability of any regime to reshape its underlying culture is rather limited.[42]

Democratic governments have no other option but to cope with the current diversity, ambiguity, and uncertainty in a tolerant and flexible manner. In short, there is no need to abandon the ideal of a consensual government. This does not mean giving in to all demands of noisy groups and passionate minorities. Nor does it mean abandoning moral grounds and legal discipline. As Guido Lenzi rightly put it: "Today as yesterday, the much demanded leadership must respond to a common moral inspiration and rely on impartial and well-established rules of behavior. It would be prudent to ensure that values which have matured for centuries in the Western conscience are put forth without imposition. If not all values, at least the methods and procedures must be commonly accepted."[43]

These remarks are equally applicable to domestic and international affairs. Foreign and security policies of the Union and its member states will need to find acceptance from the increasingly heterogeneous and fragmented electorates. But this should not necessarily imply an aimless policy of constant change without any sense of direction. If foreign and security policies ignore broader strategic considerations and give in to local partisan pressures then the result will be anarchy and chaos. But if grassroots calls are constantly ignored then apathy, banalization, and introversion may take over and the lowest common denominator will prevail. A skillful balancing is therefore needed to maintain a sense of strategic purpose in responding to the demands and expectations of the increasingly pluralistic European electorates.

The instrumental attitude of European citizens will also require a skillful balancing of long-term and short-term international concerns. Similar balancing acts will be required in order to accommodate humanitarian concerns as countries compete for power and the fulfillment of national interests. Of course, the danger is that balancing will imply a policy of "hanging on" without any sense of moral or strategic direction. But efforts to impose any moral, ideological, or geopolitical dogmas on a new Europe or the wider world would be destabilizing and condemned to failure.

In sum, there is not so much a crisis of democratic culture, as a profound cultural and moral change. Democracies may benefit from the new environment provided that they are able to recognize new social patterns and learn to operate according to them. However, this will not be an easy task in view of the representation problems caused by the cartelization of political parties and television politics. Transnational global pressures will also complicate democratic restructuring. I now turn to the latter matter.

GLOBALIZATION AND DEMOCRATIC EFFECTIVENESS

Democracies have always been under external pressures but they have managed to cope with them quite well. When the city state found itself in trouble, largely because of external pressures, democracy did not die, but was transferred to a larger unit better suited to cope with these pressures: the nation state.[44] Democracy as such has also changed in this process; it became a representative democracy rather than an assembly democracy known at the level of the city state. Today, the evidence is growing that the nation state is no longer able to withstand the new wave of external pressures usually labeled as transnational interdependence and globalization.[45] Does this imply another type of democratic crisis that incapacitates European governments? Will democracy abandon the nation state and move to a larger unit better suited to cope with globalization? Will the Union become that new democratic unit? How will democracy look after the shift? And what are the implications of all this for security and foreign affairs?

The impact of globalization on the capacity of states to act in the traditional way is most pronounced in the field of economy and finance. National economic sovereignty is being eroded by massive international labor and capital flows that constrain governments' abilities to defend their countries' economic interests.[46] The usual tools of economic policy, such as taxes, public borrowing and spending, exchange and interest rates, and capital and credit controls can no longer be used without impunity by any European state. For instance, if a government was to try now to reduce interest rates below the international level, the result would no longer be a rise in job-creating real investments, but an outflow of capital, devaluation, and an increased inflation rate. Likewise if a government was to try to tax its businesses more heavily than in other countries, firms will simply shift their production elsewhere. As William Brock argued: "In a global economy, the nation state increasingly lacks the capacity to control events. When a trillion dollars changes hands in nanoseconds in a given day, when your whole economy is based on information and technology, not on muscle power and sweat, the ability of governments to control events within geographic boundaries is increasingly limited. Governments will try to intervene because that is a normal political response, and as they try to intervene, that may make matters worse."[47]

Globalization pressures also affect other fields including security and foreign affairs. None of the European nation states is able to provide security on its own at present. Even nuclear Britain and France no longer have the military capability to defend themselves from any hypothetical aggressor. More importantly, none of the European states is able to provide stability in a broader regional context.[48] It is also increasingly difficult to prevent refugees, spies, arms smugglers, and ordinary criminals from crossing borders. Nor is there a national solution to cope with the so-called 21st century threats, such as environmental degradation or AIDS.

Diplomacy is equally affected by globalization and transnational interdependence. Governments can no longer negotiate merely among themselves; they also have to negotiate with domestic and foreign firms and a plethora of NGO's and international lobbyists.[49] Moreover, they have to adjust to the consequences of various deals between firms, between firms and NGO's, and between NGO's and other governments. This "triangular diplomacy," to use Susan Strange's term, reduces the relative significance of decisions and actions made by individual governments and intergovernmental institutions.[50] Today as never before in the history of modern Europe major trends are prompted by the decisions of multinational firms, lobbyists, and NGO's, and not chiefly or merely by European nation states.

The erosion of national power and control is thus undeniable.[51] The question is, nevertheless, how much erosion? Does this erosion effectively paralyze European governments? The answer is: yes, but only to a certain degree. As Wolfgang C. Müller and Vincent Wright put it: "Western European states, at both international and European Union level, remain central actors – arguably the central actors, even if they are increasingly prisoners of an interlocking network of bargained situations: they are not by-passed or eliminated but rather more constrained."[52] The central position of European states is underlined by their control of the armed forces and major arsenals of defense, by their high if somewhat diminished profile in the financial and commercial markets, and by their ability to pull intergovernmental forces to cope with external global pressures.[53] In this context, the creation and development of the European Union is of particular importance. There is a vast body of evidence showing that the Union has been created and subsequently developed not as a means of dismantling European nation states, but as a means for rescuing them to resist being dismantled.[54]

But does the Union represent an effective solution to global pressures? And does it benefit or hamper democracy in Europe? The answer to the first question is rather ambivalent. For instance, it is legitimate to see a regional organization as only partly equipped to cope with pressures that are global *sui generis*, and thus broader than a regional reach and perspective.[55] Moreover, it is one thing to endorse a common European policy in the field of defense, and another to endorse a common European army with no common language, tradition, training, and armaments.

The second question strikes at the heart of our problem. The Union may well rescue European nation states, but it may be about dismantling rather than rescuing democracy on the continent. After all, the larger the democratic unit, the less the chances for democratic participation of the citizens.[56] And as Giovanni Sartori has rightly argued, *"real democracy* can only be, and must be, participatory democracy...Participation and localism grow in unison."[57] The problem is that small units that are, in principle, well suited to guarantee full-fledged citizens' participation have become largely ineffective in dealing with global pressures; they are particularly vulnerable to global market machinations, regional instability, and power politics in either economic or security terms.[58]

This applies not only to local communities, but also (and increasingly so) to European nation states, small ones in particular. And thus, citizens of a European country such as France, United Kingdom, or Denmark, for instance, may well resist delegating more powers to the European Union on the assumption that this would reduce their democratic rights to control the government. However, this would imply that some important, if not the most important, matters will be beyond the capacity of national governments to deal with effectively. On the other hand, if they chose to give more powers to the European Union on the assumption that this is helpful in tackling global pressures, their power to control the activity of their (by now European) government would be severely curbed.

And thus democracy is confronted by a seemingly unsolvable dilemma: should it opt for system effectiveness or for citizen participation?[59] Democracy will obviously be doomed if it neglects the principle of effectiveness, but can it survive by compromising the principle of representation? So far, an effort is made to escape from this black and white dichotomy by pursuing a two-track policy. More and more powers are delegated to the European level without dismantling nation states and local units. Likewise, the "inferior" democracy at the Union level is being treated as a supplement and not as a replacement for democracy at lower levels. Of course, democracy cannot always have it both ways, but as Robert A. Dahl rightly argued: "The larger scale of decisions need not lead inevitably to a widening sense of powerlessness, provided citizens can exercise significant control over decisions on the smaller scale of matters important in their daily lives: education, public health, town and city planning."[60] In other words, the transfer of power and democratic process from nation states to the Union requires, where possible, strengthening rather than weakening of citizen participation at the local and nation state levels.[61]

Moreover, democracy at the Union level can also be made less "inferior." A growing sense of a true European cultural identity combined with a legal framework for European citizenship could help to create a surrogate European *demos*.[62] Development of a truly European party system, next to the existing national party systems, could offer a more meaningful choice to the voters taking part in the European elections.[63] The European Parliament itself, could be given more power at the expense of the European Council.[64] All these would hardly offer European citizens more democratic control than is the case in the present-day European nation state. The alternatives, however, are even worse. The idea that in the age of globalization effective policies should be left in the hands of unelected and unaccountable officials is as unattractive as the idea that we disperse democratic procedures towards a limitless global world.[65]

One should keep in mind, however, that more and more decisions will be made not by any European or national governments but by international markets. Those markets are not necessarily driven by rich speculators, but also by millions of small investors, consumers, and borrowers. Moreover, when those markets effectively punish irresponsible governments the net beneficiary is a European citizen.[66] But the problem with markets is that they have a peculiar notion of justice, not to mention their indifference towards such social values as solidarity, loyalty, or compassion.[67] And thus Europe and its citizens cannot do without some sort of corrective government that would reflect both their drive towards economic growth and their sense of social order and justice. Such a government is also needed to cope with a global civil society and not merely with global markets.[68]

In conclusion, the reason that European governments seem at times paralyzed in domestic and foreign affairs is partly a reflection of their growing inability to cope with global pressures. This does not imply that governments are totally powerless, but efforts to enhance their effectiveness in dealing with these global pressures are not without a price. Delegating more power to the European Union may well be helpful in terms of effectiveness, but it is clearly deficient in terms of democratic representation. While there are ways to ease the tension between incompatible demands of efficiency and citizen participation, regular problems are to be expected on both fields, causing upheaval, inefficiency, and contention.

DEMOCRACY AND FOREIGN POLICY

So far the argument has been based on the assumption that domestic and foreign policies are very much alike and both are closely tied to good and bad fortunes of democracy. Moreover, international issues are today largely domesticated, while domestic issues are internationalized. This is particularly clear when seen from a macro perspective dominated by cross-cutting interdependence, erosion of national borders, and globalization.[69] But the linkage between domestic and foreign issues is also evident when seen from a micro perspective of individual leaders considering the utility and implications of particular actions. As Bruce Russett rightly argued:

> For elected leaders (and those who try to keep them in office, and those who would take their places) foreign and security policy is, in large degree, domestic politics. In a democracy, the political leader who ignores domestic politics hamstrings his or her ability to get things done internationally, risks repudiation domestically, and ignores a set of resources – real or symbolic success abroad – that could help bring success at home also.[70]

While the linkage between domestic and foreign policies is now widely accepted, the same cannot be said about the linkage between democratic policies and foreign policies, let alone between democratic policies and security ones. There are many who would argue that democratic politics should not be applied to foreign and security affairs. So the issue at stake here is different than in the three previous sections. I will look at the rationale behind democratic control over foreign policies rather than at the question of how the failings of democracy paralyze foreign policies. Yet, the latter question can hardly be answered properly without looking at the former question. Moreover, if democratic policies are largely incompatible with foreign policies, then it is difficult to argue that the alleged crisis of democracy has a paralyzing impact on foreign policies.

Two basic arguments are raised to justify the alleged incompatibility between the three: democracy – security – diplomacy. First, security and foreign affairs concern the most vital interests of states and their citizens. We are talking about issues related to life and death, survival or collapse of nation states, and major shifts in power configurations. Such vital interests cannot fall prey to the usual partisan politics and the uncertainties of democratic bargaining. Coherence, continuity, and even secrecy are needed to make any foreign and security policy work.

Secondly, running foreign and security policy requires special talents and expertise which are not found among a general public that is emotional, uninformed, volatile, and predisposed to manipulation. In fact, the special character of foreign and security issues suggests that they are run by a small group of governmental experts, not even by parliaments consisting of democratically elected representatives.[71]

Some of these arguments cannot be easily dismissed. The technical complexity of weapons and strategies, the speed of response required in times of crisis, and the necessity of diplomatic bargaining, all these factors render democratic processes awkward, if not ineffective altogether. Should parliaments be allowed to debate highly classified war plans and conceived levels of military preparedness? Can ordinary parliamentarians, let alone a broader public, have a competent opinion about the most sophisticated modern weaponry? Should governments involved in complex diplomatic negotiations reveal their bargaining position to their electorates? And will the public and its parliamentary representatives follow the hard conclusions of strategic reasoning rather than try to have it the easy way? Back in 1955, Walter Lippmann gave a straight answer to some of these questions:

> The unhappy truth is that the prevailing public opinion has been destructively wrong at the critical juncture. The people have imposed a veto upon the judgment of informed and responsible officials. They have compelled the governments, which usually knew what would have been wiser, or was necessary, or was more expedient, to be too late with too little or too long with too much, too pacifist in peace and too bellicose in war, too neutralist or too appeasing in negotiation, or too intransigent. Mass opinion has acquired mounting power in this century. It has shown itself to be a dangerous master of decisions when the stakes are life and death.[72]

The major problem with Lippmann's statement is that governments are not always, or even usually, wiser than their respective electorates. History reveals many cases of misjudgment and misconduct of the executive branch of government.[73] The more secrecy surrounding foreign and security operations, the more chances for misconceived policies to prevail. Foreign policy elites who proclaim special competence are hardly immune to the ancient human afflictions of ambition, presumption, and overconfidence. At the same time, the general public is not as ignorant, emotional, and fickle as Walter Lippmann seems to suggest. There is a large body of evidence suggesting the public's ability to form discriminating and stable opinions.[74]

Of course, ordinary citizens cannot be expected to have the experts' technical knowledge necessary for drafting international treaties or shaping strategic doctrines. But experts have no right to claim a monopoly on making decisions concerning basic foreign policy ends, let alone on making moral decisions for millions of their fellow countrymen.[75] The fact that foreign and security issues often touch upon the most vital national interests argues for a greater, rather than a lesser, democratic involvement of the public in the decision-making process. Why should the most important issues be decided by a small group of unelected officials operating in secret ways? Why should some vital decisions about citizens' life and death be exempted from democratic scrutiny? As Robert A. Dahl put it: "It is true that a democratic regime runs the risk that the people will make mistakes. But the risk exists in all regimes in the real world, and the worst blunders of this century have been made by leaders in non-democratic regimes."[76]

More democracy is thus desirable within the CFSP framework, but can one find a workable solution for addressing the democratic deficit within the Union? Can such a solution accommodate the conflicting requirements of security and democracy?

Referenda are often seen as the best solution for improving the EU's democratic record: wrongly so, I would argue! A referendum creates a conflict-maximizing mechanism that makes it difficult to establish policies in a consensual, bi-partisan manner. As Giovanni Sartori so accurately put it: "referendum democracy represents not only perfect but also the most unintelligent incarnation of a systematic *majority tyranny*," based on "an outright *zero-sum mechanism* of decision making: the winning majority takes all, the minority loses all."[77] Moreover, a referendum forces politicians to present complicated international questions in simplistic black and white terms which obviously rewards populist politics and demagoguery. As said earlier, democracy is basically about procedures and institutions of representation. Democracy is not about people's direct rule over all possible matters.

The problem is, nevertheless, that the representation system within the Union does not function very well and this is particularly true in the field of international affairs. National parliaments in individual EU countries have little influence on the shape of foreign and security policies drawn up either by their respective governments or the Union. Valentine Herman looked at the issue in many different countries and concluded: "Whatever the system, the part played by Parliament in the conduct and control of foreign affairs appears to be small...While at best it may be able to insist on a particular orientation of foreign policy, Parliament is denied a meaningful role in the making of that policy."[78]

For instance, budgetary prerogatives of national parliaments within the Union are often irrelevant as most of the urgent foreign and security expenditures are unpredictable and thus are not reflected in any actual parliamentary budget. Legislative prerogatives of parliaments are constrained by the fact that international treaties are usually presented for ratification in the form of "package deals" that can hardly be renegotiated. Moreover, many important international agreements do not take the form of formal treaties and thus are never submitted for parliamentary ratification. Some important information concerning the governmental conduct of foreign affairs and security is never made available to ordinary MPs.

The situation does not look better when one shifts from the national to the European level. The European Parliament in Strasbourg has even less influence on foreign and security policies than respective national parliaments. Formally, the EU Presidency is obliged to consult the European Parliament on the main aspects and the basic choices of the CFSP and ensure that the views of the Parliament are duly taken into consideration.[79] In practice, however, common foreign and security policies of the Union are very much an exclusively intergovernmental affair, with the European Parliament exercising little if any democratic control over them.

The problem is not so much in the catalogue of formal powers bestowed on the European Parliament, but rather in the peculiar nature of the European parliamentary game. The European Parliament has neither a ruling party nor a ruling coalition, it has neither a governing cabinet nor a governing program to sustain or oppose. Moreover, the Parliament, the Commission, and the Council are created more or less independently, therefore the element of "fusion" that is usually observed between cabinets and their parliamentary majority does not exist. Cleavages within the European Parliament break along national "boundaries," and not along party affiliations or ideologies. And major decisions of the European Union rely on the legitimacy of national parliaments rather than the legitimacy of the European Parliament.[80] Although members of the European Parliament are now directly elected to five-year terms, these elections tend to serve as popularity contests for the ruling national governments and, as such, do little to enhance the legitimacy of European governance.[81] The essence of the problem is that there is no European public space at present, let alone a European demos.[82]

Of course, certain institutional and procedural reforms can improve the situation. For instance, the creation of a standing "committee of committees" on foreign policy, grouping national foreign affairs committees and the European Parliament's Committee on foreign policy, security, and defense would enhance democratic scrutiny of the CFSP. Moreover, as the CFSP budget progressively increases, so will the European Parliament's *real* power over the CFSP budget and therefore its long-term direction.[83] But the fact remains that it is difficult to construct a workable system of parliamentary control over foreign and security policies, and this is even more true at the European level than at the national one. It is one thing to debunk governmental (or intergovernmental) myths about their special predisposition to manage international affairs; but quite another to find a proper institutional solution that would democratize rather than paralyze the CFSP. It is one thing to argue for greater openness in foreign affairs, but another to insist on serious public hearings (debates) before allowing any serious response to a crisis. It is one thing to believe that "no national entity can secure itself by itself;" and another to shift powers from national governments to the European Parliament without support of the (non-existent) European demos.[84]

All this does not necessarily mean that democracy and foreign policy are incompatible. There are different ways in which the public and its parliamentary representatives can exercise democratic controls over the executive branch of government. Regular elections induce "self-censorship" on foreign and defense ministries. Secret pacts and negotiations are sooner or later leaked to the media.[85] Nor are parliaments totally helpless in facing assertive executive policies. In The Netherlands, for instance, the Parliament forced the Cabinet to produce several official *nota's* dealing with such sensitive matters as disarmament, human rights, development aid, arms export, the United Nations, and the military draft. When asked about the degree of their influence over foreign and defense issues, half of the MPs questioned claimed to have "much" or even "very much" influence.[86]

It is also clear that most of the arguments against extensive democratic control apply to defense issues and not to diplomatic ones. In fact, the majority of diplomatic issues could well be seen as domestic issues *sui generis* and treated accordingly in terms of democratic scrutiny.

That said, democracy, defense, and some types of diplomacy are to remain strange bedfellows. Technological innovation in the defense field can hardly be matched by innovations in democratic "techniques." Diplomatic and security priorities will continue to differ from democratic priorities. And there will always be areas of international politics where democratic logic and principles can only be applied with grave difficulty.[87]

Before new ways of democratic representation are developed the best solution is to increase transparency of foreign policy making in the Union and allow for a more informed public discourse on the CFSP questions.[88] After all, democracy basically means that actors (that is, states or the Union) arrive at decisions through a process of disclosure and deliberation. Representative government ought to be accountable. Moreover, without such disclosure and deliberation policies can hardly enjoy democratic legitimacy. Democratic governments should therefore restrict their actions and positions to those that are publicly visible and defensible. In foreign affairs this need not necessarily imply openness of all tactical operations and deliberations. However, basic strategic options should certainly be revealed to the public and no final choice should be made without a genuine public debate on the merits of different options. MPs and government officials at national and European levels should be compelled to explain why certain policies are indeed in the public's interest while others are not. Some of the issues susceptible to disclosure and deliberation have already been mentioned in the previous chapters. For instance, Union officials should be able to identify and publicly discuss a strategy of further eastward enlargement. Likewise they should be able to state clearly their case for or against the Union's acquisition of defense capabilities. The European public should have a say concerning such important matters as the Union's future borders, purpose, and functions.

The solution suggested above differs from the Union's official policy on transparency. The Union tries to promote procedural changes that would enhance the accessibility and intelligibility of draft legislation.[89] The Union hardly tries to enhance transparency of the policies themselves, especially those of strategic importance. It neither says how far it is prepared to enlarge, nor precisely what the CFSP's basic instruments and functions are. As Juliet Lodge rightly argued, "the substance of the transparency argument must not be neglected given that the transparency initiatives are portrayed as a dissatisfaction with, and arguably alienation from, the EC. Public acceptance of, indifference towards and acquiescence in European integration cannot be taken for granted any longer. Reconciling effectiveness, diversity and democracy cannot be achieved credibly by administrative and procedural measures."[90] The EU is overly complex, de-personalized, and secretive. The system of representation within the Union is much weaker in comparison to its member states. While it is difficult to expect a dramatic change in its formal structure of accountability and representation, it is right to argue for a greater disclosure and deliberation of its basic strategic considerations. The Draft Treaty of Amsterdam clears the way for the Union to adopt "common strategies," and one would hope that such strategies will indeed be regularly brought forward, discussed, and adopted.[91] One should also hope that such strategies will deal with truly "strategic," rather than symbolic, matters.

Greater transparency and openness cannot by itself eliminate the democratic deficit, but it can represent an intermediate solution for legitimizing some of the Union's current projects. Revealing all tactical maneuvers and operational details might be quite damaging for the CFSP, but revealing and discussing the substance of the Union's international strategies can only benefit the CFSP.

CONCLUSIONS

Cynics may say that a possible democratic crisis would not be terribly detrimental to foreign and security policies. Has it not been shown that assertive democratic controls may at times prevent or paralyze sensible international policies? However, such a conclusion would be based on a peculiar notion of "sensible policies." "Sensible" policies should combine effectiveness with a public purpose, and the latter is difficult to establish without referring to democracy. Democracy should allow application of effective security and diplomatic means. But means should not determine ends in any policy field without exception. In short, the point is not to choose between democracy and security, but to shape security and foreign policies in a democratic fashion, keeping in mind all possible complications.[92]

Besides, and more importantly, a healthy democratic system can greatly benefit foreign and security policies. A predictable, impartial, and legitimate system of democratic representation creates a better framework for successful foreign policies than a corrupt, volatile, and illegitimate system. Foreign policies can also benefit from a democratic culture based on trust, compromise, and solidarity. Widespread public cynicism, selfishness, and fragmentation also make it difficult for governments to shape and implement policies, including those in the field of defense and diplomacy. And if democracy succeeds in coping with global pressures this is clearly good news for Europe's economic, but also diplomatic and security interests.

The overall conclusion of this chapter is that the Union's common foreign and security policies can hardly get off the ground as long as there is no improvement in democratic representation, no revival of democratic culture, and no progress in democratic ability to deal with interdependence and globalization.[93] I have not rushed to proclaim a crisis of Europe's democracy, but have shown democracy's difficulties in responding to a series of structural environmental changes in society, culture, economy, and politics.

What is necessary for democracy to overcome the above-mentioned difficulties? This chapter has suggested several concrete, but rather trivial measures. First, there is a need to rebuild the linkage between political parties and their electorates, basically by reviving grassroots activism and doing away with the entertainment politics of the media. Secondly, there is a need for democracy to maintain a consensual style of government amidst growing cultural diversity, social individualism, and moral relativism. Thirdly, in searching for a workable compromise between system effectiveness and citizen participation, democracy has to learn to operate at various cosmopolitan, European, nation state, and local community levels.

All these suggestions are hardly original or controversial, and yet they are not really being implemented in present-day Europe. Of course, it is always easier to prescribe than to implement general policies. But the reasons for inertia can also be found in the climate of triumphant self-confidence that has been dominant since the aftermath of the Cold War era. The Soviet challenge to democracy has failed, why should democracy embark on a risky road of reform and adaptation? Any dramatic prognoses about a forthcoming democratic crisis do not sound credible in this climate. Besides, such prognoses are usually grossly overstated, and only contribute to inertia and self-confidence. Moreover, it is important to acknowledge that the traditional discourse on democracy used to be about procedures and institutions of a nation state. It is now difficult to shift this discourse to the area of culture, television, and global interdependence. New terms, concepts, and assumptions are needed in order to grasp the required nature of democratic change.

In principle there is no reason why democracy would be unable to adapt to the new circumstances the way it has often done in the past. But adaptation will not happen by itself, it must be the product of a certain degree of public awareness and political determination. Today, the danger is not so much in the rise of dictatorial alternatives to democracy. The danger is in conformity, relativism, and benign neglect. Democracy in Europe is not likely to be abolished, but it can well be made dysfunctional, self-serving, and altogether irrelevant. As such, it would be unable to legitimize the foreign policies of the Union and provide them with a widely endorsed public purpose.

Developing new forms of democratic representation cannot but be a long and complicated process. However, democratic legitimacy of the Union can be enhanced immediately by greater disclosure and deliberation of the Union's mainstream policies. In the field of international politics openness and transparency have some clear limits, especially in so far as tactical and operational questions are concerned. But the Union is in a good position to identify and make public its basic strategic options in terms of aims, functions, and geography. The Union should therefore start a serious debate about the depth of its future enlargement and about the nature (civilian versus military) of its global ambitions. The long-standing policy of keeping the EU's international purpose vague and ambiguous has proved to be detrimental in terms of democratic accountability and legitimacy. It deprives the CFSP of any genuine public backing.

NOTES

1. Students of international relations have a long tradition of separating domestic and international developments. See David Singer, "The Level-of-Analysis Problem in International Relations", in *The International System: Theoretical Essays*, Klaus Knorr and Sidney Verba, eds. (Princeton: Princeton University Press, 1961), pp. 77–92.
2. As Jack Hayward put it: "It would now be generally accepted that the interdependence of domestic and foreign policies has become so intricate that, although they may be (with difficulty) distinguished, they can seldom be separated". See Jack Hayward, "Governing the New Europe", in *Governing the New Europe*, Jack Hayward and Edward C. Page, eds. (Cambridge: Polity Press, 1995), p. 405. See also Wolfram F. Hanrieder, "Dissolving International Politics: Reflections on the Nation state", *The American Political Science Review*, Vol. 72, No. 4 (December 1978), pp. 1276–87.
3. The problem looks even graver if a country holding the EU presidency is in a political crisis undermining its democratic machinery. See, e.g., Andrea di Robilant, "Italy Takes It On the Chin for Poor Presidential Leadership: Europe's Stability May Be a Spur for Much-Needed Constitutional Reform at Home", *The European*, February 22–28, 1996, p. 8.

4. Joseph A. Schumpeter, *Capitalism, Socialism and Democracy* (New York: Harper, 1947), second edition, p. 269.

5. Hans-Georg Betz, *Radical Right-Wing Populism in Western Europe* (London: Macmillan 1994), p. 37, also Jean-Marie Guéhenno, *La fin de la démocratie* (Flammarion: Paris, 1993), as well as Herman van Gunsteren and Rudy Andeweg, *Het Grote Ongenoegen: Over de Kloof Tussen Burgers en politiek* (Haarlem: Aramith Uitgevers, 1994).

6. The sources are Hans-Joachim Veen, Norbert Lepszy and Peter Mnich, *The Republikaner Party in Germany: Right-Wing Menance or Protest Catchall?* (Westport: Praeger, 1993), p. 45 (*Washington Papers* No. 162), and *the Guardian*, September 20, 1993. As Flora Lewis observed: "Politicians in practically all industrial democracies are in trouble. People dislike and disdain them, as though they were a special, inferior breed with less than the minimum of virtues possessed by ordinary mortals." See Flora Lewis, "Politics, Like It or Not, Requires Human Involvement", *International Herald Tribune*, November 5–6, 1994.

7. *The Economist*, September 17, 1994.

8. See *The Economist*, January 6, 1996. For a comprehensive analysis of the problem see Yves Mény, *La Corruption de la République* (Paris: Fayard, 1992).

9. If we add to this the fact that three new parties entered Parliament and that a Cabinet emerged based on an unprecedented combination of parties then the results are even more dramatic. See Galen A. Irwin, "The Dutch Parliamentary Election of 1994", *Electoral Studies*, Vol. 14, No. 1 (March 1995), pp. 72–6. For a detailed analysis of electoral change see Mark N. Franklin, Thomas T. Mackie, Henry Valen et al., eds, *Electoral Change. Responses to Evolving Social and Attitudinal Structures in Western Countries* (Cambridge: Cambridge University Press, 1992), especially pp. 406–27.

10. Peter Mair, *Party Democracies and Their Difficulties* (Leiden: University of Leiden, 1994), p. 10. Also see Peter Mair, "Myths of Electoral Change and the Survival of Traditional Parties: the 1992 Stein Rokkan Lecture", *European Journal of Political Research*, Vol. 24, No. 2 (1993), pp. 121–33.

11. See Dieter Fuchs and Hans-Dieter Klingemann, "Citizens and the State: A Relationship Transformed", in *Citizens and the State*, Dieter Fuchs and Hans-Dieter Klingemann, eds. (Oxford: Oxford University Press, 1995), p. 427. The data were available for thirteen countries over a fifteen-year period: 1976–91.

12. *Eurobarometer*, No. 41 (July 1994), pp. 2–3.

13. Peter Mair, *Party Democracies and Their Difficulties*, op. cit., pp. 5 and 13. See also Richard S. Katz and Peter Mair, "Changing Models of Party Organization and Party Democracy: The Emergence of the Cartel Party", *Party Politics*, No. 1 (1995), pp. 5–28.

14. In Germany, for instance, state subsidies account for a sum that is more than ten times greater than that accounted for by other sources. In Ireland party income has more than doubled within the last twenty years, while in Austria it has increased four-fold. Full details of party finances and membership in twelve countries are reported in Richard S. Katz and

Peter Mair, eds. *Party Organizations: A Data Handbook on Party Organizations in Western Democracies, 1960–90* (London: Sage, 1992).

15. As Alan Ware put it: "The growing dependence of parties on the state, and their greater identity with it, left them more open than they had been earlier to adverse reaction by voters who believed that the state was not 'delivering' what they wanted. Whatever its advantages to the parties, the possible price of cartelization was that it made it more difficult for the parties to distance themselves from policy failure." See Alan Ware, "The Party Systems of the Established Liberal Democracies in the 1990s: Is This a Decade of Transformation?", *Government and Opposition*, Vol. 30, No. 3 (1995), p. 323.

16. Dieter Fuchs and Hans-Dieter Klingemann established that the linkage between economic growth and citizen support for democracy is to be detected in Western Europe since 1989 and not earlier. See Dieter Fuchs and Hans-Dieter Klingemann, "Citizens and the State: A Relationship Transformed", in *Citizens and the State*, op. cit., p. 441.

17. As Jack Hayward argued: "Kinship and clientelism have disintegrated into piecemeal links between factions of catch-all political parties and specific firms or localities, dismembering public interest concerns for the satisfaction of private business or partisan interests. In such a context, it is seldom clear whether specific interests are colonizing parts of government or vice versa. See Jack Hayward, "Organized Interests and Public Policies", in *Governing the New Europe*, Jack Hayward and Edward C. Page, eds. (Oxford: Oxford Polity Press, 1995), p. 247.

18. *Eurobarometer*, No. 41 (July 1994), p. 9. See also Ignacio Ramonet, "Médias en danger", *Le Monde Diplomatique*, February 1996, p. 1.

19. For a comprehensive analysis of this problem see Michael J. O'Neill, *The Roar of the Crowd: How Television and People Power Are Changing the World* (New York: Times Books, 1992).

20. David Webster, "New Communications Technology and the International Political Process", in *The Media and Foreign Policy*, Simon Serfaty, ed. (New York: St Martin's Press, 1991), p. 223.

21. As Richard Cohen put it: "News has become entertainment, something to watch on television, usually more violent and horrible than standard programming, but no more threatening." See Richard Cohen, "Waiting for New Meaning in a Post-Cold War World", *International Herald Tribune*, October 27, 1993.

22. Giovanni Sartori, *Comparative Constitutional Engineering* (London: Macmillan, 1994), pp. 149–50.

23. See Alain Minc, *L'ivresse démocratique* (Paris: Gallimard, 1995), p. 97. The polls conducted by or with the cooperation of the media industry should not be confused with serious statistical analysis conducted by academic centers. The value of evidence provided by the latter can also be disputed as we have seen earlier in this chapter, however, academic studies usually comply with some basic methodological rigors that are often ignored by media-sponsored poll taking.

24. Here I draw heavily on Giovanni Sartori's, "Video-power", *Government and Opposition*, Vol. 24, No. 1 (1989), pp. 48–9.

25. As a British MP lamented: "Newspaper, BBC and other broadcasting editors, who now determine what can and cannot be read and heard are, in effect, operating a form of censorship at the expense of the voters by seeking to replace Parliament as the main forum, setting themselves up as the only legitimate opposition... Government's future should be decided in the House of Commons and by the electors on the basis of its record and not by a self-appointed élite who are now running their own campaigns and are politically accountable to no one." See Tony Benn, "Shallow Media Coverage of Politics", *The Times*, May 14, 1994.

26. As David R. Gergen put it: "Increasingly during the 1980s, government officials have shaped their policies with an eye toward generating positive and timely television coverage and securing public approval. What too often counts is how well the policy will "play," how the pictures will look, whether the right signals are being sent, and whether the public will be impressed by the swiftness of the government's response." See David R. Gergen, "Diplomacy in a Television Age: The Dangers of Teledemocracy", in *The Media and Foreign Policy*, Simon Serfaty, ed. (New York: St Martin's Press, 1991), pp. 48–9.

27. See Bob Franklin, "Televising the British House of Commons: Issues and Developments", in *Televising Democracies* Bob Franklin, ed. (London: Routledge, 1992), p. 7.

28. One should appreciate Ralf Dahrendorf's contention that "Democracy is a form of government, not a steam bath of popular feelings." See Ralf Dahrendorf, *Reflections on the Revolution in Europe* (London: Chatto & Windus, 1990), p. 10. That said, one can still agree with Francis Fukuyama's argument that "social engineering on the level of institutions has hit a massive brick wall: experiences of the past century have taught most democracies that ambitious rearrangements of institutions often cause more unanticipated problems than they solve. By contrast, the real difficulties affecting the quality of life in modern democracies have to do with social and cultural pathologies that seem safely beyond the reach of institutional solutions, and hence of public policy. The chief issue is quickly becoming one of culture." See Francis Fukuyama, "The Primacy of Culture", *Journal of Democracy*, Vol. 6, No. 1 (January 1995), pp. 7–14. See also Seymour Martin Lipset, "The Social Requisites of Democracy Revisited", *American Sociological Review*, Vol. 59 (February 1994), pp. 3–5.

29. As Geoff Mulgan put it: "What then explains the [democratic] malaise? The simplest cause is that a huge gap has arisen between democracy as an ethos and culture and democracy as a set of institutions. The first is about equality, empowerment, the rights of all to determine their lives and express their beliefs. It fits the long-term value shifts of Western societies towards self-direction and feminization and away from traditional authority and the needs of warfare. The second is about an increasingly professionalized sphere that gives little chance for influence, little sense of belonging." See Geoff Mulgan, "Party-Free Politics", *New Statesman and Society*, April 15, 1994, p. 16.

30. Max Kaase and Kenneth Newton, "Theories of Crisis and Catastrophe, Change and Transformation," in *Beliefs in Government*, Max Kaase

and Kenneth Newton, eds. (Oxford: Oxford University Press, 1995), p. 29.

31. Jacques Thomassen, "Support for Democratic Values", in *Citizens and the State*, op. cit., p. 413. See also Robert D. Putnam, Robert Leonardi and Raffaella Y. Nanetti, *Making Democracy Work: Civic Traditions in Modern Italy* (Princeton: Princeton University Press, 1993), p. 88.

32. This was well argued in Arend Lijphard, *Democracies: Patterns of Majoritarian and Consensus Government in Twenty-One Countries* (New Haven: Yale University Press, 1984), especially p. 229.

33. See especially Ronald Inglehart, *Culture Shift in Advanced Industrial Society* (Princeton: Princeton University Press, 1990), p. 484.

34. See especially Jan W. Van Deth and Elinor Scarbrough, "Introduction: The Impact of Values", in *The Impact of Values*, Jan W. Van Deth and Elinor Scarbrough, eds. (Oxford: Oxford University Press, 1995), pp. 4–5.

35. The role of the media should once again be emphasized here. As Zbigniew Brzezinski put it: "Until rather recently, values – political or otherwise – were transferred from generation to generation, first by the family, then by the school, and then by the church, roughly in that sequence. Today, values are transferred from generation to generation, primarily in advanced countries, by mass communication, especially television. Each of us can run a simple test as to what kind of values are being transmitted by watching television for 24 hours." Quoted in *CSIS News*, Vol. 10, No. 1 (Spring 1994), p. 8.

36. Mattei Dogan, "Comparing the Decline of Nationalisms in Western Europe: the Generation Dynamic", *International Social Science Journal*, No. 136 (May 1993), p. 189.

37. Mattei Dogan, op. cit., p. 191.

38. Reasons for the growth of the instrumental orientation are complex and range from the disintegration of traditional social milieu to individualization of life situations due to societal modernization and rationalization process. See Wolfgang Streeck, "Vielfalt und Interdependenz: Überlegungen zur Rolle von intermediaren Organisationen in sich ändernden Umwelten", *Kölner Zeitschrift für Soziologie und Sozialpsychologie*, Vol. 39 (1987), pp. 471–95, U. Beck, *Risk Society: Towards a New Modernity* (London: Sage, 1992), S. Crook, J. Pakulski and M. Waters, *Postmodernisation: Change in Advanced Society* (London: Sage, 1992).

39. In extreme cases it leads to what Zbigniew Brzezinski termed "permissive cornucopia": combination of the erosion of moral criteria in defining personal conduct with the emphasis on material goods resulting both in permissiveness on the level of action and in material greed on the level of motivation. See Zbigniew Brzezinski, *Out of Control. Global Turmoil on the Eve of the Twenty-First Century*, (New York: Robert Steward, 1993), p. 65.

40. Ignacio Ramonet, "Agonie de la morale", *Le Monde Diplomatique*, Vol. 41, No. 487 (October 1994), p. 1. Charles S. Maier spoke in equally dramatic terms. See Charles S. Maier, "Democracy and Its Discontents", *Foreign Affairs*, Vol. 73, No. 4 (July/August 1994), pp. 48ff.

41. See especially Loek Halman, "Is There a Moral Decline? A Cross-National Inquiry into Morality in Contemporary Society", *International Social Science Journal*, No. 145 (September 1995), pp. 419–39.

42. Consider, for instance, the German case: the basic cultural values of the two German societies remained relatively similar despite 45 years of diametrically opposed regimes. See Ronald Inglehart, "Changing Values, Economic Development and Political Change", *International Social Science Journal*, No. 145 (September 1995), pp. 394–5.

43. Guido Lenzi, "Reforming the International System: Between Leadership and Power-Sharing", *Internationale Spectator*, Vol. 30, No. 2 (April–June 1995), pp. 49–69.

44. The historical evolution of the democratic order has been analyzed, e.g., by David Held in "Democracy: From City-States to a Cosmopolitan Order?", in *Prospects for Democracy*, David Held, ed. (Oxford: Polity Press, 1993), pp. 13–52.

45. Of course, globalization affects a variety of institutions and political actors changing the substance and form of political discourse in Western Europe. Ian Davidson grasped the problem very well by asking: "The global economy may mean that national prosperity slips out of the grasp of national governments; so what will political parties promise instead? Law and order, and repression of unemployed criminal classes? Exclusion of foreigners and xenophobia? National populism? Regional separatism? Patronage for their clients?" See Ian Davidson, "Rethink in the West", *Financial Times*, April 13, 1994.

46. According to Robert B. Reich, the very concept of national interest is also becoming obsolete: "As the borders of cities, states, and even nations no longer come to signify special domains of economic interdependence, Tocqueville's principle of enlightened self-interest is less compelling. Nations are becoming regions of a global economy; their citizens, laborers in a global market. National corporations are turning into global webs whose high-volume, standardized activities are undertaken wherever labor is cheapest worldwide, and whose most profitable activities are carried out wherever skilled and talented people can best conceptualize new problems and solutions. Under such circumstances, economic sacrifice and restraint exercised within a nation's borders is less likely to come full circle than it was in a more closed economy." See Robert B. Reich, *The Work of Nations* (New York: Alfred A. Knopf, 1991), p. 304. See also Geraint Parry, ed., *Politics in an Interdependent World: Essays Presented to Ghiţa Ionescu* (Cheltenham: Edward Elgar, 1994), p. 208.

47. William Brock quoted in *CSIS News*, Vol. 10, No. 1 (Spring 1994), p. 8.

48. Jean-Marie Guéhenno provides some powerful arguments in support of this statement. See Jean-Marie Guéhenno, *La fin de la démocracie* op cit., p. 32.

49. See Ronnie D. Lipschutz, "Reconstructing World Politics: The Emergence of Global Civil Society", *Millennium*, Vol. 21, No. 3 (1992), pp. 389–420, or Peter J. Spiro, "New Global Communities: Nongovernmental Organizations in International Decision-Making Institutions", *The Washington Quarterly*, Vol. 18, No. 1 (Winter 1995), pp. 45–55. See also a

classical study by Samuel P. Huntington, "Transnational Organizations in World Politics", *World Politics*, Vol. 25, No. 3 (April 1973), pp. 333–68.

50. Susan Strange, "The Limits of Politics", *Government and Opposition*, Vol. 30, No. 3 (1995), p. 298. Non-governmental pressures on the functioning of the European Union are analyzed by, e.g., Justin Greenwood and Karsten Ronit, "Interest Groups in the European Community: Newly Emerging Dynamics and Forms", *West European Politics*, Vol. 17, No. 1 (January 1994), pp. 31–52, or Andrew M. McLaughlin and Justin Greenwood, "The Management of Interest Representation in the European Union", *Journal of Common Market Studies*, Vol. 33, No. 1 (March 1995), pp. 143–56.

51. One should keep in mind that the erosion of the power of a European nation state also takes place in response to inward rather than merely outward pressures. R.A.W. Rhodes, for instance identifies four different factors which caused "the hollowing out" of the British state: (1) Privatization and limiting the scope and forms of public intervention; (2) The loss of functions by central and local governments to alternative delivery systems (such as agencies); (3) The loss of functions by British government to European Union institutions; (4) Limiting the discretion of public servants through the new public management, with its emphasis on managerial accountability, and clearer political control through a sharper distinction between politics and administration. See R.A.W. Rhodes, "The Hollowing Out of the State", *Political Quarterly*, Vol. 65, No. 2 (1994), pp. 138–9. See also Patrick Dunleavy, "The Globalization of Public Services Production: Can Government be 'Best in the World'?", *Public Policy and Administration*, Vol. 9, No. 2 (Summer 1994), pp. 36–64.

52. Wolfgang C. Müller and Vincent Wright, "Reshaping the State in Western Europe: the Limits to Retreat", *West European Politics*, special issue on "The State in Western Europe: Retreat or Redefinition", Vol. 17, No. 3 (July 1994), pp. 7–8.

53. As the editorial article of *The Economist* argued: "The world has changed, the global economy has indeed arrived: nonetheless, the emasculated state is a myth. Start with the simplest gauge of the state's involvement in the economy...since 1980 the public-spending ratio has increased, on average, from 36% of GDP to 40%. In Germany it is 49%, in Sweden 68%.". See "The Myth of the Powerless State", *The Economist*, October 7, 1995, p. 13.

54. A powerful historical argument for the latter hypothesis is provided by Alan Milward, *The European Rescue of the Nation State* (London: Routledge, 1992), pp. 18ff.

55. See Ernst B. Haas, "Turbulent Fields and the Theory of Regional Integration", *International Organization*, Vol. 30, No. 2 (1976), pp. 173–212.

56. Not to mention the painful question of the existence of a truly European *Demos*. See J.H.H. Weiler with Ulrich R. Haltern and Franz C. Mayer, "European Democracy and Its Critique", *West European Politics*, special issue on "The Crisis of Representation in Europe", Vol. 18, No. 3 (July 1995), pp. 9–10.

57. Giovanni Sartori, "Video-Power," *Government and Opposition*, Vol. 24, No. 1 (1989), pp. 39–40. See also Benjamin Barber, *Strong Democracy: Participatory Politics for a New Age*, (Berkeley: University of California Press, 1994). Max Gallo has put it differently: "The nation has become – and remains – the place where a democratic control is possible. At the European level, political and technocratic networks impose their will. Can we, in these circumstances, hope that the people will actively support this construction? The nation still is and will be so for a long time, the place where one can exercise democracy, where social relations and arbitrations take place, where the citizen has the best opportunity to be a party to decisions." See Max Gallo, "Oublier les nations, un mirage dangereux," *Le Monde Diplomatique*, No. 22, May 1994.

58. Trevor Smith looks at the problem of efficiency from a different angle, and talks about "de-coupling of polity and economy which, despite various attempts to forge a closer relationship, has been increasing over the last seventy years." See Trevor Smith, "Post-Modern Politics and the Case for Constitutional Renewal", *Political Quarterly*, Vol. 65, No. 2 (1994), p. 128. Dominque Wolton also raises the question of how far the economy will drag politics forward? See Dominique Wolton, *La dernière utopie: naissance de l'Europe démocratique* (Paris: Flammarion, 1993), pp. 76–7.

59. This dilemma is brilliantly analyzed in Robert A. Dahl, "A Democratic Dilemma: System Effectiveness versus Citizen Participation", *Political Science Quarterly*, Vol. 109, No. 1 (1994), pp. 23–34.

60. Robert A. Dahl, op. cit., p. 33. In an earlier work Dahl pointed out that the argument over the optimal unit goes in circles, as with a set of Chinese boxes: any unit you choose smaller than the globe itself can be shown to be smaller than the boundaries of an urgent problem. Yet the larger the unit, the greater the cost of uniform rules, the larger the minorities who cannot prevail, and the more watered down the control of the individual citizen. Since any conceivable unit has its merits and drawbacks, the important thing is to treat them in their distinctiveness. See Robert A. Dahl, "Democracy and the Chinese Boxes", in *Frontiers of Democratic Theory* H.S. Kariel, ed, (New York: Random House, 1970), pp. 372–3.

61. John Hoffman put it even more strongly: "Just as liberalism provides a necessary platform for democracy, so the state is indispensable to state-lessness. A cosmopolitan democracy can consolidate itself as a post-statist order only as states themselves recognize that the only way in which they can secure order and justice is to yield up power to regional, local and global bodies. What makes the 'seconded' force of states self-dissolving is the fact that it has to be employed only to underpin resource distributions and participatory schemes which entrench and extend common interests. States therefore have a key role to play in converting their sovereign power into local, national, regional and global government. The logic of democracy itself demands it.". See John Hoffman, *Beyond the State* (Oxford: Oxford Polity Press, 1995), p. 213.

62. See, e.g., Elizabeth Meehan, *Citizenship and the European Community* (London: Sage, 1993).

63. As Rudy Andeweg rightly argued: "The problem with political representation within the European Union lies less with the much discussed 'democratic deficit' than with the lack of a party system that offers a meaningful choice to the voters and reflects this choice in the European Parliament. The current transnational political groups in the European Parliament are unstable and heterogeneous alliances of national parties. These national parties fight European elections on national issues." See Rudy Andeweg, "The Reshaping of National Party Systems", *West European Politics*, special issue on the Crisis of Representation in Europe, Vol. 18, No. 3 (July 1995), p. 58.

64. See, e.g., M. Westlake, "The European Parliament, the National Parliaments and the 1996 Intergovernmental Conference", *Political Quarterly*, Vol. 20, No. 1 (1994), p. 7. Also Jean-Claude Piris, "After Maastricht, Are the Community Institutions More Efficacious, More Democratic and More Transparent", *European Law Review*, Vol. 19, No. 5 (October 1994), pp. 449–87.

65. A more modest argument would be that a "cosmopolitan model of democracy" as advocated by David Held, is not a visible option either. See David Held, "Democracy: From City-States to a Cosmopolitan Order?", in *Prospects for Democracy*, David Held, ed. (Oxford: Oxford Polity Press, 1993) pp. 37–44.

66. Jason Alexander went even further with the following argument: "Do non-elected and ever-more-powerful financial markets pose a threat to democracy? There is no evidence that they do; indeed in some ways, capital markets, driven by the decisions of millions of investors and borrowers are highly 'democratic.' They act like a rolling 24–hour opinion poll. Moreover, they increase politicians accountability by making voters more aware of governments' performance. Financial markets have much sharper eyes than voters.... Markets make a more effective job of showing up government's economic errors than opposition parties and journalists." See Jason Alexander, "Power Politics", *The Economist*, A Survey of the World Economy, 7 October 1995, p. 44.

67. This is well argued in Robert B. Reich, *The Work of Nations* (New York: Alfred A. Knopf, 1991), pp. 305–7.

68. This is well argued in Michael Walzer, "The Concept of Civil Society" (or the introduction) in *Toward a Global Civil Society*, Michael Walzer, ed, (Providence and Oxford: Berghahn Books, 1995), pp. 1–4 and 7–28.

69. See Wolfram F. Hanrieder, "Dissolving International Politics", in *Perspectives on World Politics*, Michael Smith, Richard Little and Michael Shackleton, eds. (London: Croom Helm, 1981), pp. 137–8.

70. Bruce Russett, *Controlling the Sword. The Democratic Governance of National Security* (Cambridge, MA: Harvard University Press, 1990), p. 1.

71. Parliaments hardly ever possess the required expertise and they are often prisoners of their volatile electorates. Moreover, parliaments' predilection to curbing powers of the executives is detrimental to the smooth functioning of foreign and security policy. Foreign policies should not be guided by sectarian institutional interests but by the national interest only. This requires, it is argued, the concentration of

power in the executive branch of the government. See, e.g., T. Clifton Morgan and Sally Howard Campbell, "Domestic Structure, Decisional Constraints, and War: So Why Can't Democracies Fight?", in *Journal of Conflict Resolution*, Vol. 35, No. 2 (1991), special issue – Democracy and Foreign Policy: Community and Constraint, Bruce J. Bueno de Mesquita, Robert W. Jackman and Randolph M. Siverson, eds., pp. 187–212, or Antonio Cassese, ed., *Parliamentary Control Over Foreign Policy: Legal Essays* (Alphen aan den Rijn: Sijthoff and Noordhoff, 1980).

72. Walter Lippmann, *The Public Philosophy* (Boston: Little, Brown, 1955), p. 20.

73. For a historical overview of the problem see Barbara Tuchman, *The March of Folly: From Troy to Vietnam* (Glasgow: Abacus, 1985). Modern cases are discussed, e.g., in David P. Forsythe, "Democracy, War and Covert Action", *Journal of Peace Research*, Vol. 29, No. 4 (1992), pp. 385–95.

74. See Ole Holsti, "Public Opinion and Foreign Policy: Challenges to the Almond-Lippmann Consensus", *International Studies Quarterly*, Vol. 36, No. 4 (1992), pp. 439–66. As far as specific European case studies are concerned see, e.g., Philip P. Everts, ed., *Controversies at Home. Domestic Factors in the Foreign Policy of The Netherlands* (Dordrecht: Martinus Nijhoff, 1985), p. 363, or Kjell Goldman, Sten Berglund and Gunnar Sjöstedt, eds., *Democracy and Foreign Policy: The Case of Sweden* (Aldershot: Gower, 1986), p. 206.

75. Although one should agree with Robert C. Johansen's argument that "Ends and means as well as moral issues and technical knowledge are inextricably related. Because means have a way of determining ends, it is simply not possible to say that the public should decide policy ends and the technicians will find the appropriate means." See Robert C. Johansen, "Military Policies and the State System as Impediments to Democracy", in *Prospects for Democracy*, David Held, ed. (Oxford: Oxford Polity Press, 1993), p. 218.

76. Robert A. Dahl, *Controlling Nuclear Weapons: Democracy versus Guardianship* (Syracuse: Syracuse University Press, 1985), p. 51.

77. Giovanni Sartori, *The Theory of Democracy Revisited*, Part One: *The Contemporary Debate* (Chatham, NJ: Chatham House Publishers, 1987), p. 115. A consultative referendum is not any better, as the government feels compelled anyway by the results of such a consultative referendum.

78. Valentine Herman, *Parliaments of the World: A Reference Compendium* (London: Macmillan, 1976), p. 879. For a more recent illustration of this argument see Stelios Stavridis, "The "Second" Democratic Deficit in the EC: The Process of European Political Cooperation," in *International Relations and Pan-Europe*, Frank R. Pfetsch, ed. (Müster and Hamburg: Lit Verlag, 1993), p. 174.

79. Article J.11 of the Draft Treaty of Amsterdam. The article also states that the European Parliament may question or make recommendations to the Council. It shall also hold an annual debate on the progress in implementing the common foreign and security policy. In general, the

Draft Treaty of Amsterdam increased the powers of the European Parliament, but not in the CFSP field.

80. A special Draft Protocol attached to the Draft Treaty of Amsterdam obliges the Commission to submit "promptly" its documents such as green and white papers and communications to national legislatures, and demands that the Council wait six weeks before considering them, so that national parliaments can make their views known.

81. Elections to the European Parliament have been branded "second order" elections, with a turnout lower and the protest vote higher than in "first order" national elections. For example, in the 1994 elections to the European Parliament, little more than half of the electorate across the EU turned out to vote, and in The Netherlands, Portugal, and the United Kingdom turnout represented only about one-third of the electorate. See Michael Gallagher, "Electoral Systems and Voting Behaviour," in *Developments in West European Politics*, Martin Rhodes, Paul Heywood and Vincent Wright, eds. (London: Macmillan, 1997), p. 128.

82. The lack of a European *demos* is probably most visible in the field of diplomacy and defense. The point is well argued in Stelios Stavridis, "The Democratic Control of the CFSP," in *Common Foreign and Security Policy. The Record and Reforms*, Martin Holland, ed., (London and Washington: Pinter, 1997), pp. 137–40. See also Joseph H.H. Weiler, *The European Parliament and Its Foreign Affairs Committees* (New York: Oceana Publ, 1982), p. 58. Discrepancies between national public opinions are well illustrated in *Eurobarometer* No. 41 (July 1994), pp. A12–13.

83. In terms of the sums involved, EC/EU budget expenditure for external action has quadrupled between 1988 and 1994. There was also a 13.3 percent increase between 1994 and 1995, and the reserves for emergency aid jumped by over 50 percent.

84. As Robert C. Johansen argued: "A 'national democracy' is gradually becoming a contradiction in terms, just as 'national security' is a dubious concept because in an age of interdependence no *national* entity can secure itself by itself. To overstate only slightly, national democrats are like apartheid democrats: they want democracy for their own group, yet they want it achieved separately from other groups. However, by trying to nationalize democracy they segregate people artificially and without their consent, even though the different groups are functionally interdependent." See Robert C. Johansen, "Military Policies and the State System as Impediments to Democracy," op. cit., p. 229.

85. One cannot but agree with Christopher Hill's argument that the public has often more indirect control over foreign policies drawn up by the Union than by their member states: CFSP may well be conducted behind closed doors, but it is seldom secret: there is simply no way of keeping discussions secret among no less than 15 EU members. The Union's public announcements of its policy and its regular reports made to the European Parliament are under tight media scrutiny. Each European summit gathers thousands of European journalists reporting and speculating about EU policy debates. Finally, the CFSP is more a matter of "grand diplomatic strategy" than "fine-grained tactics," and the latter is

clearly more susceptible to an open public discourse than the former. See Christopher Hill, "European Foreign Policy: Power Bloc, Civilian Model or Flop?" in *The Evolution of an International Actor: Western Europe's New Assertiveness*, Reinhardt Rummel, ed. (Boulder: Westview, 1990), pp. 46–7.

86. See Philip Everts, *Laat dat maar aan ons over. Democratie, buitenlands beleid en vrede* (Leiden: DSWO Press 1996), pp. 111–27.

87. Most notably, this is the case in the nuclear field because the more widely and democratically the powers of deliberation and decision making are spread, the less effective the nuclear deterrent may be. See Robert A. Dahl, *Controlling Nuclear Weapons: Democracy versus Guardianship*, op. cit., p. 3.

88. Philippe C. Schmitter suggests an elaborate set of measures aimed at enhancing citizenship, representation and democratic decision making in the Union. They include, among other things, universal presence in the European Parliament, differential representation in comités, control over party funds/nominations and support for Euro-associations and movements. See Philippe C. Schmitter, "An Alternative Strategy for the Future of European Integration: Democratization," Paper presented at an EUI Robert Schuman Centre seminar in Florence, February 25, 1997, p. 12.

89. See Commission of the European Communities, *Increased Transparency in the Work of the Commission*, SEC(92) 2274, Brussels, 1992, or Commission of the European Communities, *Openness in the Community*, COM (93) 258, Brussels, 1993.

90. Juliet Lodge, "Transparency and Democratic Legitimacy", *Journal of Common Market Studies*, Vol. 32, No. 3 (September 1994), p. 355.

91. Article J.2 of the Draft Treaty.

92. The Cold War dilemma – "Better red or dead?" – reflected the simplistic dichotomy between security and democracy. The answer given by the Western states was "neither!" And it proved to be the right answer as seen from the historical perspective, and so there is no reason to indulge in similar simplistic thinking in the post-Cold War period.

93. Philippe C. Schmitter goes even further and argues that an overtly political strategy of democratization might be the only effective way of renewing the course of European integration that has been lost with the adoption of the Maastricht treaty. This is because, as he put it: "the "Monnet Method" of exploiting the spill-overs between functionally related issues-arenas to advance the level and scope of integrative institutions has exhausted its potential, precisely because of increased citizen awareness and further politicization." See Philippe C. Schmitter, "An Alternative Strategy", op. cit., p. 15.

5 Weak institutions

Common foreign and security policy is a victim of ill-suited institutional arrangements within the European Union. No doubt, this is the most common explanation of the evolving *Euro-paralysis*. Both friends and foes of European integration willingly admit that the diffusion of authority within the Union and the disaggregated policy process of permanent intergovernmental bargaining prevent the Union from meeting its foreign and security objectives. The Union has powerful economic and political leverage, a huge bureaucracy and an ever-spreading network of diplomatic missions all over the world. Yet, when it comes to making decisions and acting, the Union is often unable to cope, even with trivial things.

Problems range from an incapacity to deliver proper policy planning, to an inability to reach any timely and meaningful collective decisions about elementary problems of policy implementation. The coherence of the system is undermined by the so-called "three pillar structure", separating trade and economics from internal affairs and foreign policy. The pillars are subject to two different institutional regimes, one more communitarian (EEC, Euratom, and ECSC in the first pillar), and the other two more intergovernmental (CFSP in the second pillar; justice and internal affairs in the third). Moreover, the link between means and ends of policy is largely broken: the CFSP has very few policy instruments at its disposal. These are either to be found in the first pillar of the Union or outside the Union structure, in the Western European Union, for instance. The disaggregation of actors and institutions produces inertia, resistance to change, and artificial compartmentalization of policy. The decision-making process based on the principle of unanimity cannot avoid being slow, conflict-ridden, and subject to the lowest common denominator. Thus the whole institutional system lacks clarity, hierarchy, and coherence, and it comes as no surprise to learn that it hardly ever works in an accountable and effective manner, especially when coping with crises.[1]

The range of institutional problems hampering common policies is thus enormous, and so is the range of solutions seen as a possible remedy. Some of them are modest. For instance, the recent Draft Treaty of Amsterdam created the office of the High Representative for the Common Foreign and Security Policy, which is meant to

177

enhance continuity and order in the CFSP representation system and contribute to basic policy planning. Other solutions are less modest: nothing short of full incorporation of the CFSP into the first communitarian pillar, with a qualified majority voting can provide a coherent, transparent, and effective foreign policy. There are also solutions that are clear, comprehensive, and logical, but immodest in the sense that they suggest doing away with the "awkward" pillars and "upside-down" assignments of competencies agreed upon in the treaties of Rome and Maastricht.[2] Edward Mortimer expressed this idea in the aftermath of Maastricht:

> I should like to see a European union with a federal constitution, in which certain clearly defined powers would be exercised by a federal executive responsible to a federal parliament, and everything else would be left to member states, or indeed to smaller units of government – which, as I understand it, is what "subsidiarity" is all about. The federation would have just enough power to ensure genuine freedom of movement for people, goods and services within the geographical space that it covered, and to conduct an effective common foreign and defense policy.[3]

The federal solutions may well be the most clear, coherent, and logical, but they directly encroach upon such sensitive areas of politics as power, legitimacy, and sovereignty. Technical solutions, such as "the High Representative" are more neutral in political terms, but they obviously improve things only marginally. In between, there is a huge variety of arrangement cocktails that are probably neither transparent nor logical, legitimate or effective. This chapter will try to grasp the complexity of institutional problems affecting common foreign and security policies. It will also look into the rationale behind various solutions for improving the existing institutional structure of the CFSP. I will first evaluate the wisdom of the political compromise struck on the eve of the integration process some 40 years ago which stated: integration should proceed step by step and start in areas where national sovereignty is not seriously threatened. And thus, no serious institutional arrangements in the sensitive fields of diplomacy and defense were to be forged, but it was hoped that the integration in the field of trade and commerce ("low politics") would in due time spill over to the field of defense and diplomacy ("high politics"). Were there good reasons to hope for such a spill-over? Can "high politics" be effectively separated from "low politics"? Can the Union act credibly and efficiently in accordance with its self-proclaimed norms and international power status without curbing member states' freedom in foreign affairs and defense?

Second, I will examine the internal institutional structure of the CFSP. Who are the Union's major institutional actors in the field of foreign and security policy? How are decisions being prepared, made, and implemented? What is the interplay between politics and policy within the CFSP framework? And why has the CFSP institutional structure been repeatedly criticized as being slow, unaccountable, incoherent, and ineffective?

Third, I will examine the division of foreign and security tasks between different international institutions. After all, not all foreign and security problems have to be dealt with by the CFSP. How did we arrive at the current division of tasks between NATO, WEU, EU, and OSCE, through cooperation or conflict? Is the current system inter-locking or interblocking? And which institution has acquired a domin-ant position?

Fourth, I will try to assess the impact of institutional engineering on common foreign and security policy. Can tinkering with institutional frameworks compensate for the lack of political will to have a common foreign and security policy? Are we not being confronted with what Philip Zelikow named "the masque of institutions: all-too diverting entertainment"?[4] In short, do institutions really matter, and if yes, why?

Fifth, I will look into ways of improving the existing institutional structure. After all, even if institutions influence policies marginally, they can still be made to work better. An effective, transparent, and legitimate institutional framework can help to get a common foreign and security policy off the ground, while there is little good to be done by institutions that are illegitimate and ineffective.

My conclusion will show the rather limited utility of institutional engineering and a spill-over process that is erratic, unpredictable, and weak. The Union has "lost" the post-Cold War institutional competi-tion with NATO and is unable to assert its leading role in shaping the events in defense and diplomacy. The major institutional problem is not so much a lack of the necessary means, but an inability to create a collective will for the organization. Put differently, the Union is hardly ever able to make up its mind and articulate its decisions. Changing this, I will argue, would require giving up some sovereignty dogmas in the sensitive field of diplomacy. It would also require endorsing a new type of foreign policy, based on political and economic rather than military ends and means. It would also require a new, more flexible approach to the issue of collective decision making, implementation, and burden sharing. In short, I will argue that overcoming the paralysis in the CFSP institutional field would require more than the bureaucratic reorganizations and procedural readjustments that are usually at the center of the institutional discourse in Brussels.

THE SPILL-OVER ILLUSION?

Robert Schuman, in his May 9, 1950 Declaration introducing the proposal for the new Community, outlined a strategy that was to shape the subsequent process of European integration. He said:

> Europe will not be made all at once, or according to a single, general plan. It will be built through concrete achievements, which first create a *de facto* solidarity... The pooling of coal and steel production will immediately provide for the setting-up of common bases for economic development as a first step in the federation of Europe.[5]

Thus the integration was to be a politically motivated exercise in institution building, ultimately leading to a European federation. Yet the road to a federation was not to be short or straight: no quick and comprehensive constitutional arrangements were to be expected which would curb the sovereignty of member states in the field of security and foreign affairs.[6] The move forward was to be concealed, ambiguous, incremental, and primarily in areas where national sovereignty would not be threatened – trade and commerce in particular. However, the assumption was that a slow gradual progress in the areas of economics and welfare would spill over to other, more sensitive areas, such as security and foreign affairs. Successful integration in the areas of lesser salience would produce more interlinkage and interdependence, and these in turn would produce changes in attitudes and enmesh each national political and economic system with the others. The public and the policy-makers who initially objected to the transfer of power to a new center would gradually come to the conclusion that integration in the area of high politics is, after all, the best way of furthering their own interests.

Of course, there have been different versions of this spill-over argument under different functionalist and neo-functionalist labels.[7] Some versions have put more emphasis on reinforcement of common institutions, others on socialization, education, and learning. Some have focused on independent pressure groups, others on governmental elites. Some have used deterministic terms such as "the necessary logic" and the "functional imperative," others have used more cautious terms such as "softening attitudes," "gradual recognition of common needs," and "overcoming the resistance of national governments." Some have talked about states losing sovereignty, others about sovereignty becoming more and more irrelevant. Yet despite all these differences and variations, the spill-over argument has rested on the assumption that sustaining international cooperation in the economic and welfare sectors would in time result in a situation "whereby political actors in several distinct national settings are persuaded to shift their loyalties, expectations, and political activities towards a new and larger center, whose institutions possess or demand jurisdiction over the pre-existing national states."[8] This would unavoidably include a common policy in the field of security and foreign affairs.[9]

The spill-over argument has been subject to heavy criticism, but it has maintained a great deal of appeal for many years partly because of its own merits, and partly because of the absence of any other positive alternative. In the early 1950s, for instance, a head-on approach to integration was tried and it failed. I refer to the attempt to set up a European Defense Community (EDC) with full-fledged federal institutions and a quasi-federal constitution.[10] The EDC Treaty was, in fact, ratified by West Germany and the Benelux countries, with the Italian parliament waiting for French ratification. The latter, however, never materialized, and the whole project came to naught.

Some merits of the spill-over argument also seem to have been vindicated in practice. Expansion of economic integration has been accompanied by incremental progress in foreign and defense cooperation. In the 1960s, cooperation in the foreign and security field was still taboo within the EC, but in the early 1970s, the European Political Cooperation (EPC) framework was developed. In 1987 the EPC was incorporated into a binding treaty: the Single Act.[11] And as Stephen George observed in 1990: "Although EPC does not include defense, it has become such an effective method of coordinating national foreign policy positions that it is often counted as the biggest success in EC integration over the last fifteen years."[12] By 1992 the EPC had again been upgraded and renamed the Common Foreign and Security Policy. In the meantime, the Union has assumed a major role in coordinating Western aid to Eastern Europe and has begun to be an active player in such important international meetings as the Group of Seven. A rapid proliferation of EU diplomacy has followed. In the late 1980s the European Commission had a handful of officers dealing with

Eastern Europe, but by the early 1990s there were already several hundred of them. The frequency of various EU meetings on foreign and security issues proliferated, not only between foreign ministers but also between ministers of defense. Joint reporting, and joint preparation of declarations and actions has become the order of the day. In short, foreign and security issues have gradually become an integral part of the EU's daily work; a dramatic development compared to the early stages of integration. Moreover, the Union has increasingly used its civilian instruments (including trade and aid) to bolster political and security objectives in Eastern Europe and other parts of the world.

That said, however, the more "substantive" integrative effects of the spill-over have proved to be very modest.[13] Frequent meetings and intensive communication has not molded 15 national policies into one. The intergovernmental character of the decision-making process has not been abandoned. And the CFSP has not been merged with external (economic) policies of the Union.[14] Moreover, the enormous acceleration of history since 1989 has raised the question whether the gradual process of institutional adjustment in the area of defense and diplomacy would be sufficient to cope with the magnitude and pace of post-Cold War pressures. And the post-Maastricht frustration with the integration process in the field of economics and welfare has raised suspicion that there is a reverse spill-over effect taking place.[15] What went wrong? Was the spill-over argument misleading from the start? Can we identify clear limits to integration in security and foreign affairs?

Three possible explanations have been given for the relative weakness of the spill-over effect in our area of concern.[16] The first one looks at various sectors of integration and suggests that some of them are more susceptible to the spill-over effect than others. While there is certainly some spill-over in the domain of "low politics," there is little or none in the domain of "high politics." This is because "high politics" is about the most sensitive issues, like war, power, and sovereignty, which are subject to a different logic and rules than the areas of trade and commerce. As Stanley Hoffman argued in the 1960s:

> In some sectors, the spill-over has turned into a trickle ... When the functions are concerned with the ineffable and intangible issues of *Grosspolitik*, when grandeur and prestige, rank and security, domination and dependence are at stake, we are fully within the realm of traditional interstate politics. There are no actors, no constituents, other than governments. The discontinuity between the

'material' realm and that of military and foreign policy among the Six has been striking...In the area of high politics, the subject matter is composed of discrete issues, among which there may be discontinuity and which show no or little solidarity among contenders. Thus here politics as usual – Machiavellian or Bismarckian or Gaullist – prevails without any of the subtle tributes which vice elsewhere is forced to pay to virtue.[17]

The second explanation looks at the types of integrative engineering and suggests that certain types of engineering generate the spill-over effect better than others. While the first explanation rests on a political argument – high politics versus low politics – the second explanation rests on a technocratic one. The spill-over is caused by the cumulative effects of the so-called "negative integration" that produce, in due time, the positive integration. Negative integration which is about eliminating national restraints is much easier to generate in the field of economics (e.g., removing tariffs, quotas, obstacles to competition or to mobility) than in the field of defense and foreign policy.[18] As measures of negative integration are multiplied, governments' abilities to perform their traditional roles shrink. They are increasingly compelled to upgrade decision making and management of issues to a higher communitarian level. But integration in the field of security and foreign affairs is all about the positive integration that requires political determination and popular legitimacy; neither of which is generated by negative integration measures. In other words, there is little in the preceding history of integration to impinge upon decision makers' abilities to manage diplomatic and defense issues and thus force them eventually to accept the desirability of creating a communitarian institutional regime in this field.

The third explanation looks at the major actors behind the integration process and points out that, as far as defense and diplomacy are concerned, there are hardly any interest groups wishing that the spill-over effect will succeed. The spill-over argument assumes that a central role is given to pressure groups behind the process of European integration, but it is difficult to identify such groups in the domain of diplomacy and defense.[19] This is partly because diplomacy and defense are about intangible costs and benefits as compared to economics and welfare. The whole public debate about diplomacy and defense is not concrete but symbolic, moralistic, and ideological and as such can merely generate volatile public movements, such as peace movements or human rights advocates. These movements are not as professional and determined as pressure groups in the field of economics and welfare. Besides, they are not particularly interested in European integration. This lack of effective pro-European pressure groups is skillfully being exploited by nationalist politicians and governments. As Andrew Moravcsik put it:

> The inherent incalculability of gains and losses in these policy areas accounts for a troubling neo-functionalist anomaly, namely the manifest importance of ideologically motivated heads of state ("dramatic-political" actors) in matters of foreign policy and institutional reform. The difficulty of mobilizing interest groups under conditions of general uncertainty about specific winners and losers permits the positions of governments, particularly larger ones, on questions of European institutions and common foreign policy, to reflect the ideologies and personal commitments of leading executive and parliamentary politicians, as well as interest-based conceptions of the national interest. This may help explain the ability and willingness of nationalists like Charles de Gaulle and Margaret Thatcher to adopt an uncompromising position toward the dilution of national sovereignty.[20]

All three explanations shed light on the limited utility of the spillover argument, but the explanations themselves are not flawless either. The distinction between "low" and "high" politics is flawed because the quest for power and glory is often about economics and not merely about diplomatic and military matters. Moreover, governments are today under similar democratic pressures in both the fields of "high" and "low" politics. "High" and "low" politics are, in fact, closely interconnected, if not effectively merged.[21]

The distinction between "positive" and "negative" integration is sound, but we could nevertheless see that positive integration is possible in some areas such as welfare without having been preceded by the negative integration there. Moreover, as Fritz Scharpf has indicated, the impact of negative integration is not always that beneficial because it paralyzes national and subnational problem solving that can hardly be compensated by positive integration measures.[22]

The third explanation either assumes that the public is ignorant about defense and foreign issues or that its pressure can only be generated by material concerns. Both these assumptions seem to be wrong. Public opinion research has repeatedly shown that foreign affairs and security issues cannot be treated as low salience issues about which the public knows little and cares little.[23] Moreover, there is enough evidence to argue that the public is not merely motivated by instrumental calculations of material interests, but also by some idealistic or altruistic motivations of a more communitarian nature.[24] It is also wrong to identify the "true" public pressures with the activity of interest groups rather than political parties. In sharp contrast to the situation in the United States, political parties in Europe are more dynamic pressure actors than interest groups, and they are often committed advocates of integration in the field of security and foreign affairs.

The spill-over argument has at times cherished the illusion of a linear, if not automatic, march towards an integrative structure, and it probably has been overly optimistic about proclaimed time-schedules. But it is difficult to deny that some spill-over is certainly at work even in the sensitive field of security and foreign affairs. However, one should also recognize various factors and forces that reduce the spill-over effect. It is therefore better to look at integration as a process that emerges out of tension between opposing forces and not as a natural movement in a single direction.[25] While it is wrong to assume that resistance to integration in the field of security and foreign policy must inevitably bow to spill-over pressures, it is equally wrong to assume that this particular field is totally immune to the spill-over effects from the preceding stages of integration.[26] However erratic and unpredictable the process may be, there are no grounds for declaring the spill-over effect to be an illusion or a myth.

THE INSTITUTIONAL LABYRINTH

All institutions face a choice of priorities between width and depth, coherence and diversity, openness and exclusiveness. They all have to make choices concerning basic aims and instruments, internal rules, hierarchy and decision-making procedures. The problem with the European Union is that such choices are hardly ever made in a consistent, unambiguous and transparent manner. All institutional arrangements have been products of hard and delicate political bargaining that had to satisfy each of the diverse participants and their conflicting, if not eccentric, agendas. Moreover, the system has been constantly in flux, with new deals being negotiated and re-negotiated with an ever-growing number of actors in response to an ever-changing international environment. The result is a "post-national, un-sovereign, poly-centric, non-conterminous and neo-medieval" arrangement, to use Philippe C. Schmitter's words, with a built-in ambiguity, volatility, inconsistency, duplication, and gaps.[27] The European Union lacks a clearly defined supreme authority, an established, central hierarchy of offices, a pre-defined and distinctive sphere of competence and a fixed membership. There is no clear separation of powers within the Union. The allocation of power between the EU and member state institutions is also unclear. And so is the division of powers between the Union and other European institutions such as NATO, WEU or OSCE.

The CFSP institutional arrangement is obviously a part of this complex and confusing picture. The final text of the Treaty on the European Union (TEU), negotiated in Maastricht, represented a compromise between the advocates of a community (supranational) approach and those in favor of an inter-governmental approach. The price of including "high-politics" in the scope of the Union was that it would be subject to a different and weaker institutional regime. A three-pillar structure was thus established which ensured that supranational arrangements would govern the decisions on economics and trade (the first pillar) while a largely inter-governmental approach would be used to determine CFSP (the second pillar) and the Union's policies on justice and internal affairs (the third pillar). The treaty also tried to diffuse a dispute between the so-called "Atlanticists" and "Europeanists" on the question of common defense by adopting a vague and open-ended phrase: "The common foreign and security policy shall include all questions related to security of the Union, including the eventual framing of a common defense policy, which might in time lead to a common defense."[28] The Western European Union has been defined as both "the defense component of the European Union" and as the instrument "to strengthen the European pillar" of NATO.

The inter-governmental character of the CFSP was underlined by assigning all crucial powers to a traditional guardian of member states' independence: the European Council. The Council was meant to define the CFSP's principles and general guidelines. Policy initiatives, representation, and implementation were explicitly reserved for the rotating Council Presidency, assisted if need be by the previous and next member states to hold the Presidency (the so-called "troika"). However, the Treaty also made some concessions to supranationalism by assuring that the Commission would be "fully associated" and "the views of the European Parliament...duly taken into consideration."

Moreover, the Commission was given the right to make proposals concerning the CFSP in the same way as member states.

The Draft Treaty of Amsterdam has not introduced major changes to the CFSP structure. The CFSP remains in the second, intergovernmental pillar, although the third pillar – dealing with justice and internal affairs – has been flagged for a gradual merger with the first pillar. The Western European Union has been kept separate from the EU, but integration of the two institutions has been made possible "should the European Council so decide."[29] The Council, with its rotating Presidency, remains in the driver's seat. Moreover, the Council's Secretary-General will also serve as the High Representative for Common Foreign and Security Policy. The Council also has the power to appoint special representatives to deal with particular policy issues as they arise. According to the Draft Treaty, the Commission will still be "fully associated" with the work of the CFSP.

Although the formal powers of the Commission are much weaker than those of the Council, its actual influence should not be underestimated. The Commission has manpower and expertise which the Council and its relatively small Secretariat clearly lack. While the Council is in a position to make some big strategic decisions, it is clearly unable to micro-manage. The (General Affairs) Council meets only once a month for one day and is always confronted with a long agenda. Furthermore, the Commission is an institution that provides continuity through the Union's changing presidencies. And one should keep in mind that some presidencies are pretty ineffective, either because the country holding the presidency is small and without sufficient diplomatic leverage, or because it is preoccupied with domestic problems. Consider for instance, the six-month presidency held by Italy in 1996, which coincided with a political crisis and a general election campaign in the country.[30] Moreover, the Commission has maintained its privileged position with respect to the external trade relations of the Union, which means that it continues to be actively involved in applying the most important CFSP instruments, such as humanitarian aid, preferential trade agreements, and economic sanctions.

Thus the Council, which is formally given the power to make all major decisions, has no other choice but to rely upon the assistance of its "supranational" rival – the Commission – especially as far as policy implementation is concerned.[31] But it comes as no surprise to learn that the Commission is not always eager to implement the decisions of the Council on which it has had little or no influence. As Hellen

Wallace rightly argued: "The Commission lacks the political resources to mediate between competing interests, because its policy competencies are constrained and it has no direct political mandate. The Council is both a European institution and the prisoner of the member states, or perhaps rather of the member governments. Such collective identity as it has developed is fragile and always vulnerable to competition between member governments, as well as competition with the Commission."[32]

The products of such an awkward institutional set-up are either chaos or immobility or both. Chaos and immobility are also caused by decision-making procedures existing within the Council. Most Council decisions require unanimity. In the Treaty of Maastricht a qualified majority vote was only allowed if "the principle of joint action on a specific issue has been agreed," and as such it has been seldom applied in practice. The Draft Treaty of Amsterdam envisages that support of a qualified majority is necessary when adopting joint actions, common positions, or taking any other decision on the basis of the so-called "common strategy." However, if a Council member declares an intent to oppose, for important and stated reasons of national policy, a particular decision that requires support of a qualified majority, the vote shall not be conducted. The consensus principle means that all important decisions are to be born of hard bargaining. Given the diversified (and ever-growing) membership of the Council such bargaining cannot but be chaotic. Immobility is, however, the most likely end result of the bargaining process because the consensus principle pushes the member states into settling with the lowest common denominator.

The CFSP decision-making process resembles what Fritz Scharpf called in another context a "joint decision trap," caused by a combination of the unanimity rule and a bargaining impetus.[33] The Council is unable to move from negotiation (in which each member state defends or promotes its own national interest in a zero-sum fashion) to collective problem solving. The decision-making process becomes so complex and involves so many actors that efficiency suffers. If this were true, Euro-paralysis is not so much a product of obsessive nationalism or excessive power games, but rather of the "pathological decision logic inherent in its basic institutional arrangements."[34]

The system becomes even more unworkable if the Union attempts to use the WEU military force. It takes unanimity for the European Council to request WEU to act, unanimity for WEU to act, and the consent of the individual nations to do so. If a single veto is used at any stage of this complex procedure, a "coalition of willing" EU countries is not allowed to go ahead with any action on its own. Again, it comes as no surprise to learn that the WEU has hardly ever been called to action by the European Council.[35]

The last example also highlights three other institutional problems mentioned earlier. The first is the segmentation of policy areas: external economic policy, foreign policy *sui generis*, and defense policy are run under three different institutional regimes. The second is disaggregation of the three decision-making stages: planning, decision making proper, and implementation. While decision making is firmly in the hands of the Council, implementation and planning are not. Implementation, in particular, requires the cooperation of actors that are only loosely linked to the EU system. The third problem is decoupling the means from the ends of policy: while CFSP decisions are made under the second pillar, all the important instruments for implementing foreign and security policy are either in the first pillar or potentially in the WEU. As a result, the CFSP is largely declaratory.

The above-mentioned flaws in the EU institutional structure are also reflected in, or even reinforced by, an internal division of tasks between the Commission and the Council. For instance, the segmentation of policy areas is reflected in a division of competence between different EU Commissioners and their respective DGs. Trade matters fall under the "jurisdiction" of the DGI, development under the DGVIII, and political affairs under the DGIA. Since none of these areas is easy to distinguish in practice, the system is a source of permanent bureaucratic in-fighting between individual Commissioners and their DGs. Martin Holland has shown how three Commissioners – Van den Broek, Brittan, and Marin – were involved in a competence conflict over the EU policy *vis-à-vis* South Africa, unable to establish whether South Africa represents a "political" issue, "trade" issue, or "development" issue.[36] Jacques Santer tried to reduce the above-mentioned conflict by assigning a geographical responsibility to the three commissioners at DGI, only to learn that new conflicts are emerging between DGI commissioners with geographical responsibility and other commissioners with functional responsibility for steel, textiles, agriculture, transport, and other matters.

Disaggregation of the three policy-making stages is reflected in an uneasy competence division between the Political Committee of the Council, which is the main decision-making body of the Council but meets only once a month, and the COREPER which meets every week but is unable to "fill in" the decision-making "gap" between the monthly meetings of the Council's Political Committee.

Decoupling the means from the ends of policy is manifested not only by the distinct pillar structure and the independent position of the WEU. It is also reflected by the confusion over the relationship between the CFSP budget line as such, and budget lines for the Community activities that may support actions under the CFSP.[37]

In 1995 Juliet Lodge observed that it is often assumed within the Union that all disputes between members will be solved peacefully through "discussion, negotiation, trade-offs, consultation, compromise, mutual assistance and acceptance of the idea of creating a balance of advantages, and of costs and benefits."[38] However, our description of the CFSP's institutional problems clearly runs against such optimistic assumptions. The system is conflict-prone, disaggregated, and unbalanced. The planning is accidental and sketchy, the actual decision making is slow and cumbersome, and the implementation either non-existent or ineffective.

That said, it is unfair to submit the CFSP's institutional set-up to absolute judgments. Decision making is unavoidably slow and cumbersome in all international organizations. Imperfect procedures, inadequate instruments, and competence conflicts are not distinctly European deficiencies; most national and international bureaucracies have similar problems. Foreign policy of any national or international actor is usually reactive rather than pro-active – it is better at diplomatic networking than at responding to sudden crises. One should not expect the Union to change the nature of foreign policy-making altogether. If certain instruments, such as sanctions, do not work when applied by the Union, it does not mean that sanctions applied by other actors would work any better. In short, the institutional performance of the Union should be judged in relative rather than absolute terms. The best test for the CFSP institutional performance is done through comparisons with nation states and other international actors. The question is: does the CFSP institutional structure allow the Union to perform certain foreign and security tasks better than these other actors? If the Union is indeed taking over foreign and security competence from other actors, does it offer a more effective system of governance? This leads us to the issue of the division of tasks between the Union and other international actors.

THE BATTLE OF INSTITUTIONS

It was never assumed that the Union should perform all foreign and security tasks. In fact, for a long time it was assumed that the role of the Union would merely be supplementary to organizations like NATO, UN, WEU, and CSCE. Thus the picture of the EU institutional design is incomplete without looking at the formal and informal division of tasks between these five organizations and their mutual performance in peace and crisis. Are they able to work in tandem? Do they complement each other or compete with each other? And what about the mechanism of inter-institutional coordination?

When the Berlin Wall fell, the division of tasks between various international institutions seemed clear-cut. NATO was seen as the Western pillar for collective defense; indispensable for maintaining Western European welfare and freedom. The Conference of Security and Cooperation (CSCE) was seen as a pan-European pillar for collective security cooperation, understood in broad terms including human rights, East-West trade, disarmament, and confidence-building measures. The European Community was mainly about external trade and about coordination of diplomatic policy among EC members – the latter within the EPC framework. WEU was basically a non-active institution revived in 1987 in order to make an out-of-area European intervention in the Gulf legally possible, (permitted by the WEU Treaty, but not by the NATO one).[39] The sensitive task of international peace keeping has traditionally been seen as belonging to the United Nations.[40]

But then, with the end of the Cold War, perceptions quickly changed and everybody began to talk about a new institutional architecture for Europe.[41] The official aim was to create a system of "interlocking" institutions, NATO, CSCE, EU, and WEU, which were to complement each other and each had a role to play if instability was to be prevented.[42] Yet it was difficult to conceal the reality of intense, if not nasty institutional competition. Competition evolved in three major fields within foreign affairs and security. The first race was about leadership in crafting a new security and cooperation system for the entire continent. The second was about leadership in managing local European conflicts. The third was about leadership in collective defense for what used to be Western Europe. The Union competed hard in all three races, but it was NATO which each time emerged the winner.

Initially it was the CSCE that seemed to win the first, most important, race. Its major strength was its all-inclusiveness: all Western and

Eastern European countries plus the United States and Canada were members.[43] Moreover, the CSCE had a successful record in handling a variety of difficult diplomatic and security issues across the East-West divide for 25 years.[44] In 1990, the CSCE states adopted the *Charter of Paris* for a new Europe, a historic document laying down the principles for a new pan-European cooperation. In addition the CSCE adopted a document on Confidence and Security Building Measures (CSBMs) and a document on the creation of institutions for the CSCE: a Parliamentary Assembly, a Council consisting of foreign ministers, a committee to prepare and carry out the work of the Council, a Secretariat based in Prague, a Conflict Prevention Center in Vienna, and the Office for Democratic Institutions and Human Rights in Warsaw. In Berlin a CSCE emergency mechanism was established in 1991 to ensure the speedy response to possible crises, and a year later a CSCE High Commissioner for National Minorities was appointed to secure action on minority issues before they reach the stage of violent conflict. The CSCE had thus become a full-fledged international organization, and was renamed accordingly the Organization for Security and Cooperation in Europe (OSCE).

The EU's claim to a leading role in the future pan-European security and cooperation framework was based on economic assets, and the pacifying record of the 40 year-old integration. The EU was in a position to offer what the countries in Eastern Europe seemed to need the most: economic aid and integration with a neighborly zone of peace and prosperity. Was not the original post-war integrative effort about inducing peace and cooperation among members of the European Community, including such long-time enemies as Germany and France?[45] Could not the enlarged European Union act as a vehicle of peace and cooperation in the eastern part of the continent? The answer was positive in both cases and the Union assumed a leading role in coordinating and providing Western help to Eastern Europe.[46] It also began signing Association Agreements with a series of Eastern European countries aimed at creating favorable conditions for its eventual eastward enlargement.

When violence in the former Yugoslavia erupted, the EU also rushed in to play a leading role in the management of the conflict. The UN Secretary General at the time bluntly stated that Slovenia is not an independent UN member, and therefore the UN has no role in the conflict, while the US spokesman conceded: "After all, it's not our problem, it's a European problem."[47] And the EU was ready to meet the challenge: "This is the hour of Europe," was the triumphant announcement of Jacques Poos, one of the three EC foreign ministers who had flown to Yugoslavia soon after the war had started.

Encouraged by the positive changes on the continent, the EC began also to think about a higher profile in collective defense. Christoph Bertram expressed the opinion of many European governments in the early 1990s by saying:

> As a result of the changes in the Soviet Union, for the first time in forty years we can consider risking a bit of Atlantic security for the sake of gaining closer European political union, relying less on nuclear deterrence for the sake of gaining what inevitably will be an imperfect, embryonic cooperation in security and defense.[48]

It was in this spirit that the pre-Maastricht negotiations were held. France and Germany in particular argued for the inclusion of defense in the treaty on political union, and an explicit link between WEU and EC.

Initially, NATO seemed to be in serious trouble. As the Soviet empire began to crumble so did the basic rationale for the old-style collective defense institution. A painful question was being asked over and over again: against whom does Europe need defenses provided by NATO? Of course, NATO could still perform important military tasks in diffusing local conflicts, but its treaty precluded out-of-area intervention, and its two most powerful members, Germany and the US, openly refused to commit their ground forces to the bloody conflict in the Balkans (albeit for different reasons and later changed their minds). Since NATO's superior competence was basically in the military sphere, and not in diplomacy or economics, the institution seemed unsuited for embracing the nascent democracies of the former Soviet-bloc. Moreover, despite all the on-going changes NATO was still being demonized in some Eastern European quarters – if not some Western ones like Dublin, Madrid, and Paris.

At a certain point it looked as if NATO would have no option but to agree to act as the CSCE's sub-contractor (a Dutch government proposal), or else dissolve itself because of the lack of any purposeful mission. Yet the US leadership in NATO wasted no time in making sure that their most important institutional bridge to Europe would take on new and more ambitious tasks, even if this would mean putting other institutions out of a job. And so NATO created the North Atlantic Cooperation Council to provide a pan-European security dialogue; a job that was supposed to belong to the CSCE. NATO and US officials also made it plain that they are not in favor of any stronger, not to say independent, European defense identity. In February 1991, for instance, the US administration sent a memorandum to 11 EC governments (which were also NATO members) warning of the damage that could be done to the Atlantic Alliance by the institution of a European defense caucus. After long hesitation, the US also decided to let NATO prove its superior quality in managing local conflicts. This meant that US ground troops were, after all, to be sent to Bosnia, a move welcomed by the European Union. However, when dealing with the Balkan crisis the US repeatedly ignored not only EU envoys (David Owen in particular), but also the EU Presidency (the Greek one in particular), and instead talked to individual EU member states (Germany, France, and UK in particular).

In practice, NATO has proved to be successful on all possible fronts. In Bosnia NATO succeeded where the EC and the CSCE failed.[49] In Maastricht, the idea of a European defense identity was not endorsed by the Treaty chiefly because of the resistance of pro-NATO EU members such as Great Britain and The Netherlands. Most importantly, the Treaty did not subordinate the WEU to the Union. The WEU has not returned to its comatose state, however it has begun acting as a pillar of the so-called "European defense and security identity" (ESDI) within NATO.[50] Following the principles for Combined Joint Task Forces (CJTF), a new concept agreed within NATO, the WEU can now undertake humanitarian or peace-keeping missions beyond the Alliance's borders using NATO's military assets. However, it is the US, not the EU that maintains an effective veto over European use of NATO assets for missions that it does not approve.[51]

NATO under American leadership also succeeded on other fronts. NACC and its successor, Partnership for Peace, have been endorsed by not only post-communist, but also neutral European countries. And many Eastern Europeans have made it clear that if forced to make a choice they would rather join NATO than the EC. In the end, even France, a long-time *enfant-terrible* within NATO has decided to re-join its Military Committee after an absence of two decades.[52]

And so, NATO became an "all-round" international player able to operate in many different areas of foreign affairs and security. In fact NATO's officials have begun to present their institution as Europe's crucial and indispensable pacifier; a guarantor of successful European integration. As NATO's Secretary General put it:

> One of the greatest achievements of the Atlantic Alliance has been to put an end to the bad habits of European power politics. Once

NATO provided an Atlantic framework, there was simply no need for secret pacts and cordial or not-so-cordial ententes. The American presence provided for a stable balance between former rivals and enemies. This framework even made it possible to bring about German unification without a major crisis in Western European politics.

By contrast, the dissolution of the Alliance and the disengagement of the United States from Europe could undermine the European integration process. This would be damaging not only for Western Europe and the United States, but would also gravely affect the political and economic transition of the countries of Central-Eastern Europe, which urgently look for links to the political, economic and military institutions of the West.[53]

NATO's "victory" in the post-Cold War institutional competition has brought about many advantages. Most importantly, it settled the on-going disputes and allowed for a new intra-Alliance consensus. It is also evident that NATO's victory has demonstrated its determination, power, and efficiency; a fact that can be put to good use by Europeans and Americans alike. Besides, despite NATO's crushing victory there is still enough space for other European institutions to fill. The OSCE, for instance, had lost its role as the primary forum for negotiating security and cooperation in Europe, but it found another one in helping to defuse minority and human rights crises.[54] Nevertheless, in the context of our discussion it is important to stress that NATO's victory presents the CFSP with a series of institutional dilemmas. First, it is now quite unlikely that the Union will develop any serious competence in matters of defense and hard-core security. This confines the Union to the status of a "civilian power" only. Cynics may say that the major mission of the Union from now on is to pay the bills for Western operations under the American leadership. After all, the Union has merely economic means at its disposal and has to rely on the American defense and security capabilities assigned to NATO.

Second, it would be difficult to enhance the institutional coherence of the Union because the WEU is now much more involved in the work of NATO than that of the EU. The WEU is formally an integral part of the development of the European Union, but the fact is that its officials hardly ever care to be represented at meetings of the European Council.[55] Instead they rush to attend various meetings within NATO. Even the exchange of documents and the cross-participation of secretariats between EU and WEU does not work properly.[56]

Third, several EU members would lack an institutional form of representation during the most crucial debates on Europe simply because they are not members of NATO. The result of the recent institutional competition implies that NATO, not the EU, would be the major forum for such debates, and there is no formal mechanism for coordination between the two institutions.

Fourth, more and more European issues would be seen in the military-strategic context due to the fact that they are handled by NATO rather than the EU. (Has not the Balkan experience exposed the limitations of institutions unable to apply military measures?) Needless to say, this would further aggravate the institutional inadequacy of the Union, which does better in the field of diplomacy and economics. For instance, the issue of security and cooperation in Eastern Europe is so far more a function of NATO enlargement than of EU enlargement.

Not all of this is bad news, however. The Union can still be an influential international actor without acquiring the capacity for defense and a hard-core security policy. The "civilian power" status is less of a disadvantage in a world no longer driven by bi-polar military competition. Economic and diplomatic instruments at the disposal of the Union are powerful enough to influence developments on the Union's most important borders, and possibly also in some other parts of the world. One needs only to look at how effective the EU Association Agreements with Central and Eastern European states have been in shaping the legal, institutional, economic, and political situation there.[57]

And so there is no need to assume that the Union is condemned to helplessness unless it becomes a super-state with a powerful military and global reach.[58] But one should be aware of the limitations of a "civilian power" status, especially in dealing with local violence. One should also comprehend that "losing" the "battle of institutions" to NATO deprives the Union in general, and some of its members in particular, of an important leverage in shaping European politics. One should also keep in mind a query raised in a previous chapter: will NATO continue to act as a pillar of a North Atlantic *Gemeinschaft*? This leads us to another important observation. The story about the post-Cold War institutional competition reveals one important feature of contemporary international relations. NATO has won the competition not because it had superior institutional arrangements, but because it was led by the greatest world power, the United States. One should therefore ask the question: how important are certain institutional arrangements? Are we not in the business of raising unjustified institutional expectations? As Josef Joffe put it in the aftermath of Maastricht:

> As long as there is neither an existential threat nor an existential foe, institutions do not really matter, and so Europe intends to enjoy the luxury of eclecticism – pushing the EC/WEU without eschewing NATO, trying to expand the CSCE and calling for the UN... Yet, when threats and foes materialize again, the Europeans will behave as nations have always done. They will listen to their national interests, look for like-minded partners, and launch an enterprise capable of deterrence and defence...[59]

If Joffe's skepticism is justified one should also refrain from blaming institutions for the policy failures of their individual member states. Was not the disastrous EU policy in the Balkans a reflection of the diverging policies of Germany, Great Britain, France, and other EU member states? Could better institutional arrangement produce different policy outcomes?

THE LIMITS OF INSTITUTIONAL ENGINEERING

That most debates in recent years have focused on institutions comes as no surprise. After all, European politicians have devoted most of their time and energy to this particular matter. One needs only to review inter-governmental declarations and communiqués issued after top level European meetings: they all focus on institutional questions!

How is this institutional predilection to be explained? One obvious reason is that institutions – unlike society, economy or culture – are susceptible to "political engineering" and are therefore government's prime target. Some other explanations are more sinister: institutions are used as a mask or camouflage to hide national interests and power ambitions.[60] A similar sinister explanation argues that international institutions strengthen the autonomy of national political leaders *vis-à-vis* their domestic electorates.[61] Has not the EU been used as a scapegoat for all policy failures of recent years?

However, the most frequent and credible explanation given for all the attention devoted to institutional questions is that institutions provide governments with a greater problem-solving capacity within the complex international environment. Institutions are, first of all, a useful source of information, which by itself reduces uncertainty and enhances mutual trust. Since states are usually suspicious about each other's intentions and afraid of disadvantageous outcomes of their mutual bargaining, cooperation among them can be difficult if not altogether impossible. By providing a certain degree of stability and predictability based on information, institutions are instrumental in making inter-state cooperation not only possible but also advantageous for most if not all involved states.[62] With all the information available, states are able to avoid prisoner's dilemma and zero-sum-game reasoning. They can safely devote their attention to cooperative problem solving rather than worrying about hidden intentions and drastically unequal gains.

Institutions are also useful in reducing transaction costs. They enhance the efficiency of inter-state bargaining by providing a negotiating forum with pre-established procedures, by facilitating multi-level trade-offs, side payments, and package deals and by creating a supportive bureaucratic framework. They also make cheating and defection difficult by monitoring compliance of the agreed rules and norms and, if necessary, providing a mechanism of imposing sanctions on defectors.

Thus institutions are employed by states for purely utilitarian reasons. They help do away with mutual suspicion and solve problems in a cooperative manner. But after their creation, institutions begin to take on a life of their own; they are not only instruments to be manipulated by member states, they are also great modifiers of a state's behavior.[63] They restrain a state's behavior by means of internalized legal norms as well as a process of socialization occurring among the elites interacting with each other in a multilateral framework.[64] They may sometimes achieve a degree of autonomy and influence as political actors in their own right. They may even start to compete with states for power and legitimacy by presenting themselves as the most efficient problem solving actors in a complex and interdependent post-modern setting.[65] This might at times be bad news for states as such, but it is good news for the international community. A higher profile of international institutions means less opportunity for members of the "club" for power bullying, band-wagoning, intimidation and aggression. A higher profile of international institutions means more opportunities for structured dialogue and more incentives for compromise and co-operation. Is not Europe, with its dense system of overlapping institutions, a more benign region than Asia which has no similar institutional system? If Western Europe enjoyed peace for more than five decades, is it not due to the beneficial working of international institutions? As John Gerard Ruggie put it in 1992: "Perhaps the most telling indicator of institutional bite in Europe today is the proverbial dog that has not barked: no one in any position of authority anywhere is advocating, or quietly preparing for, a return to a system of competitive bilateral alliances."[66]

However, not everyone believes that institutions are anything but useful tools in an on-going power struggle, and the adjective "useful" is also being questioned. According to John J. Mearsheimer, for instance, institutions do not have significant independent effects on states' behavior; they are merely manipulative instruments in the hands of mighty states.[67] As such they are unable to convince states to reject "power-maximizing" behavior and embark on the road of compromise, negotiations and peace. Institutions are guided by the balance-of-power logic, not by a flawed logic of collective security or any other multilateral institutional arrangements.[68] According to Mearsheimer there is no evidence that institutions can provide a more benign and peaceful international environment. Institutions failed in Bosnia, Rwanda, and Transcaucasia and there is little reason to think that those same institutions would do better in the next trouble spot.

Thus institutions can do little good, but some even argue that they can do some harm. This is especially the case with the CFSP. As Philip Zelikow put it:

> The organizations for European foreign policy making agreed at Maastricht may actually weaken the system and limit, not enhance, European assertiveness. The masque of institutions has been a diversion from the specific policy issues arising in the eastern half of Europe. It has been a diversion from direct discussion of the vital interests, regional policies and needed military readiness of the governments in the Euro-Atlantic community.[69]

These harsh words cannot be dismissed lightly. For the last couple of years we have seen European leaders devoting more energy to "internal" institutional conflicts than to the real conflicts on the ground. Was not the EU's initial involvement in the former Yugoslavia largely about lifting up the EU's international status? For the last couple of years we have also seen that institutions were used as a mask for states' unwillingness to take responsibility on their own. This was again most vivid in the case of Yugoslavia: some Union member states were passing the buck from one institution to another and blaming them for inaction. For the last couple of years we have also seen that institutions were set aside as soon as they failed to fit the power game of the mighty. Britain, Germany, and France had no hesitation to join the Contact Group on Yugoslavia, even though it marginalized EU involvement and established a new form of great power *directoire*.

And thus it is clear that institutions are affected by the power games and egoistic interests of individual member states. However, as shown in one of the previous chapters, power games within the European Union are not about "relentless security competition" as Mearsheimer would have it.[70] States are indeed concerned about relative gains and cheating, but they are equally concerned about the capacity for problem solving that may well be enhanced by institutions. As Charles A. Kupchan and Clifford A. Kupchan rightly argue, institutions offer added value: "institutions are better than no institutions...some form of regulated, institutionalized balancing is preferable to unregulated balancing under anarchy."[71] Moreover, states are not unitary actors guided by abstract power rationale, they are (like institutions) social structures that often think and act in illogical and contradictory ways. When Mearsheimer insists that governments cannot at the same time behave "according to the Machiavellian assumptions of the balance of power and the Wilsonian assumption of international organization" he is at odds with the current reality of all European governments.[72] When Zelikow insists that "institutions do not kill, governments do" he is also wrong: neither governments nor institutions but soldiers kill, acting on orders from their national or international commanders, all of them human beings and not abstract material structures.[73] One must agree with Robert O. Keohane and Lisa L. Martin that institutions are not always valuable, their impact varies depending on the nature of power and interests and they are hardly a panacea for violent conflict: claiming too much for international institutions would be a "false promise." But, as they argue, "in a world politics constrained by state power and divergent interests, and unlikely to experience effective hierarchical government, international institutions operating on the basis of reciprocity will be components of any lasting peace."[74]

That said, it is difficult to deny that some institutions are doing better than others. Moreover, the usefulness or value of a particular international institution is often a product of its internal institutional arrangements. In that sense Zelikow may still be right in claiming that the CFSP is doing more harm than good because it has been "unable to craft any coherent supranational executive capable of credibly wielding the power now supposedly brought within the EU's grasp."[75] And thus, what sort of institutional restructuring is needed for common foreign and security policy to get off the ground? If the

CFSP is to meet some of its ambitious aims what should its structure and policy making look like?

THE WAY OUT OF THE LABYRINTH

The catalogue of institutional problems presented in this chapter points to some specific areas awaiting serious improvement. The Draft Treaty of Amsterdam addressed three of them: representation, planning, and financing. The treaty created the post of High Representative for a Common Foreign and Security Policy with the intention of providing greater cohesion, consistency and visibility in the Union's foreign policies. The treaty also established a Policy Planning and Early Warning Unit.[76] Its tasks include monitoring and analyzing developments in areas relevant to the CFSP, providing assessments of the Union's foreign and security policy interests, and identifying areas where the CFSP should focus in future. The unit will also provide timely assessments and early warning of crises, and produce policy options papers containing analyses, recommendations, and strategies for the CFSP. The issue of financing common foreign policies was also touched upon in Amsterdam, resulting in the "Inter Institutional Agreement between the European Parliament, the Council and the European Commission on provisions regarding financing of the Common Foreign and Security Policy." The intention of this Agreement was to provide the CFSP with a more flexible budget allowing quick distribution of resources as crises arise.

However, all these and similar changes seem to be of a second order.[77] The most important priority is to find effective ways for formulating the Union's basic political and operational will. In other words, the Union should be given the institutional means of expressing itself. Without this there is no chance for overcoming the current paralysis.

Of course, the CFSP can well be enhanced when given more money and other instruments of policy. However, one should know for what purpose these instruments are to be applied by the Union, when, and how.[78] Similarly, one should know on what kind of mandates Union representatives are to act. One should also know what is to be planned and analyzed. In short, unless the Union finds ways of formulating and expressing its collective will all other institutional reforms will be built on sand.

There are three major solutions for helping the Union accomplish this task.[79] They all go beyond procedural and organizational readjustments and touch upon the difficult subjects of sovereignty, identity, legit-imacy, the scope of commitments, and membership rights. The first solution may be called a majoritarian solution and advocates institu-tional reforms that increase the Union's capacity for internal conflict resolution. The second may be called a conflict-avoiding solution and advocates the search for substantive and procedural strategies that are able to reduce conflict within the Union to more manageable levels. The third solution may be called a selective involvement solution and it advocates reforms that would allow some decisions and actions to be taken by only those Union members that are willing and capable of doing so.

The first solution would require the introduction of majority voting within the CFSP system. As mentioned earlier, the Draft Treaty of Amsterdam only allows for a limited, qualified-majority voting on foreign and security matters. Merging the first and the second pillars and subjecting common foreign and security policies to the same decision-making regime that exists under the first pillar would repres-ent the most obvious example of applying the majoritarian solution to the CFSP system. The argument that this step would produce a major crisis over national sovereignty is not convincing enough. Economic and trade issues currently subjected to majority voting in the Council of Ministers are often just as "sensitive" as the foreign and security issues dealt with under the CFSP provisions. For instance, can one credibly argue that a decision to dispatch teams of observers to moni-tor elections in foreign countries is more sensitive in political and legal terms than a decision on competition, agricultural subsidies, or co-hesion funds within the Union? Can one argue that the former type of decisions intrudes on state's sovereignty more than the latter? Why then not allow the Council to make decisions on dispatching electoral observers by a majority vote?

Of course, the same reasoning would not apply to defense issues which might involve major military commitments and the loss of life. But defense issues are currently outside the CFSP framework which is basically concerned with diplomacy and soft security. One needs only to look at a catalogue of joint actions adopted since 1993 to see that hardly any of the issues addressed by the CFSP could produce a major sovereignty crisis, even if dealt with in a more majoritarian decision-making manner.[80] In fact, one can hope that the introduction of majority voting on foreign and security matters would enhance con-sensus among EU members and deter excessive free-riding the way it did in the field of trade and economics.

This does not mean that the majoritarian solutions are altogether flawless. The major argument against them, however, is not sectoral but democratic (sectoral in the sense that some sectors are more sensitive than others). After all, the democratic legitimacy of European governance rests primarily on the agreement of democratically accountable national governments. Put differently, the citizens of countries whose governments are out-voted under a majoritarian decision-making system have no reason to consider such decisions as having democratic legitimation.[81]

The conflict-avoiding solutions would aim at specifying and possibly also reducing the scope of European foreign and security policy.[82] The idea is to remove from the CFSP agenda issues that are particularly prone to cause internal friction, and are of no fundamental importance to the Union as a whole. One way would be to identify essential common interests of the Union, another would be to define priority areas such as relations with Central and Eastern Europe, the Balkans, the Mediterranean, and possibly others.[83] Such a guideline would make sure that outside actors or individual member states would not attempt to impose their parochial and often conflicting agendas on the Union. If the list of priorities and objectives is also endorsed by parliaments (national and the European one) then the legitimacy of the Union's foreign policy can also be enhanced. One can go even further and officially adopt a policy of "sectoral neutrality."[84] The aim would be to prevent the Union from internal disputes on matters that are not central to its self-proclaimed mission and existence. As Curt Gasteyger put it:

> Nobody can force the Union in its present state of incomplete integration to take positions on international issues for which either consensus is out of reach or it is not equipped to deal with adequately. A decision to abstain or to remain neutral, be it limited in time or in substance, would make the Union's foreign policy more predictable. It would also protect it against unnecessary friction or wasteful energy spent on secondary issues.[85]

The problem with this solution is that a (too) specific list or catalogue of the CFSP priorities and objectives would be unable to cope with an ever-changing international environment. After all, few experts were able to predict the enormous changes that took place in Eastern Europe, South Africa, and the Middle East within a few short years. Moreover, declaring some areas as marginal from the EU's standpoint, or excluding some types of actions from the CFSP repertoire would send the wrong signal to any potential troublemakers. Adopting a broad list of priorities and objectives, however, would have little chance of eliminating potential friction in the course of decision making. In fact, the process of selecting priority areas or major EU objectives can in itself represent a source of major conflict. For instance, the year-long debate on what issues might be considered suitable for joint actions within the CFSP framework produced a series of disagreements and subsequently failed to come up with the much anticipated list: the so-called "Asolo list", named after the site of a meeting in Italy.

The selective involvement solution would permit member states wishing to take action together, to do so within the framework of the treaty. This solution can work on either an ad hoc or a more permanent basis. In the former case, actions taken by a coalition of capable and willing states would have to be conducted within the broad guidelines agreed upon by all EU members. However, member states that were not willing to participate in the joint action directly would not be able to prevent the action from taking place. Needless to say, countries participating in the joint action would have the right to make tactical and operational decisions on their own.

Another variant of this solution would allow member states to stay away from certain sectors of the CFSP on a more permanent basis. Countries such as Austria, Ireland, Finland, and Sweden might be willing to stay out of all sensitive security matters, but allow other members to go ahead with joint actions within commonly agreed upon limits. After all, it is better for neutral countries to allow Britain, France, or Germany to conduct their security policy within the EU framework than having them take unilateral actions.

As the Union embarks on the course of further enlargement the selective involvement solution seems particularly tempting. However, this solution clearly creates two (or more) categories of members: those at the center of decision making and those at the margins; those carrying major burdens and those given the benefit of a free ride. Obviously none of the countries would like to be "downgraded" to a category of "marginalized" countries, likewise none of them would like to be "upgraded" to a category of "abused and exploited" countries. And there will always be countries that attempt to have it both ways. One need only remember German pressure to send European troops to Yugoslavia, while insisting that these would not be German troops.

The selective involvement solution would also open conflicts about the content of general guidelines imposed on the coalition for action group of EU states. What would be the limits of their freedom, and how much reporting should take place? The experience with the Contact Group on Yugoslavia has shown that even countries with troops on Balkan soil, such as Italy and The Netherlands, were not properly briefed, let alone consulted by Germany, Great Britain and France (i.e., EU members within the Contact Group of Five countries). The Draft Treaty of Amsterdam envisages a kind of selective involvement, the utility of which will only be clear after some time. According to the Treaty, abstentions by member states shall not prevent the adoption of "unanimous" decisions.[86] Any Council member may abstain from voting, simply by making a formal declaration. In such cases, the abstaining member state is not obliged to apply the decision, but must accept that the decision becomes an EU commitment if it is adopted. Also, abstaining members cannot represent more than one-third of all "weighted" votes.

Thus all three solutions have their obvious draw backs. Yet the Union has no other option but to try to apply a combination of all three. Extending the majority voting procedures seems certainly required because it would induce member states to more cooperative behavior and eliminate the veto threat that can now be used concerning even the most trivial matters. The most obvious solution would be to subject the CFSP to the decision-making regime that governs trade and economic issues, and by the same token do away with the confusing pillar structure within the Union. This would certainly enhance the efficiency of the CFSP institutional system, but the problem is that it might undermine its democratic legitimacy.

As we have argued earlier on these pages, the European public has a vested interest in swift collective action, and not the usual Euro-squabble. We have also criticized the mythical notion of sovereignty that allows national diplomats and politicians to behave as they wish with little control and sanction. But we also insisted that the requirement of democratic legitimacy cannot be sacrificed for the sake of institutional efficiency as far as the most sensitive issues are concerned.[87] While it is difficult to identify a catalogue of such "truly sensitive" issues, there is no doubt that defense issues would be among them. The extension of majority voting should therefore not be applied to defense matters. To put it more strongly, defense issues should be taken away from the CFSP discussion agenda!

No doubt, it is difficult to carry on a comprehensive foreign and security policy without a defense component, however, there are at least two important arguments that support the case for separation.

First of all, EU-style foreign policy, based on trade and diplomacy, has already proved to be an asset in a post-industrial global environment. In other words, there is no need for the Union to aspire to an old-style power status with a strong military and imperial outlook. As Richard N. Rosecrance rightly argued:

> Europe has pioneered in creating and sustaining democratic "trading states" that no longer harbor aggressive territorial designs at the expense of one another but that, in contrast, seek their livelihood through economic development sustained by foreign trade ... European integration actually creates greater concentration of strength because, as opposed to alliance, it wields separate national units together in economic and industrial terms. Because that power is not military or hegemonic in nature but is rather the economic power of an association of trading states that are legally and to some degree constitutionally linked, an integrated Europe does not drive other states away (through balancing mechanisms) but instead attracts them. Its power attracts; it does not repel.[88]

Secondly one should also comprehend what a common defense policy of the Union would imply. A true common defense policy can hardly be confined to the peace-keeping tasks identified in the WEU's Petersberg declaration of June 1992; it must include the defense of vital interests against direct attack envisaged by the Article V of the Brussels Treaty.[89] It must probably also address the issue of a European nuclear deterrence capability. As long as the Union is not ready to meet such tasks there is no point in adding to the CFSP agenda the controversial question of defense policy. As long as the majority of member states prefer to see defense issues to be handled by NATO there is no need to replay a competitive battle between these two institutions.

Arguments suggesting the limitation of the Union's geographical grasp are sound in terms of identity, but not in terms of efficiency. After all, EU's involvement in such "remote" countries as South Africa produced much good on the ground without stirring up internal European conflicts.[90] The most demanding and controversial tasks are on Europe's own borders and they can hardly be removed from the EU agenda. However, if the Union seeks a more defined identity, then it should certainly limit its geographical scope of action. For the citizens of the European Union it is difficult to identify with open-ended policies without any sense of geographic direction and cultural focus.

Coalitions for action should also be allowed, but guided by clear rules on delegation, implementation, and feedback. It is all too easy to create the impression that EU policy is run by a kind of *directoire*. In the end the CFSP can only work properly if it is able to develop procedures that accommodate the basic views of both major and minor EU actors. The CFSP will be an empty slogan if not built on mutual trust, universally shared engagements, and common burden sharing.

CONCLUSIONS

This chapter confirms that a common foreign and security policy can hardly get off the ground without reforming the CFSP institutional system. The current system produces inertia, indifference, and inconsistency. The system hardly ever manages to produce "good ideas," and it largely fails to implement any sort of idea, be it good or bad. At the same time, the system is unable to overcome the persisting divergence of interests and opinions within the Union; one can even argue that the system itself generates some divergence and conflict.

It has also been found that institutions are only partly to be blamed for the misfortunes of the CFSP: institutions are victims of power politics and they are not immune to various cultural, technological, and economic pressures. The reverse side of the same argument is that institutions are not a panacea for running effective foreign and security policies. Institutions can improve only marginally the substance and form of policies. One would wish for a more specific assessment but, as this chapter bears witness, there are no easy ways of measuring the utility of international institutions. Nevertheless, in our case the bottom line is that if member states are not willing to take certain actions, there is little the CFSP institutions can do about it. And as we argued in earlier chapters, the member states' willingness is largely the function of public support of some sort of institutions. Such support is, in turn, the function of both cultural identity and democratic legitimacy. Institutional effectiveness is another crucial factor. Well-structured and well-managed institutions can perform various beneficial functions for the member countries and their people. They can reduce transaction costs, aggregate diplomatic leverage, enhance stability and predictability based on information, and enhance the legitimacy of collective action. Of course, badly managed and poorly designed institutions cannot perform all these functions; instead they absorb plenty of diplomatic energy and may even become a source of conflict.

I have argued that the CFSP institutional system needs to be further reformed in order to enhance common policies rather than hamper them as is often the case at present. The reform ought to be more fundamental than the one undertaken in Amsterdam because at the root of the CFSP institutional problems is the Union's inability to formulate its collective will. Three measures have been suggested: the CFSP should allow for more majority voting, but its scope of action should be reduced, and a provision for selective involvement ought to be enhanced. The first measure would basically eliminate the pillar structure within the Union. The second measure would postpone all plans to give the Union a clear defense identity. The third would allow a variable geometry in foreign affairs and security. All three measures have their negative aspects, but perfect institutional solutions do not exist. The problem, however, is not that these or other measures are "imperfect," but that the Union is currently unable to carry out any serious institutional reforms whatsoever. We are confronted with what Elfriede Regelsberger and Wolfgang Wessels called a "feasibility trap."[91] The Intergovernmental Conference, initiated in Turin in Spring 1996 and concluded in June 1997 in Amsterdam, indicated very well the scope of this feasibility gap: no substantial institutional changes to the CFSP system were endorsed despite an 18 month-long, and often heated, debate.

Some would argue that the Maastricht Treaty was one bridge too far: national governments have finally realized the degree of supranational intrusion into their "sacred" sovereign domain. Others would argue that the built-in intergovernmentalism within the Union prevents any substantial self-reform.[92] A single country unhappy with the prospects of institutional change can always use its veto power. It was also established earlier in this chapter that the long process of economic integration generates a spill-over effect that is weak and erratic as far as foreign policy is concerned.

At the same time I argued that the weak spill-over effect did generate some common foreign policies in the course of recent years even though the progress was unequal in different policy sectors, and it was neither linear nor automatic. I also argued in this and other chapters that the inter-play between national sovereignty and collective decision making is not a zero-sum-game. There is no reason to believe that maintaining a veto power is more important for member states than acquiring the capacity for collective management of the international arena. It is also doubtful whether the few short years of the early 1990s (pre-and post-Maastricht developments) provide a sufficient body of evidence for states' long-term hostility to any supranational arrangements in the field of security and foreign affairs.

And so the verdict on the Union's capacity for institutional self-reform is still not in. This chapter has tried to show that procedural and organizational readjustments would not be sufficient to improve the CFSP institutional system. One needs to look into the current nature of power politics, divergence, and convergence of national interests, evolution of basic international paradigms and the process of democratic legitimation.

NOTES

1. As Christopher Hill put it in the context of European Political Coopera-tion: "EPC has tended to try to define crises out of existence by ignoring them or locating them in longer-term patterns of diplomatic exchange." See Christopher Hill, "EPC's Performance in Crises", in *Towards Polit-ical Union. Planning a Common Foreign and Security Policy in the Eur-opean Community*, Reinhardt Rummel, ed. (Baden-Baden: Nomos, 1992), p. 149.
2. The governments that negotiated the Treaty of Rome not only declined to sign up to anything like a federal constitution, but they also agreed on a sort of "upside-down" assignment of competencies, in which the "high politics" of foreign policy, public order and defense were left to the member states while "low politics" of economic regulation, commerce and trade were to be transferred to Brussels. See, e.g., John Pinder, *European Community. The Building of a Union* (Oxford and New York: Oxford University Press, 1992), pp. 7–31 and 234–7.
3. Edward Mortimer, "End This Maastricht Agony", *Financial Times*, June 17, 1992, p. 19.
4. Philip Zelikow, "The Masque of Institutions", *Survival*, Vol. 38, No. 1 (Spring 1996), p. 7.
5. U. Kitzinger, *The European Common Market and Community: A Selec-tion of Contemporary Documents* (London: Routledge and Kegan Paul, 1967), pp. 37–9.
6. Alfred van Staden talks about a "striking paradox" in the history of European integration: "On the one hand, initial efforts to create greater unity in the western half of the European continent were driven to a significant extent by considerations of security. Thus, the major motive underlying the plan for the European Coal and Steel Community of the early 1950s was to guarantee a lasting peace between France and

Germany. War between the two was to be made not only 'unimaginable' but also impractical by developing webs of interdependence. On the other hand, the actual expansion of European integration evolved at the level of economic and social needs rather than at the level of high politics (i.e. foreign policy and defense)." See Alfred van Staden, "After Maastricht: Explaining the Movement Towards a Common European Defence Policy", in *European Foreign Policy. The EC and Changing Perspectives in Europe*, Walter Carlsnaes and Steven Smith, eds. (London: Sage, 1994), p. 140.

7. See in particular Ernst B. Haas, *The Uniting of Europe* (Stanford: Stanford University Press, 1958); David Mitrany, *A Working Peace System* (Chicago: Quadrangle Books, 1966); Leon Lindberg, *The Political Dynamics of European Integration* (Stanford: Stanford University Press, 1963). One should keep in mind, however, that we are here primarily concerned with the so-called "political" version of spill-over as distinct from the so-called "functional spill-over". The latter deals with inter-sectoral spill-over confined to the domain of "low politics" only. In the works of Haas, Mitrany and Lindenberg it is mainly the functional version of spill-over which receives the main attention, while the political version is expressed in vague and ambiguous terms.

8. Ernst B. Haas, "International Integration: The European and the Universal Process", *International Organization*, Vol. 15, No. 4 (Autumn 1961), p. 366.

9. As Paul Hoffman argued: "the good thing about the spirit of unity is that it ramifies out; when you cultivate habits of unity in the economic sphere, they naturally spread over to the political sphere and even to the military sphere when the need arises." See Paul Hoffman, *Peace Can Be Won* (New York: Doubleday, 1951), p. 62.

10. See especially Edward Fursdon, *The European Defence Community: A History* (London: Macmillan, 1980), pp. 192–9.

11. The importance of including the EPC into the treaty is highlighted in Renaud Dehousse and Joseph H.H. Weiler, "EPC and the Single Act: from Soft Law to Hard Law?", in *The Future of European Political Cooperation. Essays on Theory and Practice*, Martin Holland, ed. (London: Macmillan, 1991), pp. 121–42.

12. See Stephen George, *Politics and Policy in the European Community* (Oxford: Clarendon Press, 1990), pp. 22–32.

13. Clearly, the spill-over worked better in some sensitive areas than others. Anne-Marie Burley and Walter Mattli, for instance, provided a powerful argument for the thesis that the legal integration of the Community corresponds remarkably closely to the original neofunctionalist model developed by Ernst Haas in the late 1950s. See Anne-Marie Burley and Walter Mattli, "Europe Before the Court: A Political Theory of Legal Integration", *International Organization*, Vol. 47 No. 1, (Winter 1993), pp. 41ff.

14. Although, as Karen Smith forcefully argued in her study of the EU's policies towards Eastern Europe, "There was certainly functional spill-over between 'external economic relations' and 'foreign policy', and it was reflected in extensive EC-EPC/CFSP collaboration. Decisions on

trade concessions and aid were taken in the context of the overall foreign policy towards Eastern Europe. 'The Council' acted simultaneously as the General Affairs Council and the Council of Foreign Ministers (EPC)." See Karen Elisabeth Smith, *The Making of Foreign Policy in the European Community/Union: The Case of Eastern Europe, 1988–1995*, PhD thesis at the London School of Economics and Political Science, London 1996, p. 355 (soon to be published by Macmillan).

15. This was well illustrated in Roger Morgan, "The Prospects for Europe's Common Foreign and Security Policy", in *International System After the Collapse of the East-West Order*, Armand Clesse, Richard Cooper and Yoshikazu Sakamoro, eds. (Dordrecht and London: Martinus Nijhoff, 1994), p. 418.

16. One can ignore those explanations that present the spill-over argument in caricatural terms as a passive policy of wait-and-see in the hope for automatic integration. In fact, the spill-over argument is basically about skillful engineering of the integration process across different sectors, through a variety of means, and with the help of different social and political forces. See, e.g., Ernst B. Haas, "Technocracy, Pluralism, and the New Europe", in *International Regionalism*, Joseph Nye, ed. (Boston: Little Brown, 1968), pp. 7ff.

17. Stanley Hoffmann, "The European Process at Atlantic Crosspurposes", *Journal of Common Market Studies*, Vol. 3, No. 1 (1965), pp. 88–90.

18. The distinction between the positive and negative integration comes primarily from the field of economics. See Jan Tinbergen, *International Economic Integration* (Amsterdam: Elsevier, 1965), second edition, pp. 85–101.

19. As Alfred van Staden argued: "Neo-functionalist explanations in the context of security and defense are flawed because European bureaucrats and technocrats played no prominent part in this arena.". See Alfred van Staden, "After Maastricht: Explaining the Movement Towards a Common European Defence Policy," in *European Foreign Policy. The EC and Changing Perspectives in Europe*, op. cit., p. 155.

20. Andrew Moravcsik, "Preferences and Power in the European Community: A Liberal Intergovernmentalist Approach", *Journal of Common Market Studies*, Vol. 31, No. 4 (December 1993), p. 494.

21. This was already well argued in the 1970s. See Roger P. Morgan, *High Politics, Low Politics: Toward a Foreign Policy for Western Europe*, (Beverly Hills: Sage Publications, 1973), p. 61.

22. See Fritz W. Scharpf, "Negative and Positive Integration in the Political Economy of European Welfare States", *Jean Monnet Chair Papers* No. 28 (Florence: The Robert Schuman Centre at the European University Institute, 1995), pp. 8–12 and 36.

23. See Ole R. Holsti, "Public Opinion and Foreign Policy: Challenges to the Almond-Lippmann Consensus", *International Studies Quarterly*, Vol. 36, No. 4 (1992), pp. 439–66.

24. See Thomas Risse-Kappen, "Exploring the Nature of the Beast: International Relations Theory and Comparative Policy Analysis Meet the European Union", *Journal of Common Market Studies*, Vol. 34, No. 1 (March 1996), pp. 53–81.

25. See Albert O. Hirschman, "Three Uses of Political Economy in Analysing European Integration", in *Essays in Trespassing. Economics to Politics and Beyond* (Cambridge: Cambridge University Press 1981), pp. 266–85.

26. Recent studies of the EU institutional system seem to vindicate some original ideas of functionalism by illustrating the power of policy networks within the EU and pointing to the limits of the state-centric approach. See John Petersen, "Decision-Making in the European Union: Towards a Framework for Analysis", *Journal of European Public Policy*, Vol. 2, No. 1 (March 1995), pp. 69–93, and Daniel Wincott, "Institutional Interaction and European Integration: Towards an Everyday Critique of Liberal Intergovernmentalism", *Journal of Common Market Studies*, Vol. 33, No. 4 (December 1995), pp. 597–609.

27. See Philippe C. Schmitter, "Imagining the Future of the Euro-Polity with the Help of New Concepts", in *Governance in the European Union*, Gary Marks, Philippe C. Schmitter and Fritz W. Scharpf, eds. (London: Sage, 1996), p. 132.

28. Article J.4.1 of the Treaty on the European Union, Maastricht, December 1991.

29. In that case, Article J.7 of the Draft Treaty stipulates that the Council shall "recommend to the member states the adoption of such a decision in accordance with their respective constitutional requirements." Moreover, the next paragraph of the Amsterdam Treaty stipulates that "the policy of the Union in accordance with this Article shall not prejudice the specific character of the security and defense policy of certain member states and shall respect the obligations of certain member states, which see their common defense realized in NATO, under the North Atlantic Treaty and be compatible with the common security and defense policy established within that framework."

30. See, e.g., Chris Endean and Victor Smart, "Rudderless Italy Drives Turin Summit Off Course", *The European*, February 22–28, 1996, p. 1.

31. Martin Holland documented this point very well in his study of the EU's policy towards South Africa. He concluded that "with the composite effect of the SEA and the Maastricht process, the Commission's role as an agenda manager has significantly increased in foreign affairs, particularly in the case of South Africa." See Martin Holland, *European Union Common Foreign Policy. From EPC to CFSP Joint Action and South Africa* (London: St Martin's Press, 1995), p. 89.

32. Helen Wallace, "The Institutions of the EU: Experience and Experiments", in *Policy-Making in the EU*, Helen Wallace and William Wallace, eds. (Oxford: Oxford University Press 1996), p. 59.

33. See Fritz Scharpf, "The Joint-Decision Trap: Lessons from German Federalism and European Integration", *Public Administration*, Vol. 66, No. 3 (Autumn 1988), pp. 239–78.

34. Fritz Scharpf, "The Joint-Decision Trap," op. cit., p. 269.

35. In Amsterdam, the European leaders adopted a special protocol as an annex to the Draft Treaty, which asks that the European Union and the WEU draw up some kind of "arrangement" for enhancing cooperation between the two institutions.

36. Martin Holland, *European Union Common Foreign Policy*, op. cit., pp. 84–9.
37. See Fraser Cameron, "Europe Towards 1996: The CFSP in Operation", in *A New Transatlantic Partnership*, The Third Castelgandolfo Colloquium on Atlantic Affairs (Rome: Centro Studi di Politica Internationale, 1995), p. 33.
38. Juliet Lodge, "Introduction", in *The European Community and the Challenge of the Future*, Juliet Lodge, ed. (London: Pinter, 1995), second edition, pp. 3–4.
39. Since the creation of the WEU in 1948 there were several rather unsuccessful efforts to breathe some life into the otherwise sleeping organization. Usually on such occasions the member states repeated their ritual statement saying that "the construction of an integrated Europe will remain incomplete as long as it does not include security and defense". A similar phrase was included in the October 1987 "Platform on European Security Interests" adopted by WEU ministers in The Hague. See *Western European Union* (London: WEU, April 1990).
40. See Shashi Tharoor, "United Nations Peacekeeping in Europe", *Survival*, Vol. 37, No. 2 (Summer 1995), pp. 121–34. For an overview of relations between the UN and the EU see Peter Schmidt, "A Complex Puzzle – the EU's Security Policy and UN Reform", *Internationale Spectator*, Vol. 29, No. 3 (July–September 1994), pp. 53–66.
41. See, e.g., Joachim Krause and Peter Schmidt, "The Evolving New European Architecture – Concepts, Problems and Pitfalls", *The Washington Quarterly*, Vol. 13, No. 4 (Autumn 1990), pp. 79–92.
42. See, e.g., the Declaration issued by the NATO Summit in Rome, on 7–8 November 1991, *NATO Review*, Vol. 39, No. 6 (1991), pp. 19–33. It was stressed that appropriate links would be established among NATO, WEU and EC to ensure that all were adequately informed about decisions that might affect their security.
43. As Christoph Bertram rightly argued: "The most important and difficult initial task for multilateral diplomacy is to gain the trust of all parties involved, to win legitimacy for interfering in the internal affairs of a sovereign state and to establish a procedure for dialogue, exploration and eventually negotiation. It is of immense advantage if all the parties are already members of the same organization." See Christoph Bertram, "Multilateral Diplomacy and Conflict Resolution", *Survival*, Vol. 37, No. 4 (Winter 1995–96), p. 75.
44. See Vojtech Mastny, *Helsinki, Human Rights, and European Security* (Durham: Duke University Press, 1986), especially pp. 6–8.
45. This was in line with Robert Schuman's basic idea that European integration would make any future war between France and Germany not merely unthinkable but materially impossible. See Robert Schuman's Declaration of May 9, 1950, quoted at endnote no. 5.
46. As Margaret Thatcher put it: "The European Community has reconciled antagonisms within Western Europe; it should now help to overcome divisions between East and West in Europe... We must bring the new democracies of Eastern Europe into closer association with the institutions of Western Europe." See Margaret Thatcher, "Shaping A New

Global Community", speech to the Aspen Institute (Aspen, Colorado, August 5, 1990).

47. As quoted in *Financial Times*, June 29–30, 1991.

48. Christoph Bertram, "The Past as Future: Towards a European Defense Community", in "Power and Plenty? From the Internal Market to Political and Security Cooperation in Europe", *Jean Monnet Chair Papers* (Florence: European University Institute, The European Policy Unit, April 1991), p. 61.

49. The all-inclusiveness of the CSCE proved to be its major weakness. When violence erupted in the Balkans the CSCE was virtually paralyzed by the persistent veto of one of its members: the Republic of Yugoslavia. The European Community has also been helpless in managing the war in the Balkans, partly because of its own institutional deficiencies, partly because of American obstruction and partly because of the complexities of the conflict as such. For a detailed analysis of the institutional involvement in the Yugoslav conflict see James Gow, "Nervous Bunnies – The International Community and the Yugoslav War of Dissolution", in *Military Intervention in European Conflicts*, Lawrence Freedman, ed. (Oxford: Blackwell, 1994), pp. 15–21, or Reneo Lukic and Allen Lynch, *Europe from the Balkans to the Urals. The Disintegration of Yugoslavia and the Soviet Union* (Oxford: Oxford University Press, 1996), pp. 252–85.

50. The WEU has also done some practical things. It sent ships to the Adriatic to enforce an arms embargo on former Yugoslavia, helped Hungary, Romania, and Bulgaria to create an effective blockade on the Danube against Serbia; and lent a police force to the Bosnian town of Mostar. For a more in-depth analysis of the WEU role in providing security for the entire EU see: Guido Lenzi and Laurence Martin eds., *The European Security Space*, Working papers by the European Strategy Group and the Institute for Security Studies of Western European Union, (Paris: Institute for Security Studies of Western European Union, 1996), pp.1–34.

51. One should keep in mind that Europeans provide 80–90 percent of NATO's conventional forces. See Nicole Gnesotto, "Common European Defence and Transatlantic Relations", *Survival*, Vol. 38, No. 1 (Spring 1996), p. 26.

52. As a condition for rejoining NATO's military wing, French President Jacques Chirac demanded that the United States relinquish to a European officer the organization's southern command, which is based in Naples and includes the US Sixth Fleet. Washington initially rejected the condition and as this book goes to print, the resolution of this long-running dispute is not in sight.

53. Manfred Wörner, "NATO's Role in a Changing Europe", *Adelphi Paper* No. 284 (1994), p. 101. In 1997 Madeleine Albright, US Secretary of State, described NATO in even more ambitious terms: "NATO's Cold War task was to contain the Soviet threat. But that is not all it did. It provided the confidence and security shattered economies needed to rebuild themselves. It helped France and Germany become reconciled, making European integration possible. With other institutions, it

brought Italy, then Germany and eventually Spain back into the family of European democracies. It denationalized allied defense policies. It has stabilized relations between Greece and Turkey. All without firing a shot. Now the new NATO can do for Europe's east what the old NATO did for Europe's west: vanquish old hatreds, promote integration, create a secure environment for prosperity, and deter violence in the region where two world wars and the Cold War began." Madeleine Albright, "Enlarging NATO: Why Bigger is Better," *The Economist*, February 15, 1997, p. 20.

54. Carl Bildt offered a very good illustration of the CSCE mediating role in diffusing the minority crisis in the Baltic countries. See Carl Bildt, "The Baltic Litmus Test", *Foreign Affairs*, Vol. 73, No. 4 (September–October 1994), pp. 72–85.

55. A former Secretary-General of the WEU, Willem Van Eekelen, admitted: "The relations with the EU have hardly developed. I was present only once in a general affairs council of the EU when we discussed former Yugoslavia, and I think my successor has not yet been there." See Niklaas Hoekstra and Auke Wenema, "Prospect of European Security Policy" (interview with Willem van Eekelen and Edmond Wellenstein), *Atlantisch Perspectief*, Vol. 19–20, No. 8/1 (1995–96), p. 19.

56. See European Commission, *Report on the Operation of the Treaty on European Union*, Brussels, May 1995, p. 69.

57. For a comprehensive analysis of this issue see Karen Smith, *Policy in the European Community/Union. The Case of Eastern Europe, 1988–1995*, op. cit.

58. Some authors take an opposite view. See e.g. Giovanni Jannuzzi, "Scope and Structure of the Community's Future Foreign Policy", in *Toward Political Union. Planning a Common Foreign and Security Policy in the European Community*, Reinhardt Rummel, ed. (Baden-Baden: Nomos, 1992), p. 289.

59. Josef Joffe, "Collective Security and the Future of Europe: Failed Dreams and Dead Ends", *Survival*, Vol. 34, No. 3 (Spring 1992), pp. 48–9.

60. A Dutch scholar, Jan Rood, put it in the most concise manner: "Het gaat om posities van macht, invloed en prestige." (It is about power, influence and prestige. See Jan Rood, "Living in a Fantasy World. Nederland en het GBVB", *Atlantisch Perspectief*, Vol. 20, No. 2 (1996), p. 4.

61. See Andrew Moravcsik, "Preferences and Power in the European Community: A Liberal Intergovernmentalist Approach", *Journal of Common Market Studies*, Vol. 31, No. 4 (December 1993), pp. 507–9. Also Robert D. Putnam, "Diplomacy and Domestic Politics", *International Organization*, Vol. 42, No. 3 (Summer 1988), pp. 427–61.

62. As Charles Pentland argued: "Important for both great and small powers are the power disparities embodied in the organization and the degree to which any working consensus created among the members is likely to be compatible with their particular interests. A good measure of the power relationship is the 'presence' of the state in the organization, reflected in its contribution of finances and personnel, its demands for

action, and its level of participation in decision-making. The degree of compatibility between the working consensus of the organization and the state's interests can be seen in the responsiveness of the organization's policy decisions and executive actions to the state's original demands." See Charles Pentland, "International Organizations and Their Roles", in *World Politics*, J. Roseneau, K. W. Thompson and G. Boyd, eds (New York: Free Press, 1976), pp. 631–56.

63. As Robert O. Keohane put it: "Institutions do not merely reflect the preferences and power of the units constituting them; the institutions themselves shape those preferences and that power." See Robert O. Keohane, "International Institutions: Two Approaches", *International Studies Quarterly*, Vol. 32, No. 4 (December 1988), p. 382.

64. See Charles Pentland, "International Organizations and Their Roles", op. cit., p. 246.

65. This may well explain the paradox of states trying hard to enhance institution-building, but stopping short of giving the institutions more autonomous powers.

66. John Gerard Ruggie, "Multilateralism: The Anatomy of an Institution", *International Organization*, Vol. 46, No. 3 (Summer 1992), p. 562.

67. See John J. Mearsheimer, "The False Promise of International Institutions", *International Security*, Vol. 19, No. 3 (Winter 1994–95), pp. 5–49, also John J. Mearsheimer, "A Realist Reply", *International Security*, Vol. 20, No. 1 (Summer 1995), pp. 82–93.

68. The collective security argument targeted by Mearsheimer was presented in Charles A. Kupchan and Clifford A. Kupchan, "Concerts, Collective Security, and the Future of Europe", *International Security*, Vol. 16, No. 1 (Summer 1991), pp. 114–62.

69. Philip Zelikow, "The Masque of Institutions", *Survival*, Vol. 38, No. 1 (Spring 1996), p. 17.

70. John J. Mearsheimer, "The False Promise of International Institutions", op. cit., p. 9.

71. Charles A. Kupchan and Clifford A. Kupchan, "The Promise of Collective Security", *International Security*, Vol. 20, No. 1 (Summer 1995), pp. 53–4.

72. John J. Mearsheimer, "The False Promise of International Institutions", op. cit., p. 35. Mearsheimer refers here to Quincy Wright, *A Study of War*, (Chicago: University of Chicago Press, 1942), vol. 2, p. 781.

73. Philip Zelikow, "The Masque of Institutions", op. cit., p. 8. Alexander Wendt provides a good argument for the claim that the fundamental structures of international politics are social rather than strictly material. See, e.g., Alexander Wendt, "The Agent-Structure Problem in International Relations Theory", *International Organization*, Vol. 41, No. 3 (Summer 1987), pp. 335–70.

74. Robert O. Keohane and Lisa L. Martin, "The Promise of Institutionalist Theory", *International Security*, Vol. 20, No. 1 (Summer 1995), p. 50.

75. Philip Zelikow, "The Masque of Institutions", op. cit., p. 9.

76. The Unit was established by a special "Declaration to the Final Act".

77. For a more detailed analysis of the CFSP reform debate see, e.g., Elfriede Regelsberger, "Reforming CFSP – An Aliby Debate or

More?", in *The European Union's Common Foreign and Security Policy. The Challenges of the Future*, Spyros A. Pappas and Sophie Vanhoonacker, eds. (Maastricht: European Institute of Public Administration, 1995), pp. 93–118.

78. As Helen Wallace put it: "Significant institutional changes are improbable unless linked to changes in the level of agreement about policy.". See Helen Wallace, "Politics and Policy in the EU: the Challenge of Governance," in *Policy Making in the European Union* Helen Wallace and William Wallace eds. (Oxford: Oxford University Press, 1996) p. 26.

79. Here I largely rely on ideas put forward by Fritz Scharpf. Althought Sharpf analysed decision-making problems in the field of social policy and welfare his arguments can also be applied to foreign and security issues. See Fritz W. Scharpf, "Negative and Positive Integration in the Political Economy of European Welfare States", *Jean Monnet Chair Papers* No. 28 (Florence: The Robert Schuman Centre at the European University Institute, 1995), pp. 20ff.

80. Such a catalogue is provided by the European Commission. See *Intergovernmental Conference 1995. Commission Report for the Reflection Group*, Brussels, May 1995, p. 100.

81. This is why various ad hoc arrangements such as unanimity with "positive or constructive abstention", "unanimity minus one", "super-qualified majority", qualified majority with dispensation of the minority, general platforms of decisions taken by unanimity to be followed in their specifics by qualified-majority voting will probably not work. Put simply, they will be incomprehensible to the European electorate.

82. See Reinhardt Rummel, "Integration, Disintegration, and Security in Europe – Preparing the Community for a Multi-Institutional Response", *International Journal*, Vol. XLVII, No. 1 (Winter 1991), pp. 64–92.

83. As advocated by one DG1A official. See Fraser Cameron, "Developing the Common Foreign and Security Policy of Europe", *Brassey's Defence Yearbook* (London: Brassey's, 1996), p. 135.

84. As advocated in Curt Gasteyger, *An Ambiguous Power. The European Union in a Changing World* (Gütersloh: Bertelsmann Foundation Publishers, 1996), pp. 132–4.

85. Ibidem, pp. 132–3.

86. Art. J.13. The Draft Treaty of Amsterdam.

87. As I argued in another chapter, democracy at the Union level is, in principle, weaker than at a nation state level, even though democracy at the Union level might be more efficient. For a more detailed argument see Robert A. Dahl, "A Democracy Dilemma: System Efficiency versus Citizen Participation", *Political Science Quarterly*, Vol. 109, No. 1 (1994), pp. 23–34.

88. See Richard Rosecrance, "Trading States in a New Concert of Europe", in *America and Europe in an Era of Change*, Helga Haftendorn, ed. (Boulder, CO: Westeview Press, 1993), pp. 128 and 131.

89. This is well argued in Lawrence Martin and John Roper, eds., *Towards a Common Defence Policy*. A Study by the European Strategy Group and the Institute for Security Studies of Western European Union (Paris: Institute for Security Studies of WEU, 1995), p. 2.

90.   This was well argued in Martin Holland, "Bridging the Capability-Expectation Gap: A Case Study of the CFSP Joint Action on South Africa", *Journal of Common Market Studies*, Vol. 33, No. 4 (December 1995), p. 569.

91.   Elfriede Regelsberger and Wolfgang Wessels, "The CFSP Institutions and Procedures: A Third Way for the Second Pillar", *European Foreign Affairs Review*, Vol. I, No. 1 (July 1996), p. 32.

92.   See Gerald Schneider, "The Limits of Self-Reform: Institution-Building in the European Union", *European Journal of International Relations*, Vol. 1, No. 1 (1995), pp. 59–86.

Conclusions: The choices to be made

In this book I have offered five possible explanations for Euro-paralysis. Not one, but all five explanations have turned out to be valid, but usually in a different sense than initially asserted. Put more bluntly; the five most frequently cited "truths" about European foreign policies have proved to be only half truths, if not misleading fallacies in some cases. And thus I have found that hegemonic "atavism" rather than hegemonic politics *sui generis* is the problem at present. None of the major European states aspires to political hegemony and military preponderance on the continent. EU states compete with each other in terms of economics rather than territorial acquisition or military asser-tiveness. And the key terms in this competition are "diffusion" rather than "concentration" of power, "down-sizing" rather than "up-sizing" of the government, "cooperation with" rather than "domination over" EU neighbors. The growing network of mutual interdependence between EU states, the decreasing salience of territorial issues, the presence of multi-sectoral institutional arrangements and the restrain-ing effect of nuclear weapons suggest that old-style power politics is unlikely to return. However, some of the countries still cultivate imperial images and global pretensions, they indulge in bad habits of "playing off," "ganging-up," and parochial "bullying," they still pursue the politics of glory and pride. I named this behavior hegemonic atavism, and of course it undermines common foreign and security endeavors. But atavism remains what it is – a resemblance to a remote hegemonic ancestor – and does not imply a "back to the future" scenario for the continent.

I have also shown that the persistent divergence of national policies hampers the CFSP, but have found that despite all this divergence national policies of EU states are increasingly geared towards Europe. For individual European states, EU institutions are becoming the most important means for coping with global pressures and local problems. The EU political agenda increasingly dictates national agendas, and not the other way around. The EU framework has become the central point where most agreements and disagreements are being debated and made. But this process of pulling together different national foreign policies is being hampered by the preponderance of national loyalties, self images, and traditions cultivated by the citizens of individual EU states. It is not the alleged conflict of national interests but the reassertion of national identities that drives common policies apart. National identities are proving to be less convergent, less flexible, and less susceptible to European engineering than national interests.[1] Amidst growing uncertainty, complexity, and change Europeans stick to the only solid binding factor: national culture. The identity of the Union is novel, vague, and abstract, and as such it can hardly represent a surrogate for the existing national identities. In recent years we have even seen a falling away from multiple identities on the continent. If distinct national identities demand distinct national policies, a democratic body politic cannot but respond to this request, regardless of all global and modern pressures that suggest moving to common rather than separate policies.

I have also observed that the end of the Cold War proved to be a source of enormous conceptual confusion paralyzing common European policies. European policy makers have lost the sense of strategic purpose that is needed for steering the Union in a coherent and predictable manner. They appear to have problems identifying basic foreign and security risks and crafting suitable responses to address them. They have been unable to liberate themselves from ideological prejudices, dysfunctional concepts, and misleading terminology. Some are still trying to run a new Europe with an old mind-set and out-dated rhetoric. But I also found that the dramatic and unexpected end of the Cold War is only one of many factors behind the current confusion. The challenge is more structural and fundamental which means that clarity will not return with a slower pace of events in Europe or with some personnel changes within governments. The entire hierarchy of interests and values guiding Western security thinking is now being questioned. Several basic principles of international relations are being found to be irrelevant or obsolete. Even some basic rational assumptions behind foreign policies are now under fire. In short, to solve the current conceptual confusion, the basic norms and procedures guiding international efforts need to be re-examined and the social and civic factors that make some policies fail and others triumph must be identified. Foreign policies of the Union cannot operate in a normative and social vacuum without regard to civil society and the European polity.

There is no fundamental crisis of democracy in Europe as initially asserted: this is another finding of this book. That said, democracies clearly have problems in adapting to rapid changes in the domestic and international environments. This undermines all sorts of policies, including foreign policies run by the Union. The system of democratic representation is under strain because of the assertion of television politics and the cartelization of political parties. Democracies also have problems coping with new political attitudes and cultural trends. And the impact of global pressure forces them to make difficult choices between effectiveness and representation. Delegating more powers to the European Union may be helpful in terms of effectiveness, but it is clearly deficient in terms of representation. Democracy's problems are doing more harm than good to European foreign policies. I do not endorse the view claiming that a strong democracy and effective foreign policy are basically incompatible. Policies cannot acquire a public purpose without referring to democracy. It is also difficult to run foreign policies amidst widespread public apathy, cynicism, and selfishness. And since the Union does not enjoy spontaneous public endorsement rooted in cultural affinity, democracy could be a major source of legitimation for the Union and its policies. That said, the easy coexistence of foreign policy and democracy requires special types of arrangements that allow for disclosure and deliberation of all strategic choices at the Union level.

Finally, I confirmed that the current CFSP institutional set-up undermines common foreign policies, but I also found that the role of institutions should not be overstated. Institutions can improve or damage policies only marginally. If the people of Europe and their governments are unwilling to underwrite certain policies there is little the CFSP institutions can do about it. But of course, if well structured and well managed, the CFSP institutional structures could perform various beneficial functions for the Union. It could reduce costs of international transactions, aggregate the Union's diplomatic leverage, and enhance international stability and predictability by providing information. Above all, a well-functioning institutional structure could help the Union gain legitimacy for its foreign and security policies. Unfortunately, the current structure cannot perform all these beneficial functions, since it is poorly designed and badly managed. The decision-making system based on the principle of unanimity is slow, conflict-ridden, and subject to the lowest common denominator. The disaggregation of actors and institutions produces inertia, resistance to change, and artificial compartmentalization of policy. The link between the means and the ends of policy is largely broken. The Union also lacks an easily identifiable representation. I have argued that the reasons for this state of affairs is the Union's refusal to face basic institutional choices about its width and depth, coherence and diversity, and openness and exclusiveness. Nor is the Union prepared to state clearly its basic policy aims, instruments, internal rules, and decision-making procedures. Instead the tendency has been to rely on a spill-over effect generated by the initial negative integration in the field of economics and foreign trade. However, the spill-over argument proved overly optimistic about time schedules and patterns of progress. And so we are faced with a system that finds it extremely difficult to act and to reform itself. In order to improve the system one would need to go beyond procedural and organizational readjustment and take some bold decisions about the Union's basic purpose, geographic reach, instruments, and functions.

THE HEART OF THE MATTER

Euro-paralysis is not caused by a single factor, but some problems have clearly proved to be more serious than others, and there are one or two issues that really matter. What are they? The answer is *democracy* and *identity*, and they both can be grouped under the label of *legitimacy*, understood in cultural and civic terms.[2] Traditional foreign policy concerns such as power, institutions, and national interests were found to be less crucial in explaining the CFSP failures. In my view, common policies of the Union do not work because they do not really enjoy genuine legitimacy. Europeans do not have a high degree of natural affinity towards these policies and they have hardly any chance to control them. The CFSP is not based on spontaneous social links, communal solidarity, and shared traditions that would justify broader, cross-national support. It is not very clear who the "consumers" and "producers" of these policies are, just as it is unclear what their broader strategic purpose is. How can Europeans treat these policies as truly "theirs"? And if people in various countries do not identify with European policies, their governments can hardly allow these policies to get off the ground, especially when the other factors indicated in this book press in the same direction.

This is not to suggest that governments must blindly follow their electorates, but to insist that European foreign policies must command a minimum degree of legitimacy and respect. This is not to suggest that legitimate foreign policies are only those endorsed by the public, but to argue that legitimacy is primarily a function of democracy and identity rather than mere effectiveness. This is not to suggest that policies of nation states are always seen as legitimate, but to say that the legitimacy problem of the Union is much greater than the one of member states. This is not to suggest that Europeans are utterly opposed to common international efforts, but to underline a difference between general and genuine public support. People need to be ready to underwrite important policies with their check books, if not "blood, sweat, and tears." Public support for the CFSP can hardly be measured by the general and vague results of the Eurobarometer.[3] Since we lack reliable statistical evidence, we need to rely on deductive rather than empirical arguments.[4] The lack of statistical data should not serve as an excuse for analytical blindness and intellectual indifference.

Foreign policies of member states may well be ineffective, but they often enjoy public backing because citizens can treat them with affection and have some role in shaping them, however indirect. Foreign policies of the Union have never even had a chance to become effective, because Europeans have good reasons for preventing these policies from getting off the ground: they are unable to identify with them in cultural terms or control them in democratic terms. In other words, CFSP enjoys neither an effective nor a civic source of legitimacy, and this in turn prevents it from acquiring a utilitarian form of legitimacy based on that effectiveness.

The lack of identity and democratic credentials is bad in itself. But there are three additional reasons for treating this problem as a special kind of challenge. First, the assertion of identity and democracy in international relations is quite novel, and so suspicion, incomprehension, and even lack of proper frame of reference is the order of the day. Diplomats and soldiers are usually insensitive towards any kind of cultural argument. Many of them are likewise reluctant to allow greater transparency, let alone public scrutiny, over their work. Besides, the identity language of culture and anthropology cannot be easily translated into the language of diplomatic negotiations and military planning. Nor is it easy to talk about security in terms of transparency, ballot box, and *demos*. The problem is that international politics used to operate according to different rules and time frames than identity and democracy. It is one thing to conclude that democracy and identity are important for common foreign policies to get off the ground, yet it is quite another to argue that identity and democracy represent the answer for coping with major international challenges. Can one say how foreign policies ought to be run from the identity and democracy perspective?

Second, neither democracy nor identity are easy targets for crafting and engineering. In other words, there is little the Union can effectively do in order to address them. Institutions can well be reformed, interests can be merged, and powers can be balanced. But culture and legitimacy cannot just be fixed by a decision, compromise, or a balancing act such as SALT or the CFE Treaty. They involve a delicate long-term relationship between the people and the policy-makers without ready-made blueprints for success. It is difficult to know how to engineer affection for a new European patria, likewise there is no reason to believe that new forms of internet or voucher democracy will enhance rather than damage the democratic credentials of the system.

Third, and most important, requirements of democracy and identity run against the requirements imposed on us by modernization and global competition. To be successful one must act very quickly, operate globally rather than locally, delegate tasks to numerous "unknown" and "impersonal" units, and accept various concentric and multi-layered arrangements. Today the most effective units must recognize complexity, flexibility, and dispersion. Effective governance requires, to use Philippe Schmitter's words "growing dissociation between authoritative allocations, territorial constituencies and functional competencies."[5] It requires opening the way for institutional diversity – "for a multitude of relatively independent European arrangements with distinct statuses, functions, resources and operating under different decision rules."[6] But identity and democracy require transparency, simplicity and a sense of belonging to a defined community. Democracy can hardly work in a complicated if not impenetrable system of multi-layered and multi-speed arrangements that are run by an ever-changing group of unidentified and unaccountable people. Likewise affection and identity can hardly develop in a complex system of open-ended arrangements, with fluid membership, variable purpose, and a net of concentric functional frames of cooperation.

The first two points indicate why it is difficult to address the legitimacy issue. The third point shows why the legitimacy issue needs to be addressed. The Union has to perform in an environment that is more and more complex, competitive, and rapidly changing. This is why the Union cannot just hope and pray that the identity and democracy problems will somehow go away. There is no reason to believe that Europeans are prepared to fall at the mercy of foreign policies that are neither shaped nor supported by them. Unless the Union is able to mitigate people's concerns about the democracy/identity deficit, it will be unable to cope with the outside world. Unless Europeans are able to treat common policies as truly "theirs" the CFSP will remain in a state of paralysis.

What can be done? How can this vicious cycle be stopped? The answer is: begin by making some strategic choices. People should be told what the foreign policy of the Union is all about. These choices are to be about the EU's basic purpose, functions, and territory. Europeans need to know whether common foreign policies are about building a "nation writ large" or about something novel.[7] They need to know whether common foreign policies will eventually include defense functions or remain confined to trade and diplomacy. They also need to know who is the subject of these policies in terms of a territorially-defined community.

Making these basic choices will do away with the comfortable ambiguity that has allowed the Union to promote integration in disguise. Making these choices will damage the chances of a negatively permissive consensus concerning integration.[8] Making these choices will catalyze conflicts between those who will lose and those who will gain as a result. Making these choices will also reduce the Union's flexibility for some years to come. But I have indicated that the kind of ambiguity and flexibility practiced by the Union in recent years proved to be a mixed blessing. Fixing the Union's moving borders will let people know who the subjects of foreign policies are and why. The EU cannot be everything for everybody. By stating clearly what its foreign policies are, the Union will restrict its action to publicly visible objectives which is, after all, an element of democratic practice.[9]

Of course, the point is not to fix everything but to look for a proper balance between the requirements of effectiveness and legitimacy. The point is to fix some issues at the strategic level in order to gain some flexibility at the operational level. It is to find a proper balance between the logic of modernity and the logic of tradition, community, and identity. It is to start making some valuable foreign policies that enjoy broad public backing. In short the point is to do away with Euro-paralysis.

But can one expect Europe's politicians to make all these difficult choices? Do Europe's politicians have any interest in taking risks by making all these difficult choices in the absence of broad public pressure? And can one expect the people of Europe to take the initiative? Identifying the sickness and prescribing the medicine is important. But will the patient take the medicine? First of all, the essence of politics is making difficult choices amidst conflicting evidence and multiple pressures. Avoiding decisions and fudging solutions is also a sort of choice, as the strategy of integration in disguise has clearly shown. Second, in the European system of representative democracy, identifying and making basic choices is the task of elected politicians. If they are presented with certain choices but fail to make them, they are held accountable by their electorates. When the failure of the CFSP project produces damaging implications, elected politicians will find it difficult to hide behind unelected bureaucrats in Brussels. Third, there is no evidence to argue that the public is basically not interested in the complexities of foreign policies, while politicians are merely interested in their short-term parochial power games. The CFSP as such may never stir up public emotions or re-educate selfish politicians. However, the argument that neither the European public nor their elected officials care about the well being of their continent and will accordingly take no medicine to improve the situation is highly cynical, naïve, and beyond comprehension.

Which choices should be made? What is the prescribed medicine? One choice is to opt for a civilian-power model for the Union, the other is to define the borders of the Union.

A CIVILIAN POWER REVISITED

When François Duchène began to promote a vision of a "civilian power" in Europe a quarter of a century ago, he was attacked from many different corners. Duchène never developed his vision into a detailed and comprehensive scheme. However, he forcefully put forward five major arguments. First, there is no point in trying to build up a European superpower. Such a superpower would need to become a nuclear, centralized state with a strong sense of collective nationalism; a distant prospect in Duchène's view. "European gaullism is a contradiction in terms," he argued.[10] A major power is not the same as a superpower: Europe's leverage cannot and should not be exerted along traditional lines.

Second, there is little point in trying to build up a European army because today there is more scope for civilian forms of action and influence. Duchène argued that the lack of military power is not the handicap it once was, and may even be an advantage because it eliminates suspicion about Europe's intentions and allows it to act as an unbiased moderator. Besides, Europe is too vulnerable in physical and psychological terms to make a military power truly self protecting.[11]

Third, Europe should try to "domesticate" relations between states by trying to inject into international relations a sense of "common responsibility" and structures of "contractual politics."[12] It must act as a model or example of a new type of interstate relationship that is able to overcome the age-old legacy of war, intimidation, and violence.

Fourth, Europe should remain true to its core characteristics which are civilian means and ends, a built-in sense of collective action, and promotion of the social values of equality, justice, and tolerance. The European Community, he argued, must be a "force for the international diffusion of civilian and democratic standards or it will itself be the victim of power politics run by powers stronger and more cohesive than itself... there is no statesmanship without generosity."[13]

Fifth, Europe can only succeed if it becomes a cohesive and purposeful international actor. Since the Community will remain a "hybrid creature" – neither a collection of disparate nations nor a full-fledged power center – a great deal will depend on the "precise degree of cohesion it can master." The Community must acquire a "sense of its corporate capacity to act."[14]

Critics accused Duchène of ignoring the significance of military power and argued that a civilian power would hardly be in a position to cope with the uncivilized world. As Dominique Moïsi put it in 1982: "In a world which is fully rediscovering the scope of strategies and the most classic aspects of power politics, Europe cannot expect to see the continuation of that civil power about which François Duchène spoke at the beginning of the seventies."[15]

Critics also argued that a civilian power Europe would be condemned to superpower domination. Hedley Bull, in particular, lamented the vulnerability of the countries of Western Europe for so long as they remain without means to provide for their own military security. He called a civilian power Europe "a contradiction in terms" and advocated a "Western European military alliance with appropriate machinery attached to it."[16]

Other critics accused Duchène of making a virtue out of necessity: Europe is unable to become a full-fledged international actor and tries to sell its failure as a success. Duchène was also found "guilty" of lacing his ideas with a large dose of moralism and utopian *naïveté*.

Some of this criticism was clearly unfair. For instance, Duchène never suggested that military power be ignored, but believed that it would not be very wise for Europe to seek military dominance.

Likewise Duchène never said that Europe cannot pursue assertive politics, he only said that Europe should rely on civilian rather than military means and on a special kind of "civilian" purpose. He also never said that Europe should be at the mercy of superpowers. He merely said that Europe could better utilize its strengths by being a civilian power rather than a military superpower or a superstate.

More importantly, the last 25 years have reinforced rather than weakened Duchène's arguments. A traditional superpower status for Europe has neither become more possible nor more desirable since the early 1970s. Europe is no longer at the mercy of superpower domination that so troubled Hedley Bull at the time of the Cold War. The Soviet Union is gone and the EU is now much less dependent on US military protection. The world has not become more civilized in recent years, but the politics of violence and brutal force have been largely confined to areas outside the Western world and do not directly threaten the wealth and integrity of the Union as such. Moreover, the character of current international competition favors civilian rather than military factors. Most of today's successful international actors have a strong economy and a legitimate government either in cultural or civic terms. Military power remains important, but its utility has clearly diminished. If all these arguments are correct there are no problems in making a virtue out of necessity. Europe is indeed unable to become a true military actor, but why should it try to become one? In this book I have argued that aspiring to military power status would be an expensive, divisive, and basically futile exercise for the Union.[17] It is time to state this very clearly so the public knows what the Union is all about.

As always, there are no costless solutions, but in this case the price is not very high. A civilian power Europe does not mean that the Union would be totally defenseless. National armies will stay in place and NATO is not to be dissolved. The Western European Union will also remain active and may even grow in strength; however, more as a European pillar within NATO than a EU defense arm. Nor should one worry that the CFSP would remain totally toothless. Economic and political leverage can well be used in a shrewd and effective manner for many international objectives. In fact, if one thinks about the three most important tasks for the CFSP – managing relations with the US, managing interstate relations within the Union, and stabilizing the Union's borders – civilian rather than military means seem to be most appropriate. Military force might prove indispensable in stabilizing the EU's borders, but so might economic help, political dialogue, and cultural cooperation. In other words, one should avoid the impression that managing local violent conflicts is the prime CFSP objective, that military means are always the most suitable for handling these conflicts, and that there is no other actor but the Union to apply force in such violent conflicts.

Divorcing foreign policies from defense policies would be a difficult if not awkward operation, but the idea is to bring together under one pillar foreign policy and external trade, which are now divided in an equally awkward manner.

Opting for a civilian power Europe would represent a change both in terms of law and image. The Maastricht Treaty prescribes an open-ended set of tasks for the Union: the CFSP "shall include all questions related to the security of the Union, including the eventual framing of a common defense policy, which might in time lead to a common defense."[18] The Draft Treaty of Amsterdam further upgraded the defense commitment albeit in a rather ambiguous manner. The Treaty no longer refers to "eventual" collective security, but now institutes "progressive" framing of a common defense policy, which might lead to common defense, "should the European Council decide so."[19]

But the problem is even more serious in the world of concepts, perceptions, and images: the Union is about many different things to many different people. There is hardly any serious analysis about the CFSP that would not bring forward the issue of defense incapacity and suggest some ways of mitigating it. There is a need to reduce if not terminate this ambiguity and confusion. Opting for a civilian power Europe would represent one of the basic strategic choices that could help the Union acquire a distinct profile – so important in terms of identity and legitimacy. Another step would be to define the borders of the European Union.

It is also crucial to establish a clear division of labor between the various European institutions. Opting for a civilian-controlled Europe would make it clear that collective defense on the continent is provided principally by NATO. The WEU would undertake only those local humanitarian and peace-keeping operations in which the United States chose not to get involved directly. The Union would concentrate on diplomatic missions, applying its enormous economic and political leverage to that aim. Since the construction of a new order in a broader Europe is principally a matter of economics and politics, the CFSP is likely to acquire paramount importance in the years to come, even without a defense component.

BORDERS OF THE UNION

If the questions of identity and democracy are at the root of Euro-paralysis, then borders are of prime importance. Identity is basically about belonging to a certain kind of community that lives on a certain territory and cherishes certain types of norms. Democratic rules and norms must also operate within a clearly-defined territory and for a territorially-defined demos. As Pierre Manent rightly put it:

> Instituting a political order, prior to consulting the will of any individuals, requires first the staking out of a common territory. A common territory is the barest requirement of a political community, to be sure, but it is also in a sense the most necessary ... What is this body politic, this "political Europe" that people talk about, when it cannot even clear the minimum hurdle of fixing a common territory ... Europe is now only a high-sounding but abstract frame for democratic individualism ... But while I readily admit that one can renounce the nation as a political form, I do not believe that people can live long within civilization alone without some sense of political belonging (which is necessarily exclusive), and thus without some definition of what is held in common.[20]

Yet the borders of the Community, and later of the Union, have been moving quite regularly due to successive waves of enlargement. At the beginning, there were six founding member states, now there are no less than 15 members, and we are openly talking about admitting the next six, ten, or more new members in the years to come. It is not suggested that this process of regular, if not indefinite enlargement, should be brought to a halt, but that it be done under certain conditions and in a special manner. A simple rejection of any new members would do more harm than good. The issue of EU's borders is as complex as it is sensitive. First of all, it is difficult to talk about the Union's boundary in merely legal and institutional terms.[21] Geopolitical, transactional, and cultural boundaries, to use Michael Smith's terms, have always been equally crucial for the EC/EU.[22] The eastern border of the EC has been the most sensitive security center point (or rather center line) in the world. After the fall of the Berlin Wall the eastern border of the Union has become a line demarcating the zone of peace with the security "gray zone," or the zone of turmoil and disorder.[23] Should the project of extending the zone of peace be abandoned? The cultural boundary, however, has been and still is particularly important for the identity of the Union in both ethnic and civic terms. One cannot make the gap between cultural and legal/institutional boundaries in Europe too wide by either including culturally alien entities into the Union or excluding from it culturally similar ones.

Second, in a Union of concentric circles and variable geometry it is difficult to talk about only one type of legal and institutional boundary. Various opt-outs negotiated by some countries in terms of social and defense policy, for instance, created internal boundaries of sorts in addition to external ones. Moreover, it is not very clear whether some neutral EU countries such as Sweden, Ireland, or Austria will always remain full-fledged CFSP actors despite all the legal/institutional arrangements. The envisaged European Monetary Union will create another type of internal boundary. A further process of enlargement will probably introduce new concentric circles and new forms of variable geometry confusing the issue of boundary even further.

Third, global and modern pressures increasingly "unbound" territoriality, making the existing borders less impermeable if not open. As John Gerard Ruggie forcefully argued, a "disjointed, mutually exclusive and fixed territoriality" is becoming an old-fashioned concept as it is impossible to control the flow of goods, capital, and services across the existing borders, not to mention international criminals, refugees, and global communication newsbreakers.[24] In the field of security it is increasingly difficult to talk about a "territorial-based defense," "national (or European) defense-industrial capacity," or about a "sovereign" right to unilateral military intervention. Borders remain as they are and they are not becoming totally unimportant. But they are more for "crossing rather than defending," and they are more prone to "adjustments" than to being "fixed" and "maintained."[25]

Fourth, keeping the prospect of enlargement open provides the Union with effective international leverage. Many countries on the continent are willing to modify their behavior along EU wishes in the hope of obtaining EU membership. Fixing borders will deprive the Union of part of its attraction and will demotivate if not frustrate countries that are left out.

Fifth, not establishing territorial boundaries might be critical to avoid antagonizing potential enemies and coaxing them to join. If Ukraine, Turkey, or even Russia have the prospect of joining the Union at some point there is less reason for them to fear successive waves of enlargement of the previously "suspicious" Western club. Moreover, one can even argue that the enticing proposition of participating in a Trans-Atlantic Free Trade Area outweighs any US suspicion of Europe's strengthened position.[26]

The project of fixing EU borders cannot ignore the above-mentioned arguments. While the identity/democracy deficit requires further definition of EU's borders one should avoid policies that are either irrelevant or counter productive. What should be done exactly? The answer is: adopt a clear policy of differentiation in the process of enlargement and elaborate a sound cooperative framework with the countries that are initially left out. Some kind of enlargement cannot and should not be avoided, but it must not further undermine the Union's cultural identity and democratic credentials. Enlargement should also reflect the civilian, non-military nature of the Union, which was discussed in the previous section.

However, the adopted policy of enlargement is clearly in conflict with such recommendations. At the December 1997 Luxembourg European Council, the Union decided to open accession negotiations with five aspiring Eastern European countries – Slovenia, Estonia, the Czech Republic, Poland, and Hungary – plus Cyprus. Bulgaria, Latvia, Lithuania, Romania, and Slovakia together with the above mentioned six "front-runners" were offered the so-called "pre-accession partnership," complete with financial aid and an annual review to see if new countries should join the negotiations. The major problem with this decision is not that the list of "front-runners" is improper, but that it presents the enlargement as a continuous process with different countries joining the Union as soon as they satisfy a set of criteria, which are unclear besides.[27] As the Agenda 2000 puts it, enlargement is "an inclusive process embracing *all* of the applicant countries," and the EU Commissioner Van den Broek added: "there are no 'ins and outs' but rather 'ins and pre-ins.'"[28] It is uncertain whether this approach will indeed satisfy, let alone motivate Eastern European candidates, but it is certain that it neglects the internal "democracy/identity" dimension that has been found to be so important on these pages. How can the cultural identity of the Union be enhanced by the prospect of an open-ended enlargement? How can democratic control be asserted over the enlargement process, which is shaped by a complicated web of negotiations between the Union and so many different states? Would it not be easier for the Union's citizens to accept an enlargement that proceeds in easily identifiable stages with only a few countries taken in the first round? Is not the enlargement model chosen by NATO an example for the EU to follow?

Fixing the scope of enlargement and a time frame may indeed frustrate those applicant countries initially left out.[29] But what about the frustration of those countries in the region that deserve "privileged" EU treatment? Besides, if the situation in Slovakia or Turkey were to deteriorate, it would be more due to the democratic deficit and economic mismanagement there rather than to the Union's failure to grant them an "entrance ticket" at a discount price. And is it not right to argue that promising EU membership *only* to undisputed economic and democratic champions creates the best incentive for the laggards to improve their records? In other words, the current ambiguity is demotivating rather than motivating. The champions are not granted adequate benefits, while the laggards are not truly deterred from "misbehaving." The Union's "soft" differentiation approach is likely to end in frustration among all candidate countries.

The current enlargement policy also ignores the civilian character of the Union: the Union lacks military capabilities, and as I argued, it would be imprudent for it to seek them in the future. This suggests that both NATO's and the EU's enlargements should proceed in parallel so that the Union is not exposed to security challenges which it cannot handle on its own. However, the list of countries chosen to join NATO in the first round does not overlap with the list of "front-runners" to the EU.[30] The latter includes Estonia with its large and assertive Russian minority, and Slovenia with its recent, albeit short, legacy of the Balkan war. This is not to suggest that Estonia and Slovenia be left at the mercy of their local hegemonds, Russia and Serbia. However, there are good reasons to believe that de-coupling NATO and EU enlargements would import insecurity into the Union rather than export security to the new members.

In short, the current EU policy of keeping the prospect of enlargement ambiguously open and decoupled from NATO enlargement does not properly address the needs of Eastern Europe, and it provides those in Western Europe who oppose *any* enlargement of the EU with ammunition to support their arguments. Public support for eastward enlargement should not be taken for granted. Failure to present the Western European public with a clear-cut, if not more modest, policy of enlargement may prove fatal to the entire project, with detrimental effects for both parts of Europe. The recommended solution would basically amount to three things. First of all, the Union should state clearly that it is going to embrace only the most "Western" countries in terms of economics, democracy, and culture. This means that the idea of building the Union from Lisbon to Vladivostok and Istanbul should be refuted and forgotten. Countries such as Belarus, Ukraine, Russia, and Turkey should be embraced in different ways than by offering EU membership. Secondly further enlargement should proceed in stages, with only three countries admitted in the first round: Hungary, Poland, and the Czech Republic; all of which will be future NATO members.[31] Including them in the Union will not produce a culture shock, it will export security rather than import insecurity, and it will not involve excessive economic costs.[32]

Thirdly, the Baltic states, Slovakia, Slovenia, Bulgaria, and Romania should be given a chance to join the Union in the second round, but only after fully consolidating their still-fragile democracies, resolving their still-acute ethnic minority problems, and getting closer to the Union in (post)modern and (post)industrial cultural terms. They should also succeed in obtaining NATO membership before EU accession.

Countries initially left out should be offered substantial trade and travel possibilities, cultural cooperation, and foreign policy assistance. As argued in one of the previous chapters, defining borders should not imply closing them. The aim is not to embark on the policy of exclusion, but on a policy of access and cooperation. The aim is to overcome the identity/democracy deficit and not to insulate the Union from its members. The aim is not to indulge in a policy of discrimination, but to adopt a policy that is digestible for the Union's electorate. A limited enlargement in stages is better than no enlargement whatsoever due to the current fuzziness, ambiguity, and paralysis.

A policy of fixing borders of the European Union would thus require skillful balancing and many complex trade-offs. This will not be easy as it is increasingly evident that one of the main political dividing lines in Europe is between those who seek to overcome geographical boundaries – a "party of globalization," as Charles S. Maier put it – and those who seek to restore and reinforce the existing boundaries – a "party of territoriality."[33] But of course, simple and costless solutions do not exist in Europe today. As Jean-Marie Guéhenno has observed:

> Stripped of the certainties of the age of nation-states, when civil society was a given – the legacy on which all sorts of political constructs could be built – we have no convenient formula for defining the scope of our solidarities. There is no legacy today that may not be contested. There is no longer any historical, social or territorial given. The definition of civil society, the delimitation of frontiers, the institution of a political entity have become our choice.[34]

The argument of this book is that the Union cannot refrain from making some basic choices, and I tried to suggest which choices ought to be made, however imperfect.

If one believes that at the core of the Union's problems is its lack of democratic legitimacy and cultural identity then it is difficult to escape questions like: What are the Union's territory and borders? Who forms the European polity? What is the Union's basic aim and purpose? What are the limits of the Union's involvement? Defining Europe's borders and adopting a civilian profile will not by itself make people love the awkward acronym: CFSP. But it may help them see and comprehend what the CFSP is all about. It may open a broader discourse about the form and content of common foreign policies. It may help to identify a set of policies that reflect the real, rather than abstract, interests of citizens across the entire Union. A genuine and lasting public support for such policies may then follow, inducing change in the behavior of Europe's politicians and of the national governments run by them.

Euro-paralysis in foreign policy is still with us despite successive political earthquakes, institutional readjustments, and leadership changes. But addressing identity and democracy issues may finally help to overcome it.

NOTES

1. As I argued earlier, national interests and national identities are interconnected but they are largely about different things. See Ch.2 n.104.
2. Anthony Smith relates the question of legitimacy to the issue of cultural identity, while Jürgen Habermas to the issue of citizenship. Joseph Weiler, on the other hand, distinguishes between "formal" (legal) and "social" (empirical) legitimacy. See Jürgen Habermas, "Citizenship and National Identity: Some Reflections on the Future of Europe", *Praxis International*, Vol. 12, No. 1 (1992), pp. 3 and 12, and Antony Smith, "National Identity and the Idea of European Unity", *International Affairs*, Vol. 68, No. 1 (1992), p. 68.
3. According to the opinion polls published in May 1994 by the *Eurobarometer*: "Over the last four years, public support for a common defense and a common foreign policy rose, now remaining at high levels (75% and 68% respectively.) See *Eurobarometer*, No. 41 (July 1994), Highlights (no page given). According to the survey conducted in November–December 1995, 69% of respondents supported a common foreign policy, while 73% expressed support for an EU-wide defense and military policy. See *Eurobarometer*, No. 44 (Spring 1996), pp. 42–44.
4. For a more in-depth analysis of problems in analyzing public opinion in the field of foreign affairs see K.J. Holsti, *International Politics – a Framework for Analysis*, (Englewood Cliffs, NJ: Prentice-Hall, 1977), p. 280.

5. Philippe C. Schmitter, "Imagining the Future of the Euro-Polity with the Help of New Concepts", in *Governance in the European Union*, Gary Marks, Fritz W. Scharpf, Philippe C. Schmitter and Wolfgang Streek, eds. (London: Sage, 1996), p. 132.

6. Ibidem, p. 127.

7. The term is borrowed from Max Kohnstamm and Wolfgang Hager, eds., *A Nation Writ Large? Foreign-Policy Problems Before the European Community* (London: Macmillan, 1973), p. 275.

8. However, one can argue that as far as the European public is concerned the permissive consensus is now working in reverse. While in the past it was possible for Eurocrats to rely on permissive consensus for forging integration, today the public is clearly happy to tolerate non-cooperation among EU member states, even at the cost of reduced effectiveness.

9. As Philippe C. Schmitter put it: "Under ideal conditions, democracies should arrive at their decisions through a process of disclosure and deliberation in which citizens – collective as well as individual – restrict their actions and positions to those that are publicly visible and defensible." (Unpublished manuscript, p. 11).

10. François Duchène, "The European Community and the Uncertainties of Interdependence", in *A Nation Writ Large? Foreign-Policy Problems Before the European Community*, op. cit., p. 11.

11. As Duchène put it: "The psychological and physical vulnerability of cramped urbanized societies to threats of nuclear attack, and the inner diversity of what would still be a politically loose agglomeration of power, would make it inconceivable for a European deterrent to be anything but self-protecting." See François Duchène, "Europe's Role in World Peace", in *Europe Tomorrow. Sixteen Europeans Look Ahead*, Richard Mayne, ed. (London: Fontana/Collins, 1972), pp. 37–8.

12. Françoise Duchène, "The European Community and Uncertainties of Interdependence", op. cit., pp. 19 and 20.

13. Ibidem, p. 20.

14. François Duchène, "Europe's Role in World Peace," op. cit., pp. 45 and 47.

15. Dominique Moïsi, "Comment", *Journal of Common Market Studies*, Vol. 21, No. 1 and 2 (September–December 1981), p. 165.

16. Hedley Bull, "Civilian Power Europe: A Contradiction in Terms?", *Journal of Common Market Studies*, Vol. 21, No. 1 and 2 (September–December 1982), p. 164.

17. Domestic problems apart, one should consider that other powers may be tempted to adopt a policy of military balancing *vis-à-vis* the Union, and may even try to prevent by force a forthcoming militarization of the Union. See, e.g., Ralf Dahrendorf, *A New World Order? Problems and Prospects of International Relations in the 1980s* (Ghana: University of Ghana, 1979), p. 46.

18. Article J.4 (1) of the Treaty of the European Union, Maastricht, December 1991. EPC only concerned the "political and economic aspects of security".

19. Art. J.7. Draft Treaty of Amsterdam.

20. Pierre Manent, "On Modern Individualism", *Journal of Democracy*, Vol. 7, No. 1 (January 1996), pp. 7–8.
21. Here, one should emphasize the difference between borders and frontiers. See Friedrich Kratochwil, "Of Systems, Boundaries and Territoriality: An Inquiry Into the Formation of the State System", *World Politics*, Vol. 34, No. 1 (October 1986), pp. 27–52.
22. See Michael Smith, "The European Union and a Changing Europe: Establishing the Boundaries of Order", *Journal of Common Market Studies*, Vol. 34, No. 1 (March 1996), p. 13.
23. The terms "zone of turmoil" and "zone of peace" have been developed in Aaron B. Wildavsky and Max Singer, *The Real World Order: Zones of Peace and Zones of Turmoil* (Chatham, NJ: Chatham House, 1993), pp. 14–35. Concerning the description of a "grey zone" see Jan Zielonka, "Le paradoxes de la politique étrangère polonaise," *Politique Étrangère*, Vol. 59, No. 1 (Spring 1994), pp. 105–6.
24. See John Gerard Ruggie, "Territoriality and Beyond: Problematizing Modernity in International Relations", *International Organization*, Vol. 47, No. 1 (Winter 1993), pp. 171–4.
25. See Michael Smith, "The European Union and a Changing Europe", op. cit., p. 23.
26. I owe this argument to Richard Rosecrance. For a more elaborated version of it see: Richard Rosecrance, "EU: a new type of international actor," in *Paradoxes of European Foreign Policy*, Jan Zielonka, ed., (London: Kluwer Law International, 1998), forthcoming.
27. As pointed out in the third chapter, Agenda 2000 provides a long list of entrance criteria, but there was no attempt to weight them or provide any system of prioritizing the numerous requirements. In the meantime, the selection of countries to enter the Union in the first stage seems to be more guided by regional power politics than by "objective" analysis of progress in meeting the entrance criteria. For instance, it is hard to deny that Estonia and Slovenia have been added to the list of front-runners in order to satisfy the need for an internal balance of power between the Northern and Southern EU countries: Slovenia was strongly supported by Italy and other Southern member states, while Scandinavian member-states insisted on the inclusion of at least one Baltic country.
28. She Hans van den Broek, "No new dividing lines," *Financial Times*, September 22, 1997. For a comprehensive analysis of the differentiation policy of enlargement see Horst Günter Krenzler, The EU and Central-East Europe: The Implications of Enlargement in Stages, *Policy Papers*, No. 97/2 (Florence: Robert Schuman Centre, 1997) or Susan Senior-Nello and Karen E. Smith, "The Consequences of Eastern Enlargement of the European Union in Stages," *EUI Working Papers*, RSC No. 97/51 (Florence: Robert Schuman Centre, 1997).
29. In fact, the Luxembourg Council's decision not to offer a "pre-accession partnership" to Turkey instantly produced an angry reaction from this country whose application to join the EU has been on table since 1963. See "Turkey and the EU: not so fast," *The Economist*, December 20, 1997, p. 30.

30. In fact it has been revealed to me by a top Swedish official that non-NATO EU member states were particularly adamant against automatically applying NATO's list of would-be members to EU enlargement; since they were not part of NATO, they could only participate in the enlargement decision through the EU.
31. The Union's policy of reviewing second-round countries' applications each year is a watered-down version of having distinct steps for enlargement. See Agenda 2000 Volume I – Communication: For a stronger and wider Union, Stasbourg, 15 July 1997. The Commission suggested to open talks with five, not three, aspiring members from Eastern Europe, and the Luxembourg European Council endorsed this Suggestion.
32. In fact, the identity of the Union may well suffer if these countries are refused admission. After all, their struggle for economic freedom and democracy exemplifies the system of values which forms the moral foundation of the European Union.
33. See Charles S. Maier, "After the Left: The Two Parties in Contemporary Democracies," a paper presented at the International Conference on "Democratic Politics: The Agenda of the Future," organized by the Institute for Human Sciences, Vienna, June 11–14, 1997, unpublished draft, pp. 11–13.
34. Jean-Marie Guéhenno, *The End of the Nation-State* (Minneapolis and London: University of Minnesota Press, 1995), p. 48.

Selected Bibliography

Adler, Emmanuel and Beverly Crawford (eds.): *Progress in Post-War International Relations*, (New York: Cambridge University Press, 1991).

Algieri, Franco and Elfriede Regelsberger (eds.): *Synergy at Work: Spain and Portugal in European Foreign Policy* (Bonn: Europa Union Verlag, 1996).

Aliboni, Roberto (ed.): *Southern European Security in the 1990s* (London: Pinter, 1992).

Allin, Dana H.: *Cold War Illusion: America, Europe and Soviet Power, 1969–1989* (New York: St Martin's Press, 1995).

Allison, Graham and Gregory Treverton (eds.): *Rethinking American Security: Beyond Cold War to New World Order* (New York: W. W. Norton, 1992).

Alting von Geusau, Frans: *De Som der delen. Europa voor en na de omwenteling* (Amsterdam: Meulenhoff, 1991).

Andeweg, Rudy: "The Reshaping of National Party Systems", *West European Politics*, Vol. 18, No. 3 (July 1995), pp. 58–79.

Aron, Raymond: *On War* (London: Secker & Warburg, 1958).

Ashley, Richard K.: "The Geopolitics of Geopolitical Space: Toward a Critical Social Theory of International Politics", *Alternatives*, Vol. XII, No. 4 (October 1987), pp. 403–34.

Bakke, Elisabeth: "Towards a European Identity?", *Arena Working Papers* No. 10 (April 1995).

Barbé, Esther: "The Barcelona Conference: Launching Pad of a Process", *Mediterranean Politics*, Vol. 1, No. 1 (Summer 1996), pp. 25–42.

Barber, Benjamin: *Strong Democracy: Participatory Politics for a New Age* (Berkeley: University of California Press, 1994).

Beck, U.: *Risk Society: Towards a New Modernity* (London: Sage, 1992).

Bertram, Christoph: "Multilateral Diplomacy and Conflict Resolution", *Survival*, Vol. 37, No. 4 (Winter 1995–96), pp. 65–82.

Bertram, Christoph: *Europe in the Balance: Securing the Peace Won in the Cold War* (Washington, DC: Carnegie Endowment for International Peace, 1995).

Betts, Richard: "Wealth, Power, and Instability: East Asia and the United States after Cold War", *International Security*, Vol. 18, No. 3 (Winter 1993/94), pp. 34–77.

Betz, Hans-Georg: *Radical Right-Wing Populism in Western Europe* (London: Macmillan, 1994).

Bildt, Carl: "The Baltic Litmus Test", *Foreign Affairs*, Vol. 73, No. 4 (September–October 1994), p. 72–85.

Binnendijk, Hans and Patrick Clawson: "New Strategic Priorities", *The Washington Quarterly*, Vol. 18, No. 2 (1995), pp. 109–26.

Blechman, Barry M.: "The Intervention Dilemma", *The Washington Quarterly*, Vol. 18, No. 3 (Summer 1995), pp. 63–73.

Bloes, Robert: *Le 'Plan Fouchet' et le problème de l'Europe politique* (Bruges: Collège d'Europe, 1970).

Bloom, William: *Personal Identity, National Identity and International Relations* (Cambridge: Cambridge University Press, 1990).

Blunden, Margaret: "Insecurity on Europe's Southern Flank", *Survival*, Vol. 36, No. 2 (Summer 1994), pp. 134–48.

Bodenheimer, Susanne J.: *Political Union: A Microcosm of European Politics 1960–1966* (Leiden: Sijthoff, 1967).

Booth, Ken: "Human Wrongs and International Relations", *International Affairs*, Vol. 71, No. 1 (1995), pp. 103–26.

Booth, Ken: "Security and Emancipation", *Review of International Studies*, Vol. 17, No. 4 (October 1991), pp. 313–26.

Booth, Ken and Peter Vale: "Security in Southern Africa: After Apartheid, Beyond Realism", *International Affairs*, Vol. 71, No. 2 (April 1995), pp. 285–304.

Bot, Bernard Rudolf: "Cooperation between the Diplomatic Missions of the Ten in Third Countries and International Organisations", *Legal Issues of European Integration*, Vol. 1 (1984), pp. 149–69.

Brands, Maarten: "The Obsolence of almost all Theories concerning International Relations," *Uhlenbeck Lecture No 14*, (Wassenaar: The Netherlands Institute for Advanced Study in the Humanities and Social Sciences, 1996), pp. 3–28.

Brands, Maarten: "Van de luwte in de drup: noodzaak van een beweeglijker Nederlands buitenlands beleid na de revolutie van 1989", *Internationale Spectator*, Vol. 47, No. 1 (January 1993), pp. 6–12.

Brands, Maarten: "Een tijd vol misvattingen: de vereiniging van Duitsland", *Internationale Spectator*, Vol. 44, No. 5 (May 1990), pp. 268–72.

Broek (van den), Hans: "Why Europe needs a common foreign and security policy", *European Foreign Affairs Review*, Vol. 1., No. 1 (July 1996), pp. 1–5.

Broek (van den), Hans: *The Common Foreign and Security Policy of the European Union – An Initial Assessment* (The Hague: Clingendael Institute, May 24, 1994).

Brown, Michael E. (ed.): *The International Dimensions of Internal Conflict* (Cambridge, MA: MIT Press, 1996).

Brzezinski, Zbigniew: *Out of Control. Global Turmoil on the Eve of the 21st Century* (New York: Maxwell Macmillan, 1993).

Buchan, Alastair: *The End of the Postwar Era* (London: Weidenfeld and Nicolson, 1974).

Bull, Hedley: "Civilian Power Europe: A Contradiction in Terms?", *Journal of Common Market Studies*, Vol. 21, Nos. 1 and 2 (September–December 1982), pp. 149–69.

Bull, Hedley and Adam Watson (eds.): *The Expansion of International Society* (Oxford: Clarendon Press, 1992).

Bulmer, Simon: "Domestic Politics and European Community Policy-Making", *Journal of Common Market Studies*, Vol. 21 (1981/1982), pp. 349–63.

Burghardt, Günther and Fraser Cameron: "The Next Enlargement of the European Union", *European Foreign Affairs Review*, Vol. 2, No. 1 (Spring 1997), pp. 7–21.

Burley, Anne-Marie and Walter Mattli: "Europe Before the Court: A Political Theory of Legal Integration", *International Organization*, Vol. 47, No. 1 (Winter 1993), pp. 41–76.

Buzan, Barry: *People, States and Fear: The National Security Problem in International Relations* (Hemel Hempstead: Harvest Wheatsheaf, 1983), first edition.

Cable, Vincent: "What Is International Economic Security?", *International Affairs*, Vol. 71, No. 2 (April 1995), pp. 305–24.

Calleo, David P.: *The German Problem Reconsidered: Germany and the World Order 1870 to the Present* (Cambridge: Cambridge University Press, 1978).

Calleo, David P.: *Europe's Future: the Grand Alternatives* (London: Hodder & Stoughton, 1967).

Carlsnaes, Walter and Steven Smith (eds.): *European Foreign Policy. The EC and Changing Perspectives in Europe* (London: Sage, 1994).

Carr, E. H.: *Nationalism and After* (London: Macmillan, 1945).

Carrington, P. A. R. C. (Lord): "European Political Cooperation: America Should Welcome It", *International Affairs*, Vol. 58, No. 1 (Winter 1981/82), pp. 1–6.

Cassese, Antonio (ed.): *Parliamentary Control Over Foreign Policy: Legal Essays* (Alphen aan den Rijn: Sijthoff and Noordhoff, 1980).

Chay, Jongsuk (ed.): *Culture and International Relations* (New York and London: Praeger, 1990).

Chevènement, Jean-Pierre: *France-Allemangne: parlons franc* (Paris: Plon, 1996).

Chipman, John: "The Future of Strategic Studies: Beyond Even Grand Strategy", *Survival*, Vol. 34, No. 1, pp.109–31.

Chipman, John: *French Power in Africa* (Oxford: Blackwell, 1989).

Clesse, Armand, Richard Cooper and Yoshikazu Sakamoro (eds.): *The International System After the Collapse of the East-West Order* (Dordrecht and London: Martinus Nijhoff, 1994).

Clesse, Armand and Raymond Vernon (eds.): *The European Community after 1992: A New Role in World Politics?* (Baden Baden: Nomos, 1991).

Constantinou, Costas M.: "NATO's Caps: European Security and the Future of the North Atlantic Alliance", *Alternatives*, Vol. 20, No. 2 (April–June 1995), pp. 147–64.

Crawford, Beverly: "The New Security Dilemma under International Economic Interdependence", *Millenium*, Vol. 23, No. 1 (Spring 1994), pp. 25–55.

Crouch, Colin: *Industrial Relations and European State Traditions* (Oxford: Clarendon Press, 1993).

Crouch, Colin and David Marquand (eds.): *Towards Greater Europe? A Continent Without an Iron Curtain*, (Oxford: Blackwell Publishers, 1992).

Dahl, Robert A.: "A Democratic Dilemma: System Effectiveness versus Citizen Participation", *Political Science Quarterly*, Vol. 109, No. 1 (Spring 1994), pp. 23–34.

Dahl, Robert A.: *Controlling Nuclear Weapons: Democracy versus Guardianship* (Syracuse: Syracuse University Press, 1985).

Dahrendorf, Ralf: *Reflections on the Revolution in Europe* (London: Chatto & Windus, 1990).

Dahrendorf, Ralf: *A New World Order? Problems and Prospects of International Relations in the 1980s* (Ghana: University of Ghana, 1979).

Danchev, Alex and Thomas Halverson (eds.): *International Perspectives on the Yugoslav Conflict* (London: Macmillan, 1996).

Dassu, Marta: "The Future of Europe: the View from Rome", *International Affairs*, Vol. 66, No. 2 (April 1990), pp. 299–312.

De Michelis, Gianni: "Reaching Out to the East", *Foreign Policy*, No. 79 (Summer 1990), pp. 44–55.

Delanty, Gerard: *Inventing Europe. Idea, Identity, Reality* (London: Macmillan, 1995).

Delors, Jacques: "European Integration and Security", *Survival*, Vol. 33, No. 2 (March/April 1991), pp. 99–110.

Delors, Jacques: "Europe's Ambitions", *Foreign Policy*, No. 80 (Fall 1990), pp. 14–27.

Der Derian, James and Michael Shapiro (eds.): *International/Intertextual Relations: Postmodern Readings of World Politics* (Lexington, MA: Lexington, 1989).

Karl W. Deutsch, S. A. Burrell *et al.*, *Political Community and the North Atlantic Area* (Princeton, NJ: Princeton University Press, 1957), p. 5.

Dogan, Mattei: "Comparing the Decline of Nationalism in Western Europe: the Generational Dynamic", *International Social Science Journal*, No. 136 (May 1993), pp. 177–98.

Doyle, Michael W.: "Kant, Liberal Legacies, and Foreign Affairs" (Part I), *Philosophy and Public Affairs*, Vol. 12, No. 3 (Summer 1983), pp. 205–35.

Dunleavy, Patrick: "The Globalisation of Public Services Production: Can Government Be 'Best in the World'?", *Public Policy and Administration*, Vol. 9, No. 2 (Summer 1994), pp. 36–64.

Economides, Spyros: "Riding the Tiger of Nationalism: the Question of Macedonia", *Oxford International Review*, Vol. IV, No. 2 (Spring 1993), pp. 27–9.

Edwards, Geoffrey: "Europe and the Falkland Crisis 1982", *Journal of Common Market Studies*, Vol. 22, No. 4 (June 1984), pp. 295–313.

Edwards, Geoffrey and Alfred Pijpers: *The Politics of European Treaty* (London: Pinter, 1997).

Eser, Thiemo W. and Martin Hallet: "Der mögliche Beitrag der EG-Regionalpolitik bei einer Ost-Erweiterung der EG: Hilfe oder Hindernis?", *Osteuropa Wirtschaft*, Vol. 38, No. 3 (1993), pp. 195–217.

Evans, Tony and Peter Wilson: "Regime Theory and the English School of International Relations: A Comparison", *Millenium*, Vol. 21, No. 3 (Winter 1992), pp. 329–52.

Everts, Philip: *Laat dat maar aan ons over. Democratie, buitenlands beleid en vrede* (Leiden: DSWO Press 1996).

Everts, Philip (ed.): *Controversies at Home. Domestic Factors in the Foreign Policy of the Netherlands* (Dordrecht: Martinus Nijhoff, 1985).

Falkenrath, Richard A.: *Shaping Europe's Military Order – The Origins and Consequences of the CFE Treaty* (Cambridge, MA: Massachusetts Institute of Technology Press and Center for Science and International Affairs, 1995).

Fisher, Markus: "Feudal Europe, 800–1300: Communal Discourse and Conflictual Practices", *International Organization*, Vol. 46, No. 2 (Spring 1992), pp. 427–66.

Fitoussi, Jean-Paul: *Le débat interdit: monnaie, Europe, pauvreté* (Paris: Arléa Le Seuil, 1995).

Forsythe, David P.: "Democracy, War and Covert Action", *Journal of Peace Research*, Vol. 29, No. 4 (1992), pp. 385–95.

Franklin, Mark N., Thomas Mackie, Henry Valen et al. (eds.): *Electoral Change. Responses to Evolving Social and Attitudinal Structures in Western Countries* (Cambridge: Cambridge University Press, 1992), pp. 406–27.

Freedman, Lawrence (ed.): *Military Intervention in European Conflicts* (Oxford: Blackwell, 1994).

Freedman, Lawrence: "Strategic Studies and the New Europe", *Adelphi Paper* No. 284 (January 1994).

Freedman, Lawrence: "Order and Disorder in the New World", *Foreign Affairs*, Vol. 71, No. 1 (1992), pp. 20–37.

Fritsch-Bournazel, Renata: *Europe and German Unification* (New York and Oxford: Berg, 1992).

Fuchs, Dieter and Hans-Dieter Klingemann (eds.): *Citizens and the State* (Oxford: Oxford University Press, 1995).

Fukuyama, Francis: "The Primacy of Culture", *Journal of Democracy*, Vol. 6, No. 1 (January 1995), pp. 7–14.

Fursdon, Edward: *The European Defence Community: A History* (London: Macmillan, 1980).

Gaddis, John Lewis: "International Relations Theory and the End of Cold War", *International Security*, Vol. 17, No. 3 (Winter 1992/93), pp. 5–58.

Gaffney, John and Eva Kolinksky (eds.): *Political Culture in France and Germany* (London: Routledge, 1990).

Gagnon, V. P. Jr.: "Ethnic Nationalism and International Conflict: The Case of Serbia", *International Security*, Vol. 19, No. 3 (Winter 1994/95), p. 130–66.

Galtung, Johan: *Europe in the Making* (New York: Crane Russak, 1989).

Garcia, Soledad (ed.): *European Identity and the Search for Legitimacy* (London: Pinter, 1993).

Gartner, Heinz: "Small States and Concepts of European Security", *European Security*, Vol. 2, No. 2 (Summer 1993), pp. 188–99.

Garton Ash, Timothy: *In Europe's Name – Germany and the Divided Continent* (London: Vintage, 1994).

Garton Ash, Timothy: "Germany's Choice", *Foreign Affairs*, Vol. 73, No. 4 (July–August 1994), p. 65–81.

Gasteyger, Curt: *An Ambiguous Power. The European Union in a Changing World* (Gütersloh: Bertelsmann Foundation Publishers, 1996).

Gellner, Ernest: *Conditions of Liberty. Civil Society and its Rivals* (London: Hamish Hamilton, 1994).

Gellner, Ernest: *Nations and Nationalism* (Oxford: Blackwell, 1983).

George, Stephen: *Politics and Policy in the European Community* (Oxford: Clarendon Press, 1990).

Gerbet, Pierre: *La construction de l'Europe* (Paris: Imprimerie nationale, 1994) second edition.

Gilpin, Robert: *War and Change in World Politics* (New York: Cambridge University Press, 1981).

Gnesotto, Nicole: "Common European Defence and Transatlantic Relations", *Survival*, Vol. 38, No. 1 (Spring 1996), pp. 19–32.

Goldman, Kjell, Sten Berglund and Gunnar Sjöstedt (eds.): *Democracy and Foreign Policy: The Case of Sweden* (Aldershot: Gower, 1986).

Gompert, David C. and Stephen F. Larrabee (eds.): *America and Europe: A Partnership For a New Era* (Santa Monica, CA: Cambridge University Press, 1997).

Gordon, Philip H.: "Recasting the Atlantic Alliance", *Survival*, Vol. 38, No. 1 (Spring 1996), pp. 32–57.

Grabbe, Heather and Kirsty Hughes, *Eastward Enlargement of the European Union* (London: The Royal Institute of International Affairs, 1997).

Grant, Charles: *Strength in Numbers: Europe's Foreign and Defence Policy* (London: Centre for European Reform, 1996).

Greenwood, Justin and Karston Ronit: "Interest Groups in the European Community: Newly Emerging Dynamics and Forms", *West European Politics*, Vol. 17, No. 1 (January 1994), pp. 31–52.

Guéhenno, Jean-Marie: *La fin de la démocratie* (Paris: Flammarion, 1993).

Gunsteren (van), Herman and Rudy Andeweg: *Het Grote Ongenoengen: Over de Kloof Tussen Burgers en Politiek* (Haarlem: Aramith Uitgevers, 1994).

Gustavsson, Sverker and Leif Lewin (eds.): *The Future of the Nation-State. Essays on Cultural Pluralism and Political Integration* (London: Routledge, 1996).

Haas, Ernst B.: "Turbulent Fields and the Theory of Regional Integration", *International Organization*, Vol. 30, No. 2 (1976), pp. 173–212.

Haas, Ernst B.: "International Integration: The European and the Universal Process", *International Organization*, Vol. 15, No. 4 (Autumn 1961), pp. 366–92.

Haas, Ernst B.: *The Uniting of Europe* (Stanford: Stanford University Press, 1958).

Habermas, Jürgen: "Citizenship and National Identity: Some Reflections on the Future of Europe", *Praxis International*, Vol. 12, No. 1 (April 1992), pp. 1–19.

Halman, Loek: "Is There a Moral Decline? A Cross-National Inquiry into Morality in Contemporary Society", *International Social Science Journal*, No. 145 (September 1995), pp. 419–40.

Ham (van), Peter: *The EC, Eastern Europe and European Unity. Discord, Collaboration and Integration Since 1947* (London: Pinter, 1993).

Hanriender, Wolfram F.: "Dissolving International Politics: Reflections on the Nation-State", *American Political Science Review*, Vol. 72, No. 4 (December 1978), pp. 1243–87.

Hansen, Niels: "Die Europäische Politische Zusammenarbeit bei den Vereinten Nationen. Die Neun suchen in New York Profil", *Europa Archiv*, Vol. 15 (1975), pp. 493–500.

Harries, Owen: "The Collapse of 'The West'", *Foreign Affairs*, Vol. 72, No. 4 (September/October 1993), pp. 41–53.

Harvey, David: *The Condition of Postmodernity* (Cambridge, MA. and Oxford: Blackwell, 1990).

Hassner, Pierre: *La Violence et la Paix: De la Bombe Atomique au Nettoyage ethnique* (Paris: Esprit, 1995).

Hassner, Pierre: "Beyond the Three Traditions: The Philosophy of War and peace in Historical Perspective", *International Affairs*, Vol. 70, No. 4 (October 1994), pp. 734–56.

Havel, Vaclav: "A Call for Sacrifice. The Co-Responsibility of the West", *Foreign Affairs*, Vol. 73, No. 2 (March/April 1994), pp. 2–7.

Havel, Vaclav: *Living in Truth* (London: Faber and Faber, 1990).

Hayward, Jack (ed.): *Elitism, Populism, and European Politics*. (Oxford: Clarendon Press, 1996).

Hayward, Jack and Edward C. Page (eds.): *Governing the New Europe* (Oxford: Oxford Polity Press, 1995).

Heisbourg, François: "Sécurité: l'Europe livrée à elle-même", *Politique Etrangère*, Vol. 59, No. 1 (Spring 1994), pp. 247–60.

Heisbourg, François: "The European-US Alliance: Valedictory Reflections on Continental Drift in the Post-Cold War Era", *International Affairs*, Vol. 68, No. 4 (October 1992), pp. 665–78.

Heisenberg, Werner (ed.): *German Unification in European Perspective* (London: Brassey's Centre for European Policy Studies, 1991).

Held, David (ed.): *Prospects for Democracy: North, South, East, West* (Oxford: Oxford Polity Press, 1993).

Herman, Valentine: *Parliaments of the World: A Reference Compendium* (London: Macmillan, 1976).

Hill, Christopher (ed.): *The Actors in Europe's Foreign Policy* (London and New York: Routledge, 1996).

Hill, Christopher: "The Capability-Expectations Gap, or Conceptualising Europe's International Role", *Journal of Common Market Studies*, Vol. 31, No. 3 (September 1993), pp. 305–29.

Hill, Christopher: "1939: The Origins of Liberal Realism," *Review of International Studies*, Vol. 15, No. 4 (October 1989), pp. 319–28.

Hill, Christopher (ed.): *National Foreign Policies and European Political Co-operation* (London: George Allen & Unwin, 1983).

Hirschman, Albert O.: *Essays In Tresspassing. Economics to Politics and Beyond* (Cambridge: Cambridge University Press 1981).

Hobsbawm, Eric J.: *Nations and Nationalism Since 1780: Programme, Myth, Reality* (Cambridge: Cambridge University Press, 1990).

Hoffman, John: *Beyond the State* (Oxford: Oxford Polity Press, 1995).

Hoffman, Paul: *Peace Can Be Won* (New York: Doubleday, 1951).

Hoffmann, Stanley: "The Politics and Ethics of Military Intervention", *Survival*, Vol. 37, No. 1 (Winter 1995–96), pp. 29–51.

Hoffmann, Stanley: "Europe's Identity Crisis Revisited", *Daedalus*, Vol. 123, No. 2 (Spring 1994), pp. 1–24.

Hoffmann, Stanley: "The European Process at Atlantic Crosspurposes", *Journal of Common Market Studies*, Vol. 3, No. 2 (February 1965), pp. 85–101.

Holland, Martin (ed.): *Common Foreign and Security Policy. The Record and Reforms* (London: Pinter, 1997).

Holland, Martin: *European Union Common Foreign Policy. From EPC to CFSP Joint Action and South Africa* (London: St Martin's Press, 1995).

Holland, Martin: "Bridging the Capability-Expectation Gap: A Case Study of the CFSP Joint Action on South Africa", *Journal of Common Market Studies*, Vol. 33, No. 4 (December 1995), pp. 555–72.

Holland, Martin (ed.): *The Future of European Political Cooperation. Essays on Theory and Practice* (London: Macmillan, 1991).

Holsti, Ole R.: "Public Opinion and Foreign Policy: Challenges to the Almond-Lippmann Consensus", *International Studies Quarterly*, Vol. 36, No. 4 (December 1992), pp. 439–66.

Holsti, K. J.: *Change in the International System. Essays on the Theory and Practice of International Relations* (Aldershot: Edward Elgar, 1991).

Holsti, K. J.: *The Dividing Discipline: Hegemony and Diversity in International Theory* (Boston: Unwin Hyman, 1985).

Hooghe, Liesbet (ed.): *Cohesion Policy and European Integration Building Multi-Level Governance*. (Oxford: Oxford University Press, 1996).

Hoonson, David (ed.): *Geography and National Identity* (Oxford: Blackwell, 1994).

Howard, Michael: *War and the Liberal Conscience* (New Brunswick, NJ: Rutgers University Press, 1986), second edition.

Howard, Michael: *The Causes of Wars* (London: Temple Smith, 1983).

Huntington, Samuel P.: "The Clash of Civilisations?", *Foreign Affairs*, Vol. 72, No. 3 (Summer 1993), pp. 22–49.

Huntington, Samuel P.: "Why International Primacy Matters", *International Security*, Vol. 17, No. 4 (Spring 1993), pp. 68–83.

Huntington, Samuel P.: "Transnational Organisations in World Politics", *World Politics*, Vol. 25, No. 3 (April 1973), pp. 333–68.

Hurd, Douglas: "Developing the Common Foreign and Security Policy", *International Affairs*, Vol. 70, No. 3 (July 1994), pp. 421–28.

Ifestos, Panayiotis: *European Political Cooperation: Towards a Framework of Supranational Diplomacy* (Aldershot: Gower, 1987).

Inglehart, Ronald: "Changing Values, Economic Development and Political Change", *International Social Science Journal*, No. 145 (September 1995), pp. 379–404.

Inglehart, Ronald: *Culture Shift in Advanced Industrial Society* (Princeton: Princeton University Press, 1990).

Irwin, Galen A.: "The Dutch Parliamentary Election of 1994", *Electoral Studies*, Vol. 14, No. 1 (March 1995), pp. 72–6.

Jahn, Egbert: *Europe, Eastern Europe, and Central Europe* (PRIF Report 1, 1989).

Jannuzzi, Giovanni: "Comunità Europea e politica estera: al di là dell' Atto Unico", *Rivista di Studi Politici Internazionali*, Vol. 227 (1990), pp. 371–80.

Joffe, Josef: "'Bismark' or 'Britain'?", *International Security*, Vol. 19, No. 4 (Spring 1995), pp. 116–17.

Joffe, Josef: "Deutsche Aussenpolitik-Postmodern", *Internationale Politik*, Vol. 50, No. 1 (January 1995), pp. 43–5.

Joffe, Josef: "The New Europe: Yesterday's Ghosts", *Foreign Affairs*, Vol. 72, No. 1, "America and the World" (1993), pp. 29–43.

Joffe, Josef: "Collective Security and the Future of Europe: Failed Dreams and Dead Ends", *Survival*, Vol. 34, No. 2 (Spring 1992), pp. 36–50.

Johnson, Alastair Iain: "Thinking about Strategic Culture", *International Security*, Vol. 19, No. 4 (Spring 1995), pp. 32–64.

Jopp, Mathias: "Die Reform der Gemeinsamen Aussen-und Sicherheitspolitik, Institutionelle Vorschläge und ihre Realisierungschancen," *Integration*, Vol. 3 (July 1995), pp. 133–43.

Jopp, Mathias: "The Strategic Implications of European Integration", *Adelphi Paper* No. 290 (July 1994).

Kaase, Max and Kenneth Newton (eds.): *Beliefs in Government* (Oxford: Oxford University Press, 1995).

Kaiser, Karl: *Deutschlands Vereinigung. Die Internationalen Aspekte* (Bergisch Gladbach: Lübbe Verlag, 1991).

Kaiser, Karl and Pierre Lellouche (eds.): *Le couple franco-allemand et la défense de l'Europe* (Paris: IFRI, 1986).

Kaldor, Mary: *The Imaginary War* (Oxford: Basil Blackwell, 1990).

Kaldor, Mary, Gerard Holden and Richard Falk (eds.): *The New Detente: Rethinking East-West Relations* (London: Verso, 1989).

Katz, Richard S. and Peter Mair: "Changing Models of Party Organisation and Party Democracy: The Emergence of the Cartel Party", *Party Politics*, No. 1 (1995), pp. 5–28.

Katz, Richard S. and Peter Mair (eds.): *Party Organisations: A Data Handbook on Party Organisations in Western Democracies, 1960–90* (London: Sage, 1992).

Keohane, Robert O.: "International Institutions: Two Approaches", *International Studies Quarterly*, Vol. 32, No. 4 (December 1988), pp. 379–96.

Keohane, Robert O. (ed.): *Neorealism and its Critics* (New York: Columbia University Press, 1986).

Keohane, Robert O. and Lisa L. Martin: "The Promise of Institutionalist Theory", *International Security*, Vol. 20, No. 1 (Summer 1995), pp. 39–51.

Keohane, Robert O. and Joseph S. Ney Jr.: "Power and Independence Revisited", *International Organization*, Vol. 41, No. 4 (Autumn 1987), pp. 725–53.

Kissinger, Henry: *Diplomacy* (New York: Simon & Schuster, 1994).

Knorr, Klaus: *Threat Perception in Historical Dimensions of National Security Problems* (Lawrence: University of Kansas Press, 1976).

Kohnstamm, Max and Wolfgang Hager (eds.): *A Nation Writ Large? Foreign-Policy Problems Before the European Community* (London: Macmillan, 1973).

Kolakowski, Leszek: *Modernity on Endless Trial* (Chicago: University of Chicago Press, 1990).

Kolboom (van), Ingo: "Dialog mit Bauchgrimmen? Die Zukunft der deutsch-französischen Beziehungen", *Europa-Archiv*, Folge 9 (1994), pp. 257–64.

Konretarris, George A. and Andreas Moschonas (eds.): *The Impact of European Integration. Political, Sociological and Economic Changes*. (Westport and London: Praeger, 1996).

Kratochwil, Friedrich: "Of Systems, Boundaries and Territoriality: An Inquiry into the Formation of the State System", *World Politics*, Vol. 34, No. 1 (October 1986), pp. 27–52.

Kratochwil, Friedrich: "On the Notion of 'Interest' in International Relations", *International Organization*, Vol. 36, No. 1 (Winter 1982), pp. 1–30.

Krause, Joachim and Peter Schmidt: "The Evolving New European Architecture–Concepts, Problems and Pitfalls", *The Washington Quarterly*, Vol. 13, No. 4 (Autumn 1990), pp. 79–92.

Krenzler, Horst G.: "A New Transatlantic Agenda", *European Foreign Affairs Review*, Vol. 1, No. 1 (July 1996), pp. 9–28.

Krenzler, Horst G.: "Die Einheitliche Europäische Akte als Schritt auf dem Wege zu einer gemeinsamen europäischen Aussenpolitik", *Europarecht*, Vol. 4 (1986), pp. 384–91.

Krenzler, Horst G.: "The EV and Central-East Europe: The Implications of Enlargement in Stages (Florence: Robert Schman Centre, 1997).

Krugman, Paul: *Development, Geography, and Economic Theory* (Cambridge, MA: The MIT Press, 1995).

Kuechler, Manfred: "Germans and 'Others': Racism, Xenophobia, or 'Legitimate Conservatism'?", *German Politics*, Vol. 3, No. 1 (April 1994), pp. 47–74.

Kupchan, Charles A.: "Reviving the West", *Foreign Affairs*, Vol. 75, No. 3 (May/June 1996), pp. 92–3.

Kupchan, Charles: *Nationalism and Nationalities in the New Europe* (New York: Council on Foreign Relations, 1995).

Kupchan, Charles and Clifford A. Kupchan: "The Promise of Collective Security", *International Security*, Vol. 20, No. 1 (Summer 1995), pp. 52–61.

Kupchan, Charles and Clifford A. Kupchan: "Concerts, Collective Security and the Future of Europe", *International Security*, Vol. 16, No. 1 (Summer 1991), pp. 114–61.

Lapid, Yosef (ed.): *Return of Culture and Identity in International Relations Theory* (Boulder: Lynne Rienner, 1996).

Laqueur, Walter: *A Continent Astray. Europe, 1970–1978* (Oxford and New York: Oxford University Press, 1979).

Lefeber, R., M. Fitzmaurice and E. W. Vierdag: *The Changing Political Structure of Europe. Aspects of International Law* (Dordrecht: Martinus Nijhoff, 1991).

Lellouche, Pierre: "France in Search of Security," *Foreign Affairs*, Vol. 72, No. 2 (Spring 1993), pp. 122–131.

Lenzi, Guido: "Reforming the International System: Between Leadership and Power-Sharing", *International Spectator*, Vol. 30, No. 2 (April–June 1995), pp. 49–70.

Lijphardt, Arend: *Democracies: Patterns of Majoritarian and Consensus Government in Twenty-One Countries* (New Haven: Yale University Press, 1984).

Lindberg, Leon: *The Political Dynamics of European Integration* (Stanford: Stanford University Press, 1963).

Lippmann, Walter: *The Public Philosophy* (Boston: Little, Brown, 1955).

Lipschultz, Ronnie D.: "Reconstructing World Politics: The Emergence of a Global Civil Society", *Millenium*, Vol. 21, No. 3 (Winter 1992), pp. 389–420.

Lipset, Seymour Martin: "The Social Requisites of Democracy Revisited", *American Sociological Review*, Vol. 59, No. 1 (February 1994), pp. 1–22.

Little, Richard and Michael Smith (eds.): *Perspectives on World Politics* (London: Routledge, 1991) second edition.

Lodge, Juliet (ed.): *The European Community and the Challenge of the Future* (London: Pinter, 1995) second edition.

Lodge, Juliet: "Transparency and Democratic Legitimacy", *Journal of Common Market Studies*, Vol. 32, No. 3 (September 1994), pp. 343–68.

Gladwyn, Hubert Miles Gladwyn Jebb (Baron) *The European Idea* (London: New English Library, 1967).

Lotter, Christoph and Susanne Peters (eds.): *The Changing European Security Environment* (Weimar: Böhlau Verlag, 1996).

Ludlow, Peter (ed.): *Europe and the Mediterranean* (London: Macmillan, 1994).

Ludlow, Peter: "Implementing the CFSP", Centre for European Policy Studies working group background paper, Brussels 1993.

Lukic, Reneo and Allen Lynch: *Europe from the Balkans to the Urals. The Disintegration of Yugoslavia and the Soviet Union* (Oxford: Oxford University Press, 1996).

Luttwak, Edward N.: "Where Are the Great Powers?", *Foreign Affairs*, Vol. 73, No. 4 (July/August 1994), pp. 23–9.

Maier, Charles S.: "Democracy and its Discontents", *Foreign Affairs*, Vol. 73, No. 4 (July/August 1994), pp. 48–64.

Mair, Peter: *Party Democracies and their Difficulties* (Leiden: University of Leiden, 1994).

Mair, Peter: "Myths of Electoral Change and the Survival of Traditional Parties: The 1992 Stein Rokkan Lecture", *European Journal of Political Research*, Vol. 24, No. 2 (1993), pp. 121–34.

Mandelbaum, Michael: *The Dawn of Peace in Europe* (New York: Twentieth Century Fund, 1996).

Mandelbaum, Michael: "Foreign Policy as Social Work", *Foreign Affairs*, Vol. 75, No. 1 (January/February 1996), pp 16–32.

Manent, Pierre: "On Modern Individualism", *Journal of Democracy*, Vol. 7, No. 1 (January 1996), pp. 3–11.

Maoz, Zeev and Bruce Russett: "Normative and Structural Causes of Democratic Peace", *American Political Science Review*, Vol. 87, No. 3 (September 1993), pp. 624–38.

Marks, Gary, Philippe C. Schmitter and Fritz W. Scharpf (eds.): *Governance in the European Union* (London: Sage, 1996).

Martin, Lawrence: "Chatam House: The Way Forward", *The World Today*, Vol. 50, No. 4 (April 1994), pp. 62–3.

Martin, Lawrence and John Roper (eds.): *Towards a Common Defence Policy. A Study by the European Strategy Group and the Institute for Security Studies of Western European Union* (Paris: Institute for Security Studies of WEU, 1995).

Martinet, Gilles: *Le Réveil des Nationalismes Français* (Paris: Editions du Seuil, 1994).

Mastny, Vojtech: *Helsinki, Human Rights, and European Security* (Durham: Duke University Press, 1986).

Maull, Hanns W.: "Germany in the Yugoslav Crisis", *Survival*, Vol. 37, No. 4 (Winter 1995–96), pp. 99–130.

Maull, Hanns W.: *Europe and World Energy* (London: Butterworths, 1980).

Maury, Jean-Pierre: *La construction européenne: la sécurité et la défense* (Paris: Presses Universitaires de France, 1996).

Mayall, James: *Nationalism and International Society* (Cambridge: Cambridge University Press, 1990).

McArdle Kelleher, Catherine: *The Future of European Security: An Interim Assessment* (Washington, DC: The Brookings Institution, 1995).

McCarthy, Patrick: *The Crisis of the Italian State: from the Origins of the Cold War to the Fall of Berlusconi* (Basingstoke: Macmillan, 1995).

McLaughlin, Andrew M. and Justin Greenwood: "The Management of Interest Representation in the European Union", *Journal of Common Market Studies*, Vol. 33, No. 1 (March 1995), pp. 143–56.

Mearsheimer, John J.: "The False Promise of International Institutions", *International Security*, Vol. 19, No. 3 (Winter 1994/1995), pp. 5–49.

Mearsheimer, John J.: "Back to the Future. Instability in Europe after the Cold War", *International Security*, Vol. 15, No. 1 (Summer 1990), pp. 5–56.

Meehan, Elisabeth: *Citizenship and the European Community* (London: Sage, 1993).

Mendras, Henri: *L'Europe des Européens* (Paris: Gallimaed, 1997).

Menon, Anand: "NATO the French Way – From Independence to Co-operation: France, NATO and European Security", *International Affairs*, Vol. 71, No. 1 (1995), pp. 19–34.

Mény, Yves: *La corruption de la République* (Paris: Fayard, 1992).

Mény, Yves, Pierre Muller, and Jean-Louis Quermonne (eds.): *Adjusting to Europe. The Impact of the EU on National Institutions and Policies*. (London and NY: Routledge, 1996).

Miall, Hugh (ed.): *Redefining Europe: New Patterns of Conflict and Cooperation* (London: Pinter Publishers for the Royal Institute of Foreign Affairs, 1994).

Michalski, Anna and Helen Wallace: *The European Community: The Challenge of Enlargement*, European Programme Special Paper (London: Royal Institute of International Affairs, 1992).

Miles, Lee (ed.): *The European Union and the Nordic Countries* (London and New York: Routledge, 1996).

Milward, Alan: *The European Rescue of the Nation-State* (London: Routledge, 1992).

Minc, Alain: *L'ivresse démocratique* (Paris: Gallimard, 1995).

Mitrany, David: *A Working Peace System* (Chicago: Quadrangle Books, 1966).

Moravcsik, Andrew: "Preferences and Power in the European Community: A Liberal Intergovernmentalist Approach", *Journal of Common Market Studies*, Vol. 31, No. 4 (December 1993), pp. 473–524.

Morgan, Clifton T. and Sally Howard Campbell: "Domestic Structure, Decisional Constraints, and War: So Why Can't Democracies Fight?", *Journal of Conflict Resolution*, Vol. 35, No. 2 (1991), pp. 187–212.

Morgan, Roger P.: *High Politics, Low Politics: Toward a Foreign Policy for Western Europe* (Beverly Hills and London: Sage, 1973).

Morgenthau, Hans J.: *Politics Among Nations. The Struggle for Power and Peace* (New York: Alfred A. Knopf, 1960).

Morse, Edward L.: "The Transformation of Foreign Policies: Modernisation, Interdependence and Externalisation", *World Politics*, Vol. XXII, No. 3 (April 1970), pp. 371–92.

Mortimer, Edward: "European Security after the Cold War", *Adelphi Paper* No. 271 (Summer 1992).

Mueller, Harald: "The Export Controls Debate in the 'New' European Community", *Arms Control Today*, Vol. 3, No. 2 (March 1993), pp. 10–13.

Muir, Richard and Ronan Paddison: *Politics, Geography and Behaviour* (London and New York: Methuen, 1981).

Muller, Wolfgang C. and Vincent Wright: "Reshaping the State in Western Europe: The Limits to Retreat", *West European Politics*, Vol. 17, No. 3 (July 1994), pp. 1–11.

Ney, Joseph S.: "Neorealism and Neoliberalism," *World Politics*, Vol. 40, No. 1 (October 1987), pp. 234–51.

Niblett, Robin: "The European Disunion: Competing Visions of Integration," *The Washington Quarterly*, Vol. 20, No. 1 (Winter 1997), pp. 91–108.

Niedermayer, Oskar and Richard Sinnott (eds.): *Public Opinion and the Internationalised Governance* (Oxford: Oxford University Press, 1995).

Nuttall, Simon J.: *European Political Cooperation* (Oxford: Clarendon Press, 1992).

Palmer, Diego A. Ruiz: "French Strategic Options in the 1990s", *Adelphi Paper* No. 260 (Summer 1991).

Pappas, Spyros A. and Sophie Vanhoonacker (eds.): *The European Union's Common Foreign and Security Policy. The Challenges of the Future* (Maastricht: European Institute of Public Administration, 1995).

Pardalis, Anastasia: "European Political Cooperation and the United States", *Journal of Common Market Studies*, Vol. 25, No. 4 (June 1987), pp. 271–94.

Parry, Geraint (ed.): *Politics in an Interdependent World: Essays Presented to Ghita Ionescu* (Cheltenham: Edward Elgar, 1994).

Petersen, John: "Decision-Making in the European Union: Towards a Framework for Analysis", *Journal of European Public Policy*, Vol. 2, No. 1 (March 1995), pp. 69–93.

Pijpers, Alfred E.: *Kanonnen en boter* (Amsterdam: Uitgeverij Jan Mets, 1996).

Pijpers, Alfred E.: *The Vicissitudes of European Political Cooperation. Towards a Realist Interpretation of the EC's Collective Diplomacy* (Leiden: University of Leiden, 1990).

Pijpers, Alfred E., Elfriede Regelsberger, Wolfgang Wessels and Geoffrey Edwards (eds.): *European Political Cooperation in the 1980s. A Common Foreign Policy for Western Europe?* (Dordrecht: Martinus Nijhoff, 1988).

Pinder, John: *European Community. The Building of a Union* (Oxford and New York: Oxford University Press, 1992).

Piris, Jean-Claude: "After Maastricht, Are the Community Institutions More Efficacious, More Democratic and More Transparent", *European Law Review*, Vol. 19, No. 5 (October 1994), pp. 449–87.

Pryce, Roy (ed.): *The Dynamics of the European Union*, (London: Croom Helm, 1989).

Putnam, Robert D.: "Diplomacy and Domestic Politics: The Logic of Two-Level Games", *International Organization*, Vol. 42, No. 3 (Summer 1988), pp. 427–60.

Putnam, Robert D., Robert Leonardi and Raffaella Y. Nanetti: *Making Democracy Work: Civic Traditions in Modern Italy* (Princeton: Princeton University Press, 1993).

Regelsberger, Elfriede and Wolfgang Wessels: "The CFSP Institutions and Procedures: A Third Way for the Second Pillar," *European Foreign Affairs Review*, Vol. 1, No. 1, (July 1996), pp. 29–54.

Regelsberger, Elfriede, Philippe de Schoutheete de Tervarent and Wolfgang Wessels: *European Policy of the European Union. From EPC to CFSP and Beyond* (Boulder: Lynne Rienner, 1997).

Reich, Robert B.: *The Work of Nations* (New York: Alfred A Knopf, 1991).

Reisch, George A.: "Chaos, History and Narrative", *History and Theory*, Vol. 30, No. 1 (1991), pp. 1–20.

Reus-Smith, Christian: "Realist and Resistance Utopias: Community, Security and Political Action in the New Europe", *Millenium*, Vol. 21, No. 1 (Spring 1992), pp. 1–28.

Rhein, Eberhard: "Europe and the Mediterranean: A Newly Emerging Geo-political Area?", *European Foreign Affairs Review*, Vol. 1, No. 1 (July 1996), pp. 79–86.

Rhodes, R. A. W.: "The Hollowing Out of the State: The Changing Nature of the Public Service in Britain", *Political Quarterly*, Vol. 65, No. 2 (April–June 1994), pp. 138–51.

Risse-Kappen, Thomas: "Exploring the Nature of the Beast: International Relations Theory and Comparative Policy Analysis Meet the European Union", *Journal of Common Market Studies*, Vol. 34, No. 1 (March 1996), pp. 53–81.

Risse-Kappen, Thomas (ed.): *Bringing Transnational Relations Back In. Non-State Actors, Domestic Structures and International Relations* (Cambridge: Cambridge University Press, 1995).

Roberts, Adam: "From San Francisco to Sarajevo: The UN and the Use of Force", *Survival*, Vol. 37, No. 4 (Winter 1995–96), pp. 7–28.

Roberts, Adam: "A New Age in International Relations", *International Affairs*, Vol. 67, No. 3 (July 1991), pp. 509–26.

Rometsch, Dietrich and Wolfgang Wessels (eds.): *The European Union and Members States. Towards Institutional Fusion?* (Manchester and NY: Manchester University Press, 1996).

Rood, Jan: "Living in a Fantasy World. Nederland en het GBVB", *Atlantisch Perspectief*, Vol. 20, No. 2 (1996), p. 4.

Rosecrance, Richard : "The Rise of the Virtual State", *Foreign Affairs*, Vol. 75, No. 4 (July–August 1996), pp. 45–61.

Rosenau, James N. and Ernst-Otto Czempiel (eds.): *Governance Without Government: Order and Change in World Politics* (Cambridge: Cambridge University Press, 1992).

Ruggie, John Gerard: "Territoriality and Beyond: Problematizing Modernity in International Relations", *International Organization*, Vol. 47, No. 1 (Winter 1993), pp. 139–74.

Ruggie, John Gerard: "Multilateralism: The Anatomy of an Institution", *International Organization*, Vol. 46, No. 3 (Summer 1992), pp. 561–98.

Rummel, Reinhardt (ed.): *Toward Political Union. Planning a Common Foreign and Security Policy in the European Community* (Baden-Baden: Nomos, 1992).

Rummel, Reinhardt: "Integration, Disintegration, and Security in Europe – Preparing the Community for a Multi-Institutional Response", *International Journal*, Vol. 47, No. 1 (Winter 1991/92), pp. 64–92.

Rummel, Reinhardt (ed.): *The Evolution of an International Actor: Western Europe's New Assertiveness* (Boulder: Westview, 1990).

Rupnik, Jacques: "Europe's New Frontiers: Remapping Europe", *Daedalus*, Vol. 123, No. 3 (Summer 1994), pp. 91–114.

Russett, Bruce: *Controlling the Sword. The Democratic Governance of National Security* (Cambridge MA: Harvard University Press, 1990).

Russett, Bruce: *Grasping the Democratic Peace: Principles for a Post-Cold War World* (Princeton: Princeton University Press, 1993).

Salmon, Trevor C.: "Testing Times for European Political Cooperation: The Gulf and Yugoslavia, 1990–1992", *International Affairs*, Vol. 68, No. 2 (April 1992), pp. 233–53.

Sartori, Giovanni: *Comparative Constitutional Engineering* (London: Macmillan, 1994).

Scharpf, Fritz W.: "Negative and Positive Integration in the Political Economy of European Welfare States", *Jean Monnet Chair Papers* No. 28 (Florence: The Robert Schuman Centre at the European University Institute, 1995).

Scharpf, Fritz W.: "The Joint-Decision Trap: Lessons from German Federalism and European Integration", *Public Administration*, Vol. 66, No. 3 (Autumn 1988), p. 239–78.

Schlör, Wolfgang F.: "German Security Policy", *Adelphi Paper* No. 277 (June 1993).

Schmidt, Peter: "A Complex Puzzle – the EU's Security Policy and UN Reform", *Internationale Spectator*, Vol. 29, No. 3 (July–September 1994), pp. 53–66.

Schneider, Gerald: "The Limits of Self-Reform: Institution-Building in the European Union", *European Journal of International Relations*, Vol. 1, No. 1 (March 1995), pp. 59–86.

Schwartz, Hans-Peter: "Germany's National and European Interests", *Daedalus*, Vol. 123, No. 2 (Spring 1994), pp. 81–107.

Schwerin, Otto Graf: "Die Solidarität der EG-Staten in der KSZE", *Europa Archiv*, Vol. 15 (1975), pp. 483–92.

Seidelmann, Reimund (ed.): *Crises Policies in Eastern Europe: Imperatives, Problems and Perspectives* (Baden-Baden: Nomos Verlagsgesellschaft, 1996).

Senior-Nello, Susarn and Karen E. Smith *The Consequences of Eastern Enlargement of the European Union in Stages* (EUI Working Papers, RSC No. 97/51) 1997.

Serfaty, Simon, (ed.): *The Media and Foreign Policy* (New York: St Martin's Press, 1991).

Serre (de la), Françoise: "La politique européenne de la France: new look or new deal?", *Politique Etrangère*, Vol. 47, No. 1 (1982), pp. 125–37.

Seton-Watson, Hugh: *Nations and States. An Enquiry into the Origins of Nations and the Politics of Nationalism* (London: Methuen, 1977).

Sharp, Jane M.O. (ed.): *Europe After an American Withdrawal* (Oxford: Oxford University Press, 1990).

Shin, Dong-Ik and Gerald Segal: "Getting Serious About Asia-Europe Security Cooperation", *Survival*, Vol. 39, No. 1 (Spring 1997), pp. 138–55.

Siccama, Jan G. and Jan Q.Th. Rood (eds.): *Grenzen aan de Europese Integratie* (Assen/Maastricht: Van Gorcum, 1992).

Smith, Anthony D.: "National Identity and the Idea of European Unity", *International Affairs*, Vol. 68, No. 1 (January 1992), pp. 55–76.

Smith, Anthony D.: *National Identity* (London: Penguin Books, 1990).

Smith, Michael: "The European Union and a Changing Europe: Establishing the Boundaries of Order", *Journal of Common Market Studies*, Vol. 34, No. 1 (March 1996), pp. 5–28.

Smith, Steve and Michael Clarke (eds.): *Foreign Policy Implementation* (London: Unwin, 1985).

Smith, Trevor: "Post-Modern Politics and the Case for Constitutional Renewal", *The Political Quarterly*, Vol. 65, No. 2 (April–June 1994), pp. 128–37.

Snyder, Jack: "Averting Anarchy in the New Europe", *International Security*, Vol. 14, No. 4 (Spring 1990), pp. 5–41.

Spencer, Claire: "The Maghreb in the 1990s", *Adelphi Paper* No. 274 (February 1993).

Spiro, Peter J.: "New Global Communities: Nongovernmental Organisations in International Decision-Making Institutions", *The Washington Quarterly*, Vol. 18, No. 1 (Winter 1995), pp. 45–55.

Staden (van), Alfred: "Politieke Wetenschap en Politiek Comentaar", *Internationale Spectator*, Vol. 51, No. 2 (February 1997), pp. 100–3.

Staden (van), Alfred: "De Veilighed van Europa in Theoretisch Perspectief", *Transaktie*, Vol. 19, No. 3 (September 1990), pp. 199–213.

Stavridis, Stelios and Christopher Hill (eds.): *Domestic Sources of Foreign Policy: West European Reactions to the Falkland Conflict* (Oxford: Berg, 1996).

Story, Jonathan (ed.): *The New Europe: Politics, Government and Economy since 1945* (Oxford: Blackwell, 1993).

Strange, Susan: *Retreat of the State. The Diffusion of Power in the World Economy* (Cambridge: Cambridge University Press, 1996).

Strange, Susan: "The Limits of Politics", *Government and Opposition*, Vol. 30, No. 3 (1995), pp. 291–311.

Streek, Wolfgang: "Vielfalt und Interdependenz: Überlegungen zur Rolle von intermediaren Organisationen in sich ändernden Umwelten", *Kolner Zeitschrift für Soziologie und Sozialpsychologie*, Vol. 39 (1987), pp. 471–95.

Taylor, Paul: *The European Union in the 1990's* (Oxford: Oxford University Press, 1996).

Tharoor, Shashi: "United Nations Peacekeeping in Europe", *Survival*, Vol. 37, No. 2 (Summer 1995), p. 121–34.

Thatcher, Margaret: *The Downing Street Years* (London: Harper Collins, 1993).

Tsakaloyannis, Panos (ed.): *Western European Security in a Changing World: From the Reactivation of the WEU to the Single European Act* (Maastricht: European Institute of Public Administration, 1988).

Tsoukalis, Loukas: *The European Community: Past, Present, and Future* (Oxford: Basil Blackwell, 1983).

Ullman, Richard (ed.): *The World and Yugoslavia's Wars* (New York: Council on Foreign Relations, 1996)

Ullman, Richard: *Securing Europe* (London: Adamantine Press, 1991).

Van Deth, Jan W. and Elinor Scarbrough (eds.): *The Impact of Values* (Oxford: Oxford University Press, 1995).

Waever, Ole: "European Security Identities", *Journal of Common Market Studies*, Vol. 34, No. 1 (March 1996), pp 103–32.

Waever, Ole: "Identity, Integration and Security. Solving the Sovereignty Puzzle in EU Studies", *Journal of International Affairs*, Vol. 48, No. 2 (Winter 1995), pp. 389–432.

Waever, Ole: "Nordic Nostalgia: Northern Europe after the Cold War", *International Affairs*, Vol. 68, No. 1 (January 1992), pp. 77–102.

Wallace, Helen and William Wallace (eds.): *Policy Making in the European Union* (Oxford: Oxford University Press, 1996).

Wallace, William: "British Foreign Policy after the Cold War", *International Affairs*, Vol. 68, No. 3 (1992), pp. 423–42.

Wallace, William: *The Transformation of Western Europe* (London: Pinter Publishers for the Royal Institute of International Relations, 1990).

Wallace, William (ed.): *The Dynamics of European Integration* (London: Pinter, 1990).

Wallace, William and William E. Pederson (eds.): *Foreign Policy-Making in Western Europe*, (Farnborough: Saxon House, 1978).

Waltz, Kenneth N.: "The Emerging Structure of International Politics", *International Security*, Vol. 18, No. 2 (Fall 1993), pp. 44–79.

Waltz, Kenneth N.: *Theory of International Politics* (Reading, MA: Addison-Wesley, 1979).

Walzer, Michael (ed.): *Toward a Global Civil Society* (Providence and Oxford: Berghahn Books, 1995).

Ware, Alan: "The Party Systems of the Established Liberal Democracies in the 1990's: Is This a Decade of Transformation?", *Government and Opposition*, Vol. 30, No. 3 (1995), pp. 312–26.

Weidenfeld, Werner and Josef Janning (eds.): *Europe in Global Change: Strategies and Options for Europe* (Gütersloh: Bertelsman Foundation Publishers, 1993).

Weidenfeld, Werner and Josef Janning (eds.): *Global Responsibilities: Europe in Tomorrow's World* (Gütersloh: Bertelsmann Foundation Publishers, 1991).

Weilemann, Peter R.: *Zwischen Nationalem Interesse und Europäischem Engagement – Innenpolitische Akzeptanz, Institutionelle Reform und die Europapolitischen Vorstellungen der Deutschen* (Bonn: Konrad Adenauer Stiftung, October 1993).

Weiler, J. H. H., Ulrich R. Haltern and Franz C. Mayer: "European Democracy and Its Critique", *West European Politics*, Vol. 18, No. 3 (July 1995), pp. 4–39.

Weiler, Joseph H. H.: "The Evolution of the Mechanisms and Institutions for a European Foreign Policy", *EUI Working Papers* No. 202/1985, Florence.

Weiler, Joseph H. H.: *The European Parliament and Its Foreign Affairs Committees* (New York: Oceana Publishers, 1982).

Wendt, Alexander: "The Agent-Structure Problem in International Relations Theory", *International Organization*, Vol. 41, No. 3 (Summer 1987), pp. 335–70.

Wendt, Alexander: "Constructing International Politics," *International Security*, Vol. 20, No. 1 (Summer 1995), pp. 71–81.

Wessels, Wolfgang: "Die Einheitliche Europäische Akte: Die europäische Zusammenarbeit in der Aussenpolitik", *Integration*, Vol. 9 (March 1986), pp. 126–32.

Westlake, M.: "The European Parliament, the National Parliaments and the 1996 Intergovernmental Conference", *Political Quarterly*, Vol. 66, No. 1 (1995), pp. 59–73.

Wight, Martin: *International Theory: The Three Traditions* (Leicester and London: Leicester University Press for the Royal Institute of International Affairs, 1991).

Wight, Martin: *Power Politics* (Harmondsworth: Penguin, 1986).

Wildavsky, Aaron B. and Singer, Max: *The Real World Order: Zones of Peace and Zones of Turmoil* (Chatham, NJ: Chatham House, 1993).

Wincott, Daniel: "Institutional Interaction and European Integration: Towards an Everyday Critique of Liberal Intergovernmentalism", *Journal of Common Market Studies*, Vol. 33, No. 4 (December 1995), pp. 597–609.

Wolton, Dominique: *La dernière utopie: naissance de l'Europe démocratique* (Paris: Flammarion, 1993).

Wörner, Manfred: "NATO's Role in a Changing Europe", *Adelphi Paper* No. 284 (1994).

Wright, Joanne: "France and European Security", *European Security*, Vol. 2, No. 1 (Spring 1993), pp. 23–43.

Zalewski, Marysia: "Well, What Is the Feminist Perspective on Bosnia", *International Affairs*, Vol. 71, No. 2 (April 1995), pp. 339–56.

Zelikow, Philip: "The Masque of Institutions", *Survival*, Vol. 38, No. 1 (Spring 1996), pp. 6–18.

Zelikow, Philip: "The New Concert of Europe", *Survival*, Vol. 34, No. 2 (Summer 1992), pp. 12–30.

Zelikow, Philip and Condoleezza Rice: *Germany Unified and Europe Transformed: A Study in Statecraft* (Cambridge, MA: Harvard University Press, 1995).

Zielonka, Jan: "Les paradoxes de la politique étrangère polonaise," *Politique Étrangère*, Vol. 59, No. 1 (Spring 1994), pp. 99–114.

Zielonka, Jan: "Security in Central Europe", *Adelphi Paper* No. 272 (1992).

Zielonka, Jan: "Europe's security: a great confusion", *International Affairs*, Vol. 67, No. 1 (January 1991), pp. 127–37.

Index